MAX TEACHING WITH READING AND WRITING:

Classroom Activities for Helping Students Learn New Subject Matter While Acquiring Literacy Skills

Mark A. Forget Ph.D.

Cover photo: Mary Williams shown conducting a preview of a textbook section while teaching a middle school science class at McConnell Middle School, Loganville, GA.

Note for Librarians: A cataloguing record for this book is available from Library and Archives Canada at www.collectionscanada.ca/amicus/index-e.html
ISBN 1-4120-0992-8

Printed in Victoria, BC, Canada. Printed on paper with minimum 30% recycled fibre. Trafford's print shop runs on "green energy" from solar, wind and other environmentally-friendly power sources.

Offices in Canada, USA, Ireland and UK
This book was published *on-demand* in cooperation with Trafford Publishing. On-demand publishing is a unique process and service of making a book available for retail sale to the public taking advantage of on-demand manufacturing and Internet marketing. On-demand publishing includes promotions, retail sales, manufacturing, order fulfilment, accounting and collecting royalties on behalf of the author.

Book sales for North America and international:
Trafford Publishing, 6E–2333 Government St.,
Victoria, BC V8T 4P4 CANADA
phone 250 383 6864 (toll-free 1 888 232 4444)
fax 250 383 6804; email to orders@trafford.com
Book sales in Europe:
Trafford Publishing (UK) Limited, 9 Park End Street, 2nd Floor
Oxford, UK OX1 1HH UNITED KINGDOM
phone 44 (0)1865 722 113 (local rate 0845 230 9601)
facsimile 44 (0)1865 722 868; info.uk@trafford.com
Order online at:
trafford.com/03-1361

20 19 18 17 16 15 14

To Kim… colleague, friend and loving wife

Table of Contents

Preface

Changing the Ways We Help Students Learn

Great teachers are good learners. It is my hope that any teacher who understands the important role that literacy — reading, writing, speaking, listening, and thinking — played in his or her own background development as a person and as an intellectual will use this work as a guide to learn how to become effective at coaching students to acquire the same skills. These skills are the same ones that all people use to make sense of text and of complex learning situations.

It is not easy to change. However, most people who see that something will greatly improve their success at what they are doing are willing to attempt to change. My experience in working with teachers over the years leads me to believe that, even though the literacy activities that I model in my workshops work well there, many teachers are reluctant to try them in their own classrooms for a variety of reasons. I am hoping that this book will help many of them get over their reluctance to take the leap.

This book is divided into two parts. Part I explains how the process works to help students acquire both course content and literacy skills at the same time. It presents to the reader three essential components of a complete reading/writing-to-learn classroom. The three components are 1) a three-step lesson framework (MAX Teaching), 2) a three-step skill acquisition model (SAM), and 3) the systematic and formulaic use of cooperative learning (CL). The three of these components combine and are interwoven to provide for and to facilitate student acquisition of both content and skills through daily practice. Each of these will be described, explained, and justified with supporting research based on what we have learned during the 20th century from cognitive psychology and through the more modern study of the human brain.

Part II describes generic lesson plans for content-literacy-based classroom instruction. It includes 23 detailed classroom activities that have been developed and researched over the last three decades. Each strategy is introduced, explained, and then presented as a generic lesson plan that could be applied to virtually any given subject area lesson. These lessons have been carefully laid out to include all three essential components, including the lesson framework, cooperative learning, and skill acquisition. Each lesson includes step-by-step instructions for generic lessons that a teacher may have open on the desk in order to reference during a class.

My work with thousands of teachers over the past 11 years has led me to see the desire for such explicitly outlined lessons. The lessons are by no means the only way to apply a particular strategy. However, each is based on years of experience with students in various subject areas and of various ages. All good teachers know that any given class is alive and changing from minute to minute, and that no formula is guaranteed to work at any given time or with any given set of students. That being said, the way the lessons in part two are presented is meant to be generic enough and flexible enough to be helpful in assisting any teacher to become comfortable with the use of reading and writing to help students acquire both content and skills.

Acknowledgments

My gratitude is owed to many people. Deena Smith first introduced me to the concept of using a reading-to-learn framework of instruction to teach my social studies subject matter. She encouraged me to participate in a train-the-trainer program which allowed me to develop a sense of expertise and of confidence in using the strategies, and she helped me enormously in the second part of that program which involved working with other teachers to help them use reading and writing in their own subject area classes. She remains a close friend and collaborator in the process of helping teachers develop as reading/writing-to-learn teachers.

I am indebted to many other colleagues with whom I worked to develop and practice many of the strategies herein. Among those are Brian Alexander and Kelly O'Dell-Vance, both of whom worked closely with me in a 9th grade content area reading/writing program called "The Model School," as well as the many other colleagues with whom we practiced peer coaching across the disciplines to focus on developing ourselves as teachers who use reading and writing strategies. Rosemarie O'Grady provided opportunities to foster and practice literacy-based practices in the foreign language classroom, and Ann Zingraff-Newton and Dave Hale provided opportunities for practicing this form of instruction in mathematics classrooms. James DiNardo III and Yogi Hightower-Boothe collaborated with me in using these classroom activities in the health and physical education classroom. Ray Morgan, of Old Dominion University, has been an inspiration and guide throughout my development as a literacy teacher, a researcher, and a staff developer.

Without my experiences at the Southern Regional Education Board, working with Gene Bottoms, and many of the other reform-minded educators in the *High Schools That Work* (*HSTW*) program, I would not have had the opportunity to become exposed to the variety of schools, school environments, and classroom experiences that helped to clarify and solidify the understandings that I have developed over the years about what works and what does not work in the classroom. My experiences at *HSTW*, and the exposure to the multitude of schools and classrooms made possible by my work there has contributed greatly to this work.

There are many researchers in the field of cognitive psychology, brain-compatible learning, and literacy-based classroom instruction who came before me and to whom I am indebted for their efforts. An enormous and growing body of knowledge supports the contentions that are made in this work. I hope that this work contributes to the growth and development of that body of knowledge that facilitates this most important aspect of the most important profession — the teaching of life-long literacy-based learning skills. I also hope this work makes it possible for more teachers to feel like they have enough knowledge to make a go of it in the classroom. Content-literacy-based instruction changed my life as a teacher, and it has changed the lives of many of my colleagues. It has also affected the lives of the thousands of students who have come through our classrooms over the years. I hope that this work helps make possible and probable the spread of that success.

Part I

MAX TEACHING:

how the process works to help students acquire content and skills

Chapter 1

Introduction

The illiterate of the 21st century will not be those who cannot read and write, but those who cannot learn, unlearn, and relearn.

Alvin Toffler

I am a schoolteacher. Since learning and refining the classroom activities presented in this book, I have taught classes in many subject areas, including algebra, algebra foundations, American history, earth science, geography, health and physical education, reading, U.S. Government, and world history. The classroom activities (which, along with a lesson framework and two other procedures, I have named *MAX Teaching*) have been effective in all of these classes. Through the systematic use of reading and writing as tools, I have seen students become engaged in mastering the content of whatever course they were taking. *MAX* is an acronym for a three-part teaching framework composed of *M*otivation to engage in learning, *A*cquisition of new information, and e*X*tension beyond the text. This book shows how it works.

Not only are MAX Teaching classroom activities effective in a range of content areas, they are effective in various types of school settings as well. Frequently, I perform modeling in the classrooms of schools where I'm invited to lead staff development programs. Thus, I have opportunities to teach in rural schools, urban schools, and suburban schools; and I teach all subject areas from 1st grade through the 12th, in both academic and vocational settings. In this range of settings, I've continued to use and appreciate the value of the classroom activities I want to share with you through this book.

Learning from Experience

My own teaching career, launched in 1974, has been the inspiration for this book. You could say that I first learned how to teach in a student-centered reading and writing classroom, using a book of carefully thought-out lesson plans not unlike Part II of this book. But that would not be entirely true. I did not learn how *to teach*; rather, I learned *how to facilitate active learning by students*. That's an altogether different thing. But I didn't learn that immediately.

My discovery of student-centered teaching techniques did not take place until my third year of teaching. I tried other classroom activities before that time. For example, when I first got out of the college of education, I wanted to imitate the best of my college professors who had been able to hold my attention for hours as they lectured about their research interests and other topics. My first classroom experience involved teaching the history of the United States. It was a great time to be teaching that subject. The Alex Haley miniseries "Roots" was on television, and there were dramatic turns occurring in U.S. politics. I was enthusiastic, and my enthusiasm carried over to my students. But it was not enough to keep students interested for long. They lacked the discipline of a college student accustomed to lectures. In addition, I had all the problems that any young teacher might have with classroom management and discipline. Results were mixed at best.

The Turning Point

By my third year, I was ready to try something new. At that time, Holt, Rinehart, and Winston had developed an "inquiry curriculum" in the social studies. Each lesson was designed by curriculum specialists at the Carnegie-Mellon Institute to use constructivist principles, leading students to *discover for themselves* new understandings. Such discoveries would take place through the use of primary source materials to write about, discuss, and set purposes for reading, reading in the classroom, and then writing about and cooperatively discussing student ideas to assist in creating meaning regarding history. Each lesson was written in a step-by-step format that any teacher could follow. If the teacher did so, students were led through a sequence of getting ready to read through thinking, writing and discussion, silent reading from various forms of text, and more discussion and writing that allowed them to systematically construct meaning from written and other sources.

What was great about this method is that it allowed students to become historians—to work as historians do. They would form opinions and make predictions about what other historians would conclude—even before they would read the history textbook. The result was that once they got into the textbook, they had sufficient knowledge and purposes for reading that allowed them to become active in processing text that otherwise might have been much less interesting. A typical lesson from the Holt curriculum might read as follows (I abbreviate it for terseness.):

1. Pass out to each student the list of laws written in 1619 in Jamestown, Virginia. Ask students to read the laws silently to themselves, thinking about how the laws reflected the society that existed there.
2. Tell students to write on their own paper what they thought Jamestown Colony might be like.
3. Share students' predictions on the chalkboard, making a list of predictions for the whole class.
4. Ask students to scan the list of predictions they have made to see if they could be organized into a few categories.
5. Lead the class through a discussion, narrowing the list to three or so categories.
6. Tell students that now that they have collectively made predictions of what the Jamestown Colony was like at the time, they have become historians. Then introduce them to the next step, looking at the textbook to see what other historians have said about the same topic.
7. And so it went. Students were engaged, the teacher was empowered to let students learn, and students routinely used literacy skills to perform higher order thinking about topics important to understanding who we are as Americans.

Coaching and Active Learning

What I learned from the pre-planned lessons created by Holt Reinhart Winston and the Carnegie-Mellon Institute was that students actually learn better when they are *coached* through a process in which *they* are active in trying to make sense of something. It is the opposite of the lecture wherein students struggle to perceive what the teacher has on his or her mind. It is also the opposite of what occurs when students are provided worksheets designed to help them learn the details of subject matter. What really occurs with most worksheets is that students simply decode the "correct" answer to fill in the spaces on the worksheets. Rarely do they get to mull over important ideas relating to what they are learning. I had now seen firsthand what works and what doesn't work if learning (in the best sense of the word) is to take place.

But then I changed jobs. I moved away from that teaching position to another state which presented the challenge of a different curriculum. I no longer had the pre-planned lessons I had found so effective in leading my students through the discovery process. My new job was to teach U. S. and Virginia Government. Although I had a reasonably good textbook, the instructor's manual did not provide for the same level of student engagement. Again, the teacher was "on stage" for most of the class. Students learned, but they learned what was on the teacher's mind rather than being led through a thought-provoking discovery of how our governmental systems work. If the teacher had a limited understanding of the topic of the day, then the students were doomed to the same.

In my fourth year as a government teacher, I was first exposed to the idea of using reading and writing to help students become engaged in their own learning. I had the opportunity to attend a summer staff development experience that taught me several classroom activities (many of which are included in this book) to use within a three-step lesson framework that helps students become actively engaged in learning virtually any subject matter. The three steps of the lesson framework that I learned that summer were "anticipation, realization, and contemplation" (Vaughan & Estes, 1986). Through the facilitation of a knowledgeable teacher, classroom students could become engaged in virtually any subject matter in such a way as to be ready for confronting new ideas in text, be equipped with strategies for gathering new information while reading, and be able to construct their own understandings so that they could think critically about the ideas afterward.

Classroom activities that Work Anywhere

No longer did I need a "canned curriculum" such as that from which I first learned that student-centered learning works best. Now, in *any* subject area, I could help students use text to become engaged in learning subject matter that probably wouldn't have interested them otherwise. I was immediately struck by the potential of these new classroom activities. And I saw what happened as soon as I put them into action. When I employed reading and writing in such a way that students became engaged in their own processing of new information, they became motivated to learn. On a daily basis, they all learned much more than I could have told them through lecture and note taking. Why? Because each student was involved in first processing the new information in his/her own unique way, followed by discussion with others, and then coming to an understanding based on collective analysis and interpretation. What had occurred in my third year of teaching — student-centered active engagement in learning from print and from each other — was now happening in my government class, even though I was designing and facilitating the lessons myself rather than following a prefabricated published guide!

It is more fun to teach in this way, and it is more fun to learn this way. I quickly made that discovery. I found that students in my classes were actively engaged and therefore not causing problems related to discipline. But an even more significant result was occurring: while my students were better learning my subject matter, they were also becoming better readers and thinkers, attaining knowledge and skills that would enhance their lives forever. They were learning to *learn* — and they were learning how to learn effectively.

Teaching Reading as Thinking

For students to become independent learners, they must practice reading in ways in which they are (a) able to monitor their own comprehension, (b) recognize when they are not comprehending, and (c) know what to do to correct the situation if comprehension fails to occur. This ability is generally not taught to students in schools.

Schools do a good job of teaching students to decode print in the early grades, but fail to follow up with comprehension instruction in the upper elementary grades and beyond. The result is that many students, who do not have parents or others who are able to sit down with them to make sense of difficult text, simply "throw in the towel" and give up on reading.

This giving up often occurs at an early age. The most common time for students to become frustrated with reading is the fourth grade. After reading mostly stories from kindergarten through the third grade, students first confront textbooks at this time. Since they often do not get instruction in how to interpret these strangely boring and seemingly complex readings, they simply quit reading. Those students from homes where parents can assist them in comprehension have a distinct advantage. Those whose homes cannot provide such support often founder.

Strategic reading is very important in the learning process. It involves planning what to think about before reading, adjusting the effort during reading, and constantly evaluating the success of the ongoing effort to make meaning from text.

The problem is that a majority of high school students in America are not aware of strategic reading or how to practice it. Many middle schools and high schools are filled with large numbers of remedial students who have difficulty making sense of their texts. These students often don't know how to identify when they are having problems in comprehension. Frequently, they think they are "just not smart" and just can't "get it." They are likely to believe that other students learn and remember things more easily simply because the others are more intelligent than they. (Unfortunately, their teachers and administrators often concur in this belief—a factor contributing to low expectations for students.) In reality, these remedial students may simply need to develop strategic reading/thinking practices that will enable them to monitor their own comprehension. The problem is that the process of strategic reading does not lend itself to explanation. Instead, the process must be modeled and practiced in the classroom throughout the school year. Hence, what is needed is an approach that allows students to internalize strategic reading gradually through regular guided practice in an environment that is conducive to learning.

Development of the Mind and Learning Processes

The human brain is physiologically developed through the use of language (Hart, 1983; Healey, 1993; Smith, 1986). This is especially true in fostering the ability to stay mentally focused, put information into perspective, reflect on meaning, plan ahead, and follow through effectively — skills frequently cited by teachers as lacking in many of today's students. Furthermore, students' deficiencies in the development of these skills are the result of three factors: (a) insufficiency of early language development brought about by limited language interaction with parents, child care providers, and others, (b) the influence of television and its characteristically one-way language which eliminates the possibility of verbal interaction, and (c) educational experiences that frequently fail to place stress on language, especially the interactive use of language, oral and written, to solve real problems (Healey, 1993).

Language shapes culture and thinking. The use of language literally influences the intellects of developing students, and this process may continue to be effectively enhanced until the late teens or early twenties. Classroom use of literacy skills helps children to reason, reflect, and respond to the world around them. The minds of many middle and high school students are being structured in language patterns antagonistic to the values of formal education because of the above mentioned poor or non-existent exposure to the forms of good, meaningful language that would enable them to relate to others, to the written word, and to their own minds (Healey, 1993). The focus of most classroom activities is on getting the right answer and remembering it. To accomplish this, little thought is usually required. Students only need to decode the print in their textbooks to find the answers to fill in spaces on worksheets. They do not have to think.

To reason effectively and solve problems, a developing mind needs to learn what it feels like to be in charge of its own thinking and learning process, actively pursuing a mental or physical trail, and inhibiting responses to distractions. Put another way, the mind needs to learn to be interactive with its own thoughts and with those of others; and reading, writing, speaking, listening, and thinking skills are the means to that end. In sum, an interactive, language-rich learning situation is superior to the passive reception of information that is experienced through television, and most often occurs in the traditional classroom.

The most effective solution to the language skill problem is teacher modeling of correct use of language and thought processes. Since this is often not accomplished either in the home or in the modern day-care situation, then it must be done in the school. If it has not been accomplished by the time a student reaches high school, then it must be done there. The problem is that the traditional classroom does not provide this modeling. Faced with the need to "cover" the material they are supposed to teach, with little regard for whether students are getting it, teachers choose pedagogical techniques such as teacher lecture, worksheet skill drills, and reading to answer end-of-chapter comprehension questions. Even teachers that employ classroom discussion as a learning tool often place themselves and their own knowledge at the focus of the learning, a practice that fails to connect with many students.

The "Matthew Effect": Why Basic Courses and Skill-focused Approaches to Teaching Reading Often Fail to Accomplish What They Set Out to Do.

Students who have been placed in lower-level courses because they lack certain abilities tend to be overdosed on skill work to the neglect of integrated reading, writing, and talking across the curriculum. Teachers of these students tend to practice a form of instruction that uses little reading, and almost no meaningful classroom interaction by students. This is especially true in working with students considered poor readers. In fact, those students who most need practice in strategies that would help them to develop as active and independent readers and learners are provided with fewer such strategies than are other students, a reversal of priorities that leads to the "Matthew Effect" (Stanovich, 1986). This term comes from the biblical book of Matthew: "Those who have, will get more until they grow rich, while those who have not, will lose even the little they have" (Matthew 25:29). Students placed in lower tracks as a result of being identified as having poor skills, fall further behind others who have been identified as successful learners.

Teachers who use a lecture and worksheet approach to teaching can claim that they have "covered" what they were supposed to cover in the curriculum. These teachers then tend to blame students for being lazy and unmotivated. Teaching that uses methods to actively engage students in reading for interpretation and discussion is all too rare within high school classrooms. Rather, reading is assigned to be done as homework; or, as has already been discussed, if it is done in class at all, it is to answer questions at the end of a chapter or to fill in spaces on dull worksheets. The result is that students perceive reading as a frustrating, often boring, learning experience in which they seldom see how different subjects relate to either reality or each other—or even how what was learned last week in a given subject area relates to what was learned this week. Often, once a test is administered, students can afford to "forget" what they heard in class or saw in print, but never really learned.

Abundant research over the last several decades substantially supports a much more active notion of the reading process than that which is generally ascribed to in our schools. Research also supports an active approach to teaching students to practice successful strategies for understanding text. However, many studies over the last several decades have shown that almost no comprehension instruction takes place in classrooms beyond the third grade. If students have not learned to be strategic readers by that time, the odds are that they never will!

The results of this are evident in the ubiquitous measures of standardized test scores. Schools are thus failing to perform a service that could open doors for their clients, the students. Merely raising standards, assigning more homework, or requiring students to take more classes (or higher-level classes) will not solve the problem. Schools need to recognize that, to help students become better readers and autonomous, life-long learners, they must provide instruction in ways that engage students in reading, writing, speaking, listening, and thinking about the subject matter they are learning. This instruction is best accomplished when not limited to the language arts classroom or the remedial reading classroom, but also practiced in the context of learning real subject matter in courses such as science, geography, welding, or mathematics — in other words — in the content areas. Any content area classroom can become a literacy club in which students get two for one. They learn new subject matter while they acquire literacy skills.

What's Different about This Book?

Most content area reading textbooks focus on theory, offering only very brief descriptions of specific reading and writing classroom activities, while leaving the details up to the practitioner. However, many teachers want something more. The vast majority of the thousands of teachers with whom I've worked as a staff developer say they would be interested in specific and detailed lesson plans that are complete in their presentation. They want some specific guidance. When they hear about classroom activities such as those I'm presenting here, they find themselves thinking, "Yes, this seems like it would work, but I'm uncertain about how exactly I might perform a given classroom activity in my own classroom. What if I don't do it right? Will I leave out an important component of the lesson that causes it to fail?"

This is a handbook designed to meet that need for guidance. What makes it different is that it makes teaching content area subjects easy by providing a detailed lesson plan for many of the most effective and commonly used content area reading and writing classroom activities to date.

Part I of this book also attempts to paint a picture of why the use of reading and writing to learn is so powerful in developing students in subject-area expertise while helping them develop as learners at the same time. Part II, on the other hand, takes the classroom reading/writing activities and breaks them down into a detailed, easy to follow lesson-plan time line for each classroom activity. A teacher can have the classroom activity lesson plan on the desk to refer to during the class period.

In other words, this book provides a generic version of the sort of detailed lesson plan that helped me to become a *facilitator of active student learning* rather than a teacher in the conventional sense of the word. As I described earlier, in my third year of teaching, I was given specific lessons to go with specific readings, but what I am presenting here goes many steps beyond that. MAX Teaching differs from that "tailored-to-specific-text-readings" approach, because each of the classroom activities chosen for this book is applicable to text or other learning experiences in a wide variety of circumstances. The classroom activities are not limited to specific portions of text only.

The classroom activities described in part II of this book are of various origins. Some are mine, and some were created by other authors that I'll be referring to at various points. It is possible that, in the case of a particular reading/writing classroom activity, my interpretation of exactly how to carry it out may differ a bit from the original authors' specifics; yet, the classroom activities are presented as I and others have used them successfully in many different classrooms and subject areas.

It is my hope that, by having such detailed lesson plans to follow, teachers who use this book will find it helpful in getting past the anxiety of trying something new. I also hope that teachers who use this book to assist them in their own development as reading/writing-to-learn teachers will change or adapt the classroom activities as they see fit in their own classrooms in the future. The literature contains hundreds of research-proven reading/writing-to-learn classroom activities, and this book does not pretend to address all or even most of them. But what I do hope is that it will assist in easing teachers into using reading and writing as a tool to (a) help students learn their subject matter and (b)develop lifelong literacy skills. I also hope that teachers thus prepared will seek out other reading/writing classroom activities to further enhance their students' development.

Using This Book

This book is designed to be used by a teacher who wishes to have a simple, easy to read blueprint for employing a variety of specific classroom activities for reading and writing. It is primarily a handbook for complete lessons using reading, writing, cooperative learning, and a skill acquisition model that coaches students as developing learners. Any teacher who only wishes a clear and detailed blueprint for specific lesson plans may wish to skip part I and go directly to any of the classroom activity descriptions.

The set of generic lesson plans that are provided can be used as blueprints for complete lessons that truly engage students in the active pursuit of knowledge through reading and writing. Teachers who choose to use this book as a "how to" manual may want to skip part I, which provides a rationale for using reading and writing in the content area classroom. Instead, they may skip directly to a particular classroom activity to find a timeline of a lesson that follows a systematic three-part paradigm designed to

- engage students in active pursuit of subject matter understandings,
- provide students with guided practice in life-long learning skills, and
- help students use cooperative learning to construct meaning from various forms of text.

All that a teacher needs to effectively use a reading/writing classroom activity is included in the description listed for that classroom activity. No prior knowledge is assumed for any of the classroom activities described. Therefore, this book can be used to accompany any of the principal content area reading textbooks. On the other hand, it doesn't have to be used in concert with any other text. It stands alone. And once a teacher has made up his/her mind to use content reading in the classroom, this book is all that is required to design powerful and effective lessons—lessons that will help students deeply learn course content in any subject area while at the same time practicing important learning and communication skills.

Once a teacher is comfortable with using reading and writing to learn, s/he can more easily go to other sources for new ideas. The number of actual reading and writing classroom activities in the literature is in the hundreds. This book by no means attempts to be all encompassing in that regard. The classroom activities described present a broad selection of those that are my favorites. Having used many different classroom activities in my own classes over the years, and having rejected many, I have found that students respond very well to the ones described herein. I can recommend them without hesitation.

In choosing the learning activities described in this book, I used five criteria:

- frequency of inclusion in content reading textbooks
- reported frequency of a classroom activity's use by surveyed teachers
- perceived effectiveness of a classroom activity as I experienced it in my own classes over 15 years of using it
- lifelong learning/study skills that a particular classroom activity teaches
- applicability of a classroom activity to the greatest number of disciplines

I can assure you that there are enough classroom activities in this text to teach for many years without ever having classes that are boring and predictable. I am not suggesting that you don't explore further — just that you will not need to.

Chapter 2

The Classroom
Every Teacher Would Like

Treat people as if they were what they ought to be, and you help them to become what they are capable of being.

Johann Wolfgang von Goethe

Would you like to learn how to get each student, every day, to come to class after having not only read the homework assignment with the assistance of an adult, but also having discussed it with two or three peers for twenty minutes on the way to school?

That's a question I have asked teachers all across the country in my work as a staff developer. I continue to ask it every time I work with a new group. And the response is always the same. First, every teacher raises a hand, signifying a yes answer. Then — they *laugh*.

Why the laughter? Because no one believes that this is going to happen in any school district in the country today. Nevertheless, I don't stop. I proceed to ask teachers, "But suppose it *were* possible. What do you think would be different in your classrooms?"

Here is a list of actual responses from teachers in some of my workshops. I've divided them into three categories of expected changes—in the classroom, among students, and among teachers.

Overall Changes in the Classroom

Classrooms would be more productive.

Dynamic, lively discussions would take place.

Energy level of class improves.

Enrichment could occur.

Fewer disturbances would occur in class.

It would be more fun for teachers and students.

Lively discussions would occur.

There would be an increase in Socratic dialog.

There would be increased cooperation, give and take, improved social skills.

They (students and teachers) would love to come to class.

We would have an energized atmosphere.

You'd have some discipline.

Changes among Students

Active learning would be the norm.
Dropout rates would go down.
Focused thinking would occur.
Grades would go up.
Graduation rates would go up.
Higher achievement would occur.
HOTS (higher order thinking skills) would be possible.
Interest would go up.
More productivity would occur.
More students would experience success.
Prior knowledge would be improved.
Retention would improve.
Student interaction would increase.
Students would be analyzing, synthesizing, and applying information.
Students would be confident and competent.
Students would be engaged.
Students would be learning by talking about stuff.
Students would be more self-directed.
Students would be prepared more for discussion.
Students would gain mastery of material.
Students would have better understanding of concepts.
Students would have more success in learning.
Students would lead in the learning process.
Students would retain more.
They would all be on the same page.
They would be responsible for their own learning.
They would teach each other.
They'd actually learn.
They'd be prepared.
They'd learn the material.
We'd have interested students.

Changes among Teachers

Finally, we would get down to interesting new stuff.
I could go in different directions.
I could move more quickly.
I could reach more students.
Less class time would be wasted.
Less time would be spent on discipline.

Our job would be easier.

There would be less teacher frustration.

There would be time for hands-on activities.

We could build on what they know.

We could go from concrete to abstract thinking.

We could have an enriched curriculum.

You would not have to reteach things as much.

Is there anything on this list that any teacher would *not* want to have take place in the classroom? Yet, what many teachers don't realize is that these goals are reachable; they can be achieved by using a variety of research-based classroom activities, some of which have been presented in the literature for as many as three decades now, while others are more recent. This book is intended to guide you in using such classroom activities in your own classroom so that you can (a) achieve the goals implied in the question that opened this chapter and (b) get the predicted results listed by the teachers.

I'll be describing systematic ways to get your students to learn the subject matter through guided practice of literacy skills—reading, writing, speaking, listening, and thinking about subject matter in your classroom. And together we'll also consider what most often takes place in grades four through twelve in urban, suburban, and rural classrooms nationwide (in other words, the "what *is*") and then compare it with what might happen in a classroom organized around the use of literacy skills to facilitate learning (the "what *could be*"). This comparison should make clear why much of traditional teaching practice does not work effectively with most students, and why using literacy skill practices should be seriously considered. There is no more effective way to help students develop subject area competencies while at the same time acquiring lifelong learning skills.

Why Haven't Most Teachers Been Using Reading/Writing to Teach Content?

There are several reasons why any given teacher may not have already been using reading-and-writing-to-learn classroom activities. First, many of the classroom activities have been newly developed over the past few years. A considerable number of teachers who are practicing today had their training and entered the classroom in the period just before most of the literature on content area reading and writing came out (the late 1970s to the present). Professors who earned their degrees during that same time period have taught most of the rest of the teachers who entered the profession later. That may help to explain why there is a lag in adopting the principles of using reading and writing in content areas. The techniques have been in existence for some time, but most teachers have not really been exposed to them.

A second reason is that many who enter the teaching profession may take literacy skills for granted, not being aware of how they themselves actually acquired the abilities to read, write, speak, listen, and think critically. Third, many teachers teach in the same ways they were taught, without questioning the classroom activities they observed and internalized.

At the same time, those who *have* been exposed to every "new and improved" technique that has come down the pike in the past 30 years may suffer from extreme skepticism when confronted with new ideas. "It's just one more educational reform idea that will run its course, so I think I'll sit this one out." Such skepticism, then, provides a fourth reason some may not use the classroom activities.

A fifth reason has to do with *timing*. When many of us learned these classroom activities, we were in undergraduate or graduate school, and we had little experience in the classroom. We were in love with our subject matter — not really focused on the *skills* we would need to help *students* connect to that subject matter and share our enthusiasm. In addition, we probably thought that if the way *we* were taught was good enough for *us,* it must be good enough for the students we were about to teach.

Sixth, we may not have attempted to use these classroom activities because we may not have seen the positive effects they can have on students in terms of developing learning skills. We may have had the perception that by using reading and writing activities in the classroom, we would be sacrificing time that could otherwise be spent teaching our precious subject matter. It is very important that teachers see that this is a misconception. The fact is that by helping students use reading and writing strategies to learn subject matter, we *do* accomplish all the above goals — helping students to master the subject matter, practice critical thinking about the subject matter, and enhance their learning skills all at the same time.

How Students Learn Most Effectively

Research suggests that we remember about 10% of what we read, 20% of what we hear, 30% of what we see, and 70% of what we ourselves discuss. How much do we remember of all the books we read in college? Is 10% a good estimate? We read the books and most likely did comprehend what we read and held onto it for a test, paper, or discussion. Most of that retention was momentary understanding but was not processed as personal knowledge for ourselves. The reason for such a low percentage of information being retained is largely related to how it was learned (or not learned). Exposure to information and long-term retention are definitely two separate entities.

Research also tells us that "85% of the knowledge and skills presented to students in school comes to them in some form of language: teachers talking, materials to read, films to watch and listen to, and so forth." If students only retain 20% of what they hear, then is frequent lecturing an effective way to teach, and is it an effective use of learners' time? On the other hand, if we remember 70% of what we *discuss*, is it any wonder that teachers who often lecture seem so knowledgeable?

Percentages aside, teachers especially know how beneficial it is to talk to someone else about subject matter. As good learners, we know from experience that when we have discussed something with someone else, we have clarified subject matter, made connections that we might not have realized before, and mentally and verbally interacted with the ideas of our partner(s) in the discussion.

These same concepts apply to our students. An interactive learning situation is superior to the passive reception of information that characterizes the traditional classroom. When students work cooperatively to construct the meaning from a piece of text, they learn more deeply, and they are helping one another learn how to learn. In order to motivate students to think about, learn, and discuss what they have read, we should use a framework of instruction that allows students to be active in their own learning.

Teaching Literacy Skills

Generally speaking, reading is not taught beyond the third grade in most school systems. Up to third grade, the focus is on decoding print and developing fluency in reading. Most of the reading is in the form of stories. Beginning about the fourth grade, most students are exposed to different forms of text, and to much more difficult text. If a student has not mastered reading comprehension skills by the fourth grade, chances are that s/he will struggle with learning in grades four through twelve. Many middle school and high school students lack the ability to use literacy skills effectively for the purpose of learning. Teachers and parents often assume that these skills will develop by themselves over time. The fact is that they rarely do.

What should be done about the problem? One solution is to use *embedded curriculum* (Kiewra, 1993; Forget & Morgan, 1997), in which learning skills are taught in conjunction with course content. In other words, the "how" of learning can be embedded within the "what" of learning. This book shows how you can put this method into action.

Your role is crucial in making this work. Students need to be provided with appropriate modeling of language and thought processes, and if this is not accomplished in the home, it must be done in the school. The problem is that all too often classrooms have not been providing this modeling. Faced with the ubiquitous pressure of standardized tests, teachers often resort to rapid "covering" of the material they are supposed to teach, with little regard for whether students are developing appropriate brain programs for learning, thinking, and problem solving. In most schools, the preferred pedagogical techniques are teacher lecture, worksheet skill drills, and reading to answer end-of-chapter comprehension questions. Teachers who use these methods can claim that they "covered" what they were supposed to cover in the curriculum. The results are that students perceive school as a passive, often boring, learning experience in which they seldom see how different subjects relate to each other or to "real life"—or even how what was learned last week relates to what was learned this week.

Textbooks and Other Text Sources

Textbooks are valuable tools. Though the textbook should not be the only information source in a class, the textbook is an often-neglected or misused tool for learning. The fact is that much of the content being measured by standardized tests is to be found in textbooks. The problem is that, even though many of the questions on standardized tests require interpretive reading, most students are not being exposed to thoughtful interpretation of text. The basic themes of a course and the vocabulary of the discipline are to be found in the text.

Any person, regardless of age, can perform higher order thinking about even the most abstract ideas if s/he has a basic understanding of the concepts involved. The fundamental concepts are presented in most textbooks, and teachers need to recognize that the fundamentals need to come first before more advanced thinking can occur. Many teachers recall the joy of the advanced, in-depth understandings that they derived from coursework at the college level or on the job. They often forget that to appreciate the deeper understandings that they achieved, they first had to grasp the basics. Textbooks can allow for acquisition of important knowledge upon which can be built greater understanding — and without which, higher order thinking will not occur. However, it is important that the textbook be used properly — as a source of context that will facilitate student interaction — and that other information sources are also used appropriately.

Teachers who think that students can't perform higher order thinking do not realize that the problem doesn't stem from inadequate mental capabilities on the part of the students. Rather, the problem lies in the students' lack of preparation for thinking about the subject matter. Once students have processed the basics, they can more readily perform higher order thinking skills about the area under discussion. Many teachers practice assumptive teaching — thinking that because they themselves understand certain concepts, the students will also understand them in the same ways. Such assumptions must be laid aside.

A Framework for Teaching Literacy Skills with Content

A framework of instruction for developing reading skills along with content area knowledge includes three-steps that facilitate active engagement of students, allowing the brain to function at its highest levels.

1. **Before reading**, teachers can help students to recall and add to their prior knowledge of the topic to be studied, and to set their own purposes for reading.
2. **During the reading**, teachers can help students maintain their purposes and learn to monitor their own comprehension.

3. **After the reading**, teachers can facilitate higher-order thinking by students, allowing for the thinking to extend beyond the text.

This three-step framework for using reading and writing to facilitate learning has been in the literature since the 1970's and has had various acronyms to characterize the three steps. As described in chapter 1, this book utilizes the acronym "MAX" (Motivation, Acquisition, and eXtension) to describe the three steps of the framework.

Interaction between student and self, student and teacher, and among students *in the context of the subject area* is critical in developing these abilities. Emphasis is on learning through guided practice in reading, writing, speaking, listening, and thinking. All these are practiced in the classroom on a daily basis, while students participate in an active process of learning from textbooks, from each other, and from other materials. Students of all ability levels, in all content areas, benefit from this form of deeper learning. In addition, the skills learned in conjunction with the content instruction are transferable to other learning experiences, because one important thing being learned is the process of learning itself. Students thus develop naturally positive brain programs that they can apply in all future learning situations.

The Other Two Components of MAX Teaching

In addition to the basic three-step framework, MAX Teaching includes two important components, which will be described in more detail in the next chapter and in subsequent chapters. These components are the systematic use of cooperative learning and a skill acquisition model to create a "literacy apprenticeship" (Kiewra, 1993; Forget and Morgan, 1997; Greenleaf, Schoenbach, Cziko, & Mueller, 2001). This literacy apprenticeship focuses on the use of reading, writing, speaking, listening, and thinking, and can become a part of any academic or vocational classroom that emphasizes teaching students subject matter while at the same time helping them develop as skilled, independent learners.

Several different content area reading frameworks of instruction have evolved over the past three decades. The acronyms that describe them include ARC, for anticipation, realization, and contemplation (Vaughan & Estes, 1986), PAR, for preparation, assistance, and reflection (Richardson & Morgan, 2003), and others. All of the frameworks have in common a *pre*-reading phase, a *during*-reading phase, and a *post*-reading phase.

What separates MAX Teaching from the others are several factors. One is the heavy emphasis on cooperative learning and skill development which is explicit and central to each lesson. An emphasis on skills turns each class into a developmental experience in which students are brought along as less skilled participants in a procedural environment that allows them to develop expertise in specific competencies related to the discipline being studied, and often transferable to other disciplines as well.

The most important difference separating MAX Teaching from the other frameworks is the emphasis on acquisition as the central feature of the process. Acquisition is different from learning (Krashen, 1996; Smith, 1983, 1988). While learning takes conscious effort on the part of the learner, acquisition occurs without the person even being aware that it is occurring, often with no effort at all. (Chapter 5 will expand on this idea.) My experiences in fifteen years of teaching using content literacy activities in my classroom suggest that the term "acquisition" best describes what is happening with students.

Acquisition is how you developed your first language. No one followed you around when you toddled about the room as a one-year-old, describing to you that every sentence must have both a subject and a predicate, and that the subject must agree with the predicate. You acquired this knowledge without even being aware that you were doing so. You did so through meaningful use of the language and through imitating people who were better than you at using it. My experiences in the content literacy classroom — in the subjects of social studies, mathematics, and science — caused me to see that this process is what was happening with my students. They were acquiring both the subject matter and the literacy skills needed to become life-long learners.

The Teacher/Student Relationship – Some Descriptive Analogies

Emphasis on practice of skills is analogous to an athletic coaching experience in which the coach and/or other players on the team have various skill levels compared to one another and are willing to share their knowledge (Forget, Morgan, & Antinarella, 1996). It is also analogous to a master/apprentice relationship (Kiewra, 1993; Forget & Morgan, 1997; Schoenbach, et al., 1999) in which the master (teacher) is the model for the apprenticed students. A third analogy is that of a club wherein a person joins to be like the other members of the club, and they, in turn, help the joiner to develop as a successful member (Smith, 1988). In all three of the analogies one thing stands out — the supportive, developmental atmosphere with the more advanced members assisting in the development of those less skilled. All humans develop in such a manner — first from parents and siblings, and then from peers and significant others.

What Classrooms Too Often Look Like

I had the opportunity to participate in technical assistance visits (TAV) in a multitude of schools over the past few years in the role of School Improvement Consultant with a nationally known whole-school reform initiative known as *High Schools That Work*, a part of the Southern Regional Education Board. In participating as a team member on many TAV's, I very quickly saw a relationship between how well a given school was doing in the various measures such as standardized tests, retention rates, dropout rates and other such measures on the one hand and classroom activities that occurred routinely in the schools on the other hand.

Figure 2-1 compares three classrooms that are characteristic of what goes on in schools across America. The first column, on the left, is characteristic of schools that had such abysmally low scores that the schools were often being taken over by their state education systems. In any given school, there were always classroom exceptions, but most classrooms in failing schools were characterized by the activities in the left column titled "The Way It Shouldn't Be."

There are a few common threads that run through the classroom activities that take place in the column showing "the way it shouldn't be":

- All activities require no more than the ability to decode print.
- No real reading or thinking is required. Students just call out words or hunt for answers.
- Cooperative learning is not possible since no real problem needs to be solved.
- All activities are teacher-centered.

Very little learning can take place in such a classroom. Students bide their time, hoping to pass out of one year's class into another similar one where little actual meaning is developed. Teachers can say that they covered the content because students went through the actions of finding answers, but little actual sense is made of anything in such a setting, and students can pass through with no development of a sense of the rich nature of the subject matter or of literacy skills and their empowering ability to enhance understanding.

The second or middle column, "the way it sometimes is," describes to a great extent my own classroom before I began to use the classroom activities and methods in this book. On any given day, three of the thirty students in my class had done the homework. So, the four of us would carry on an intelligent conversation regarding the subject matter while most students struggled to figure out what we were talking about. But I was a dedicated teacher who broke the class into several steps and used various techniques to get my content across. By the time I was finished, every student in the classroom had some concept of the content I was supposed to have taught. But none of them had developed their learning skills — because I had done all the work! The hidden message in such a classroom is this: "You don't ever have to do the homework because he's going to teach it to you anyway!" Like students subjected to the pedagogy of the first column, students taught in this environment fail to acquire literacy skills and their empowering ability to enhance understanding.

The third column, "the way it is with MAX," describes the way it can be in any classroom that systematically employs the use of literacy skills to help students learn new subject matter. By the time all the students have read the subject matter, written some notes to bring to the discussion, and then discussed the subject matter with their peers to construct meaning from the reading, intelligent discussion can occur — with all students on the same page — literally as well as figuratively! In fact, this kind of classroom takes us to exactly what any teacher wants. Instead of having a few students (who either have the support at home or the necessary self discipline to do homework) as the only participants in a topical discussion, *all* students can be interacting together in higher order thinking. The classroom comes alive, with no one left out. It is a dream come true. And it can happen for you.

Figure 2-1 – Three Classrooms Compared

The Way It Shouldn't Be	The Way It Sometimes Is	The Way It Is with *MAX*
• Students have no connection to what they are to learn because they did not read the homework assignment and they do not connect to their prior knowledge.	• 10-20 % of students have completed the assigned reading. Most students have no clue about the assignment or the concepts they should have learned from the text.	• Teacher helps students link prior knowledge to the day's lesson. Students establish their purposes for learning.
• Teacher has students copy down 15-20 vocabulary words and look up definitions for them.	• Teacher attempts to teach concepts by lecture, questions, probes for understanding, video, notes, etc.	• Students actively probe text in attempt to satisfy their need for understanding.
• Round-robin reading.		• Students help one another construct understanding of subject matter.
• Students are told to copy down notes the teacher has provided.	• All students have some level of conceptual understanding.	• Intelligent discussion occurs with all students having complete knowledge base with which to work.
• Students fill in spaces on worksheets created by textbook publisher.	• None have improved their learning skills. The teacher did all the work!	
• Students are told that this material will be on the test on Friday.		• All students use the vocabulary of the discipline.
• Little or no verbal interaction occurs, and no one learns very much, but the class is quiet and orderly.	• The hidden message is that students don't have to read – the teacher will tell them all they need to know.	• Students perform meaningful reflection for homework.

Achieving the Classroom Every Teacher Wants

What all the content area reading frameworks developed over the years have in common is this: they place *individual silent reading* at the center of the lesson. First, the teacher motivates students to *want* to read (more about that later). Then, right there in the classroom, students simply read — silently and with purpose — all the while gathering information for later discussion and critical thinking. After the reading, students extend beyond the text to perform higher order thinking over the subject matter. However, in this paradigm, the discussion is not limited to the three or four students who did their homework. Each and every student has read the text — right there in the classroom!

Thus, what happens when such a framework is used correctly is that teachers and students achieve a variation of the goal embedded in the question with which this chapter began: *Would you like to learn how to get each student, every day, to come to class after having not only read the homework assignment with the assistance of an adult, but also having discussed it with two or three peers for twenty minutes on the way to school?*

We all know that the full intent of the question will not be realized in very many places — if any — anywhere in the United States at any time soon. Most students will *not* come to school having already read their homework assignment with an adult's assistance and having spent their time on the school bus or their walk to school discussing the homework topic with their peers (who, in this hypothetical situation, would also have read the assignment).

But what you will find is that in the content area reading/writing classroom you have achieved the same thing—only *you, the teacher, are the adult doing the assisting*, and it is not on the way to school where the discussions take place but rather *in the cooperative learning groups* in the classroom. Nevertheless, the results you may expect are the ones that teachers identified when posed the question originally, and the whole classroom scene becomes different from the frustrating one we most often see in schools today.

Take a moment to look back at those predicted classroom behaviors listed by teachers as they imagined a classroom in which all students had done their homework in the manner suggested in the opening question. *What you are seeing is a list of behaviors that are characteristic of a content literacy classroom!* In such a classroom, students take ownership of the knowledge because they are empowered to become active participants in the process of making meaning about the subject matter. Chapter 3 will explain in more detail how the MAX teaching framework functions to help students acquire literacy skills while they are actually acquiring your subject matter.

Chapter 3

MAX Teaching with Reading and Writing: A Rationale and Method

The only way to learn how to read is by reading, and the only way to get students to read is by making reading easy.

Frank Smith

Literacy, in the most basic sense of the word, is the ability to read and write. But such an ability entails so much more than simply deciphering combinations of letters on a page or placing words on paper in a certain order. Literacy involves listening, thinking, and speaking in such a way that information and ideas are processed and communicated to the benefit of self and society.

Few would deny the importance of literacy skills in either the academic world or the business world. Yet, schools beyond the early grades often do not see the role they could play in developing and expanding literacy skills in students, and so they relegate that duty to others. Standardized tests such as the National Assessment of Educational Progress (NAEP) provide evidence of this failure to stimulate students to achieve higher levels of literacy skills. According to NAEP tests, a significant portion of middle grades and high school students read at or below the basic reading levels.

Disparity in Literacy Skills

The poor performance in reading scores that many American middle and high school students consistently earn on state and national tests results not from inadequate test preparation but from a lack of basic literacy skills that in other times and circumstances might have been learned at home. It is no surprise that schools situated in upper middle class neighborhoods consistently score higher than those in poorer areas, whether rural or urban. The fact of the matter is that children who come from homes in which literacy (the ability to read, write, speak, listen, and think well) is valued and practiced are the ones who consistently score higher on standardized tests. These are children who come from homes in which books are commonplace, magazines are found on the coffee table, and a newspaper lies on the driveway in the morning. They see their parents using literacy to learn, communicate, and conduct business. To such children, literacy skills tend to come easily, and thus they score highly on standardized tests. On the other hand, children from homes that have little print matter available and in which the TV and/or siblings are raising the children (often because financial circumstances require the parents, or a single parent, to be away much of the time working two jobs) tend to score lower on the same tests. Schools can make up for this disparity, but to do so, they will have to rethink how they teach children.

What Do Reading Tests Measure?

We must not be too quick to criticize elementary schools for the job they are doing. Though schools vary in their performance, early grades educators are generally doing a good job of teaching students to decode print through the use of phonics and other methods. At grade four, United States students lead the world in the ability to read (learn). It is by eighth and twelfth grades that a negative disparity is found between the scores of American students and those of other industrialized countries.

Tests conducted by the Department of Education's National Assessment of Educational Progress show that more than 60 percent of high school seniors in the United States score at or below the basic level of reading (as compared to the proficient and advanced levels). A scan of NAEP's own literature points out that what is being measured in their tests is the ability of students to perform higher order thinking while they read. The manual that NAEP publishes with their report every two years suggests that when grade level materials are used, students reading at the "basic" reading level should be able to "demonstrate an overall understanding and make some interpretations of the text." Students reading at the "proficient" level should be able to "show an overall understanding of the text which includes inferential as well as literal information." And students reading at the "advanced" level should be able to "describe more abstract themes and ideas." In addition, students reading at the advanced level should be able to "analyze [and] extend the information from the text by relating to their own experiences and to the world." (National Center for Educational Statistics, 2003).

In other words, what the NAEP is measuring is the ability of students to perform higher order thinking while learning. The question is, Are we teaching students how to think? Are we creating the conditions in our classrooms in which students are routinely enabled to analyze, apply, synthesize, and evaluate what they read?

How Schools Can Help Students Acquire Literacy Skills

What can schools do to help middle and high school students improve their achievement in learning? The systematic use of reading and writing to help students learn their subject matter is one answer. Students who are placed in an environment in which they are allowed to pursue learning through the means of reading, writing, discussing in cooperative groups, and thus manipulating ideas to construct meaning are finding that learning does not have to be difficult or boring. Rather, it can be fluid and engaging — even *exciting*. What students in such an environment learn is that, despite their background or home environment, they can succeed as learners. A collateral benefit is that, while students in content area classes read, write, and discuss in order to learn content, they actually improve the thinking skills directly related to higher performance in reading and writing.

What About Students Who Are Reading Below Grade Level?

Reading involves construction of meaning. Modern views of reading suggest that the reader, using the "set of tracks" left by the author and relating it to the reader's prior knowledge, thereby constructs a message. The good news is that students who are reading below grade level, and who do not at a given time have the skills to read a piece of text independently, can read text considerably beyond their diagnosed reading grade level when they have the support of competent peers and/or a facilitating teacher. Students practicing learning through reading in this way can in fact read text that is as much as four years above their diagnosed reading levels (Dixon-Krauss, 1996). The key is having well prepared teachers — teachers who know strategies to help students (a) interpretively process text and (b) work cooperatively to manipulate the ideas and themes of the course,

Students who have previously been frustrated by their lack of literacy skills find that they are able to develop appropriate skills and strategies that can make all the difference. The mediated literacy instruction, which employs cooperative learning, helps such students gain the ability to perform literacy skills autonomously. Stated another way — There is only one way to learn literacy skills, and that is by practicing them…and there is only one way to get students to practice literacy skills, and that is to make it easy for them to do so. That is what **MAX Teaching** is all about.

How MAX Teaching Works

MAX is an acronym that stands for the three steps of a teaching framework that any teacher can use. The acronym stands for **M**otivation, **A**cquisition, and **EX**tension. It's a way to help all students better learn their subject matter and improve their literacy skills. The essential goal of teachers who use the **MAX** teaching framework (See Figure 3-1.) is to level the playing field by raising the bar for all students. This involves creating a classroom environment that provides instruction in building skills to enable improved performance, while at the same time engaging all students in active learning from textbooks and other forms of textual matter.

<u>**M**otivation</u>: (the first step)

Much of modern research into motivation of students involves the study of two simultaneous and often competing drives within the learner – striving for success and avoidance of failure (Marzano, 2003). Everything that the teacher does in the pre-reading phase of the three-step framework of instruction is based on the awareness of these two drives.

Too often, when students receive assignments that they must read, they see the assignment as something to be avoided. Such assignments often seem like busy work that do not hold much meaning for the students. Often, when reading to find answers to questions on worksheets or study guides, or questions at the end of the chapter, students are not motivated to thoughtfully read as you are doing right now. They see such reading as an obstacle to their happiness – something to get out of the way so that they can do what they would really rather do. *The goal of a teacher who uses **MAX Teaching** is to create a situation in which the **reading becomes the solution** to a problem rather than have the reading be the problem.*

Each class begins with activities designed to motivate students to become engaged in the learning of content, even if it is content that is difficult or might not otherwise interest them. This first step is accomplished through the systematic use of both individual and cooperative activities that help the teacher…

- find out what the students already know about the topic to be studied,
- assist students in connecting to and seeing the relevance of subject matter,
- provide for increased conceptual understanding for all students,
- introduce and model a literacy-related skill that the students will use to probe text and gather information for development of new understandings, and
- help students establish concrete purposes for actively probing the text.

It is through carefully guided implementation of all of these components that students who otherwise might not have taken an interest in the learning experience are guided to feel as though they will have success in the reading, to become curious about subject matter, and to form a concrete plan for finding and gathering new information. In other words, the teacher is *facilitating* the reading process. The term "facilitate" means "to make easy."

Figure 3-1

The Three Phases of MAX Teaching

Motivation		**A**cquisition		**e**X**tension**	
Helping students strive for success	Reducing anxiety over possible failure	Threat-free opportunity to interact with text	Individual practice in a learning skill	Higher order thinking	Repetition of important concepts and vocabulary
<ul><li>Writing to think and commit to ideas</li><li>Cooperative discussion to<ul><li>Determine prior knowledge</li><li>Build prior knowledge</li></ul></li><li>Focusing on a learning skill</li><li>Setting concrete purpose for reading</li></ul>		<ul><li>Silent purposeful reading</li><li>Writing to gather information for further discussion</li><li>Individual practice in the learning skill</li><li>Individual manipulation of concepts and vocabulary</li></ul>		<ul><li>Cooperative discussion and/or debate to collectively construct meaning</li><li>Low-threat immediate feedback</li><li>Individual and group manipulation of vocabulary & concepts</li><li>Writing to reorganize information</li><li>Analysis, synthesis, application, evaluation of reading material</li><li>Reflection on use of the learning skill</li></ul>	

Acquisition: (the second step)

Once students have clear purposes for learning, the teacher facilitates guided practice in the learning skill introduced in the **M**otivation stage of the lesson. (The exact skill to be practiced varies, depending on the needs of the students, the structure and/or difficulty of the text, or on other variables.) In the **A**cquisition phase of the lesson, each student

- silently reads to interpret and gather information in writing for later discussion,
- actively probes text for acquisition of new content, and
- works toward acquisition of expertise in the practiced literacy skill.

Typically, this part of the class involves silent reading by students as they each gather information to be brought to small-group and whole-class discussion after the reading. In some cases, where student reading abilities are uniformly well below the level of the text, the teacher might read all or a part of the text aloud to the class while students read along silently. However, as early in the school year as possible, students should be allowed to practice mature silent reading to gather information through their own interpretations.

Frequent systematic guided practice in literacy related skills allows students to *acquire* them without even being aware that they are doing so. Just as a person acquires fluency in a language through the immersion process by living for some time in a place where the language is spoken, students acquire complex literacy-related skills. Acquisition is different than learning — most people who ever tried to "learn" a second language through years of course work cannot speak it. Yet people who were given the opportunity to spend lengthy periods in foreign lands often *acquire* the language without formal training. It is this less observable yet profound form of development that is occurring in a content literacy classroom through immersion in reading, writing, speaking, listening, and thinking. (The concept of acquisition is explained in much greater detail in Chapter 5.)

e**X**tension: (the third step)

The final phase of the lesson framework involves e**X**tension beyond the text. This takes place through various activities that might include debate, discussion, writing, reorganizing, or otherwise manipulating the ideas that were confronted in the reading. Students meet in small groups and as a whole class to construct meaning from the text. The teacher, in this phase of the lesson, acts as a facilitator for the higher order thinking that will allow students to (a) synthesize information, connecting new facts and ideas with what they already knew before the lesson; (b) analyze the knowledge newly gained; and (c) think about how to apply what they have learned in real-world circumstances, or even to make an evaluation of the author's argument or underlying intent. It is through such higher order thinking that students develop more complete understandings about new content. It is also through such practice in higher order thinking that students develop the skills and abilities to perform these tasks on their own as independent life-long learners. (Chapter 6 will expand on this phase of the lesson.)

The principles underlying the **MAX** teaching framework have been well researched over many years. The essential components of the use of cooperative learning throughout the first and last phases of the lesson, along with the systematic introduction of skills in which students are given guided practice in the use of language as a tool for thinking, combine to help all students learn how to become effective learners and thinkers. In addition, the **MAX** teaching framework provides a way for upper grade teachers to help compensate for the inadequate language skills development that too many children exhibit.

How Frequently Should Teachers Use Max?

All effective teachers use some form of the three steps that comprise **MAX**. At the beginning of class, most teachers use some form of an "anticipatory set" to get students thinking about the subject matter. The new information is often then "presented" in some format such as a lecture, video, teacher-led discussion, or some other way of communicating information. The presentation of new information is usually followed by some form of check, such as a worksheet or quiz.

Thus, the paradigm shift in using **MAX** as a framework of instruction is easy for most teachers who are, themselves, readers (Powell-Brown, 2004) since, with **MAX**, they now become facilitators of their students' active learning through the use of reading, writing, speaking, listening, and thinking in the middle and final phases of class. The teacher acts as a "master learner" among "apprentice learners" in a classroom wherein *the focus is on acquisition of knowledge and skills through guided practice in using literacy skills to process new subject matter.*

Using literacy skills to process new understandings can easily become the central focus of a classroom and can be used as a way to learn any new information. The variety of tested strategies available to teachers is enormous. Researched and proven strategies abound. Thus, practicing literacy skills to learn should not be a once-a-week or once-a-month activity. It can become the routine of a classroom in which students are engaged in making personal meaning from text and discussion every day.

Which Teachers Should Teach This Way?

Teachers who use the **MAX** teaching framework do not need to be reading specialists. Academic and vocational teachers from the elementary grades through high school only need to recognize that by using the concrete tools of text and student writing, along with teacher modeling and cooperative learning, they can help their students routinely achieve higher order thinking about their subject matter. Staff development in using these strategies is accomplished through hands-on demonstration and modeling. Any teacher can use these techniques. After participating in staff development in using reading and writing to learn, most teachers are immediately able to employ a variety of reading/writing strategies in their classrooms. Recent research has demonstrated that students can improve their reading levels by two or more years over a six month time period when exposed to learning through these strategies (Greenleaf, Schoenbach, Cziko, & Mueller, 2001). Which teachers would *not* want to teach this way?

All Teachers Can Help Students Better Understand Subject Matter while Improving Students' Reading Skills

The first thing any teacher needs to know is that any content area teacher can be successful at helping students learn subject matter while practicing important reading/thinking skills. However, it may require some change on the part of some teachers from what has been considered the "traditional" method of "teaching by telling." In a classroom that successfully engages students in thoughtful processing of language, several important characteristics are present:

- Reading is taught by engaging students in higher level thinking processes about text.
- The teacher acts as a master learner among apprentice learners.
- Students of varying ability levels help each other think and learn.
- Students actively construct meaning from text and other materials.
- Each class is a problem-solving experience leading to successful comprehension and application of subject matter learned.
- A systematic framework of instruction makes it easy for teachers to accomplish each of the above five characteristics.

What the data show is that this type of classroom is all too rare, even for students considered as college preparatory in nature. Most students find their classes boring and lacking any challenge.

Using Reading to Develop Higher Order Thinking Skills in High Schools

The message is clear. Real reading is thinking, and teachers need to develop higher order thinking skills in all students. Higher order thinking skills are generally characterized by abilities to create, make decisions, solve problems, visualize, reason, analyze, and interpret new information. Characteristics of critical thinkers are perseverance, flexibility, awareness of reading and learning strategies, transfer of knowledge, problem orientation, open mindedness, use of quality standards, and independence, a list that could well describe what employers in the 21st century generally are seeking in employees. The problem is that it is not possible to "teach" critical thinking. On the other hand, "acquisition" of the ability to think can be fostered through the creation of an environment in which higher order thinking can occur.

Teaching strategies that can incorporate active learning and higher order thinking have emerged from recent research on how people learn and how they solve problems. Teachers cannot *tell* students about these skills. Rather, they need to plan learning as an active process in which learners construct knowledge as a result of interaction with the physical and social environment. Learning is moving from basic skills and pure facts to linking new information with prior knowledge; from relying on a single source of authority to recognizing multiple sources of knowledge; from novice-like to expert-like problem solving. The teacher's role, then, is to act as a facilitator, helping to develop strategic learners rather than as a teacher of students. Teachers need to set up classes in which they

- help students call upon their prior knowledge to build on what they already know,
- model the strategies needed to process information and solve problems,
- allow students to acquire skills through guided practice in information processing and problem solving,
- facilitate students in extending beyond the learning experience through analysis, application, synthesis, and evaluation of what they have learned.

Any subject area class is the ideal place for this pedagogy. What is perhaps new in this scenario is that *reading* to learn new information becomes central to the lesson. The teacher can model the relationship to prior knowledge by helping students think about what they know about a topic before reading the textbook (or other printed matter) and organize that knowledge to help set a purpose to seek new information. The teacher can then model and provide guided practice in strategies used to process new knowledge from the text, followed by discussion, debate, and reorganization, and, ultimately allow students to perform guided practice in these tasks on their own. The final eXtension of the newly acquired knowledge takes place in synthesis, or evaluation, or application of the learning in the garage, computer lab, welding area, etc. Even though many teachers are not avid readers, virtually all of them have used reading within their own field of endeavor, and can readily model this behavior.

Figure 3-2

Combining the Three Phases of MAX with Cooperative Learning and the Skill Acquisition Model

	MAX	**SAM**	**CL**
Before Reading	**M**otivation Reducing Anxiety and Improving the Probability of Success in Reading	Introduction and Modeling of the Skill	Written Commitment & Small-Group Discussion
During Reading	**A**cquisition Individual Silent Reading for Personal Interpretation	Guided Practice in the Learning Skill	Individual Gathering of Data for Discussion
After Reading	e**X**tension Cooperative Construction of Meaning through Discussion, Writing, etc.	Reflection on How the Skill Worked	Attempt to Achieve Group Consensus

Cooperative Learning and Raising Expectations

If schools are going to raise expectations for students that have traditionally been assigned to basic courses and lower tracks, they are going to have to recognize that assigning students to basic level courses ought to be replaced with a somewhat more heterogeneous grouping of students in classrooms. Cooperative learning is where small groups of students learn the same subject matter by working together to solve a problem. In the literacy-based classroom, the problem to be solved is usually interpretation of some form of textual matter. The teacher acts as a facilitator in this process rather than as a dispenser of knowledge. Heterogeneous, or mixed, grouping of students according to their reading abilities helps all students achieve better.

Students of varying ability levels benefit from each others' insights, perceptions, and even misperceptions. In effect, each student receives peer tutoring from others in the group. High achievers and low achievers alike benefit from the process of helping each other come to some understanding regarding interpretation of the text. It is a well-known phenomenon that paraphrasing and/or arguing about subject matter leads to deeper understanding and greater retention. Less able students contribute as much as high achievers because their interpretations are treated as no less important than those of others. Thus, when facilitated properly by the teacher, all members of a heterogeneous cooperative group benefit from the effort to cooperatively make sense of text. Three essential steps (Forget, Morgan, and Antinarella, 1996) must be incorporated for real cooperative learning to occur:

- Individual writing on the part of each student before entering group discussion,
- Small group discussion in an effort to come to consensus as to what the text means,
- Large group, whole class discussion, with the teacher acting as mediator/arbitrator.

By having each student committed ahead of time in writing, each student has a personal stake in the discussion even before entering the group. This prevents the "smarter" person from doing all the work while the others loaf. Once students have written what they believe on paper, they tend to want to defend it in the group's discussion. The key word here is *commitment*. The effort to reach agreement among students with differing prior knowledge assures that all students, regardless of their ability levels contribute to discussion. (In many cases, students with poor literacy skills are nevertheless good thinkers, and they will contribute to group thought process once the discussion starts if they were committed beforehand.) By always entering the group discussion with some sense of commitment in writing, all students are more prone to participate.

Small group discussion is best accomplished by getting groups to try to come to a *consensus*, the key term for the second step of the process. At this stage of the process, students are helping one another construct meaning from the text. In attempting to come to consensus, as opposed to "majority rules," all students are more prone to engage in argument, especially if the teacher has modeled the process and encourages them to do so. Small group discussion becomes the sounding-board for students to try out their thinking processes in an environment that is less risky than whole-class discussion, an environment often stifling to adolescent learners. Thus, all students hear each other out in an effort to agree on some meaning. (What is really happening in the effort of a small group to come to consensus is one-on-one reading instruction — with no reading specialist in the classroom! By attempting to achieve consensus, students help each other in the fundamental process of reading – construction of meaning.)

The final step involves whole-class discussion, wherein the entire class now attempts to reach a consensus. The key term at this point is *mediation/arbitration*, and this refers to the role the teacher plays. For cooperative learning to come to its fruition, the teacher must act as a facilitator, allowing students to argue against one another, using the text to provide evidence of their small group interpretations. Here, the teacher pits one group against the other in attempting to act only as an impartial judge in helping students construct a class consensus on what the text means. The teacher's job is to moderate the discussion and to see that students are able to refer to the text to support their inferences.

The importance of student-owned discussion cannot be overemphasized here. When students hear the teacher taking over the discussion, their thinking shuts down. When they are engaged in attempting to state a case or hear the case made by other students in the classroom, they tend to be very engaged because they have a personal stake in the discussion.

How, then, can the teacher prevent the entire class from coming to some agreement about something that is not true? The answer to this lies in the role of the teacher as a part-time guide in small-group discussions that take place before the full class meets to discuss a topic. The teacher has all the opportunity to plant seeds by listening to small groups discussing the subject matter and suggesting at that time where the students might find relevant information in the text. It is only necessary to have one group with a clear understanding for the subsequent full-class discussion to be turned in the right direction. The big difference between this setting and the traditional classroom is who is doing the discussing and interpreting. Students who are engaged are students who are learning.

Thus, students have become active learners, using interpretive reading to make sense of subject matter text. The teacher has acted as a facilitator rather than as a teller of information. When students are grouped heterogeneously, and teachers employ the three steps of commitment, consensus, and mediation/arbitration in a content area reading environment, students tend to learn the subject matter better than in a teacher-centered classroom where they have little stake in the conversation and are more concerned with "being right." Each class becomes a problem-solving experience where students actively participate in constructing meaning from text.

Recent research also leads to a caution when using cooperative learning. Students need to work together to solve a problem, but each student must be held individually accountable for the learning (Stahl, 1992). Each student, in other words, must be able to pass a test, write about, or orally defend his or her own learning. (Each lesson in Part II of this book includes the three components of cooperative learning that are described here.)

Can We Expect the Average to Below-Average Student to Read 30 Books a Year?

Much of the literature from *High Schools That Work,* a whole-school reform effort that is a part of the Southern Regional Education Board, has stated that high school teachers ought to insist that high school students read the equivalent of 30 books each year. Evidence shows that students who do so achieve at the highest levels on the NAEP reading tests. The problem is, for many students, getting them to read *at all* is difficult. If they have not had success in reading or in school, they are not likely to want to pick up book number one, let alone the other 29. However, through a concerted effort by teachers who provide a "literacy apprenticeship" (Kiewra, 1993; Forget and Morgan, 1997; Greenleaf, et al., 2001) in their classrooms, many students are achieving just that.

When a teacher can hold up the science (or social studies, mathematics, welding, health, etc.) book at the end of the school year, and say to students, "You students ought to realize that, in this classroom this year, you have read this entire textbook of more than 900 pages!" that teacher is reminding students of their success in having read the equivalent of several smaller books. Most of the reading may have been done in the classroom, but a great deal of evidence is pointing to the fact that this sort of "literacy club" (Smith, 1988) or "literacy apprenticeship" or "embedded curriculum" has taken students of widely varied ability levels and shown them through experience that they can succeed at complex and difficult literacy tasks. Imagine if several teachers, including the language arts teacher, were to be affecting the same students through their own courses to do a similar quantity of reading. The goal of the *equivalent* of 30 books *is* possible—with the assistance of knowledgeable teachers.

It is hoped that Part II of this book will allow teachers to have enough confidence in their abilities to practice student-centered literacy-based teaching in their own classrooms, and that through use of the lesson plans that are in Part II they will acquire the skills and knowledge that will lead to a literacy apprenticeship for all their students. The results will be greater student retention of subject matter and acquisition of life-long learning skills — important goals desired by educational leaders in all 50 states and around the world. Chapters 4, 5, and 6 will now address in greater detail what **MAX Teaching** is all about.

Chapter 4

Motivation

…There is no such thing as a 'grade reading level'; a young person's 'reading level' and attention span will rise and fall according to his degree of interest.
Richard Peck

Teachers of students in grades four through twelve often tell me that they have many "non-readers" in their classes. I respond to them by suggesting that there are probably few, if any, "non-readers" in their classes; however, there are probably many low-performing readers. Many of these low-performing readers read below grade level — some as much as four or more years below the level of the text that is assigned to them. Over sixty percent of readers measured in grades eight and twelve are reading at or below the "basic" level, according to the National Assessment of Educational Progress (National Center for Educational Statistics, 2003).

Motivating Low-Performing Readers

The vast majority of students beyond the third grade avoid reading school-related text whenever they can do so. This is often true even for those "honor" students who excel in school. There are two basic reasons why students avoid reading. The first is that they get very little practice at real reading for learning in content area textbooks. (Most of the "reading" they are asked to do is really hunting for answers to fill in spaces on worksheets or to answer end-of-chapter comprehension questions.) The second is that, when they do get the opportunity to read, they often are not motivated to read for learning. These two problems will be discussed in this chapter, along with a prescription for both motivating and getting students ready to experience success in reading in a mature way in order to learn new subject matter.

What you will see in this chapter is that the *MAX Teaching* process, and especially what the teacher does in the *Motivation* stage of the class, has everything to do with whether students will be willing to read, how they actually go about reading during the *Acquisition* phase of the lesson, and how they E*X*tend beyond the text after they have finished the reading. Before the reading is assigned, the teacher has the opportunity to systematically improve the probability that success will occur for all students. During and after the reading, the teacher continues to provide the support that lets each student know that s/he is a successful reader – a process that motivates students to persist at difficult work. Correct use of the *MAX Teaching* framework combines with the skill acquisition model and appropriate use of cooperative learning to help students want to attempt difficult tasks and to persist at the tasks once begun.

Marzano (2003) addresses five lines of research and theory that converge to provide a fairly consistent picture of the nature of motivation. They are (1) drive theory, (2) attribution theory, (3) self-worth theory, (4) emotions, and (5) self-system. The vast majority of studies reported on motivation and achievement show significant gains in achievement for students who are motivated to learn (Marzano, 2003). This chapter will address these five lines of research and attempt to explain how what happens in the *MAX Teaching* classroom addresses what research and theory say about motivation.

Drive theory refers to the simultaneous and often competing drives in all humans — striving for success and avoidance of failure (Marzano, 2003). Both of these drives lead to emotional responses that manifest themselves in a variety of ways. Students whose focus is on striving for success derive emotional rewards from eagerly taking on new and challenging tasks.

On the other hand, students whose focus is on avoidance of failure are often behaving in response to a lifetime of failures in the task. Thus, confronted with a difficult or apparently uninteresting reading, and having had little or no success in the past with such readings, a student might choose to act out by refusing to read. A student such as this might place his head upon the desk in an exhibition of apparent fatigue. Sometimes, she might act up as the class clown. These are avoidance behaviors, and they take various forms.

Not unrelated to drive theory is **attribution theory** — student perception of the causes of success or failure and the concomitant amount of effort that results from this perception. Students who see their own efforts as the reason for success or failure are more likely to persist in efforts to succeed at a difficult task. Students who perceive the causes of success and failure as being external to their own effort are more likely to exhibit avoidance behavior when confronted with challenge.

Self-worth theory refers to the role played by one's sense of acceptance in a peer culture. "If the criterion for self-acceptance in the classroom is high academic accomplishment relative to others, then by definition, only a few high-performing students can obtain a sense of self-worth."(p. 147). Teachers who are aware of this phenomenon make sure that other criteria for success are part of each learning opportunity in the classroom.

Self-system involves a network of interrelated goals or desires that help one to decide whether to engage in a new task. In a sense, self-system combines the factors of drive, attribution, and self-worth theories to form in the student a sense of self-definition that corresponds to a hierarchy of needs starting from basic survival needs and progressing to self-actualization (Marzano, 2003). Consider Csikszentmihalyi's (1990) four factors critical to successful completion of self-actualizing experiences:

1. the freedom to set clear goals that are highly meaningful to the individual,
2. having the resources to carry out the goals and becoming immersed in the act of trying to accomplish them,
3. paying attention to what is happening and making changes when necessary, and
4. enjoying immediate short-term successes while keeping an eye on the ultimate goal (Marzano, p. 148).

As will be seen, MAX Teaching, done properly, permits each of these four factors to become routine in the classroom.

The important role played by **emotion** will be discussed below in the section on neuropsychology and affect. Establishing a brain-compatible learning environment is crucial to motivating students to read. (Indeed, the two words motivate and emotion have the same Latin root.) Teachers who are aware of how the brain works with regard to emotions and learning can take advantage of this knowledge to motivate students to read.

The focus in this chapter is on post-primary-grade readers who are not motivated to read. It will attempt to explain why they avoid reading, and list several steps that content area teachers can use in the motivation phase of the class to help students see that they can succeed in reading "boring, difficult text" in order to learn new subject matter. It is important to note here that the form of reading that is being discussed in this chapter, as well as throughout this book, is a mature form of reading that involves engaging and thoughtful processing of text for the purposes of making meaning and manipulating ideas — as *you* are doing right now. (Answering questions on worksheets or questions at the end of the chapter do not lead to the type of reading discussed herein.)

In order to see how *Motivation* works, I will first explain two cycles of failure that often prevent real reading for learning from occurring. One is the cycle of reading failure experienced by low-performing middle and secondary level readers, and the other is the cycle of pedagogical failure that teachers often experience by simply not knowing what they could do to motivate students to read. Then I will describe what teachers can do in the before-reading stage of the lesson to get students to want to read, and what teachers can do during and after the reading to maintain the motivation of students in learning from text.

The Nature of Text — Boring, Difficult , but Valuable

When I first work with students in content area classrooms, I frequently ask them two related questions at the beginning of the class. The first is, "By a show of hands, how many of you love to read this textbook?" Their hands remain on their desks and they look at me as if I were crazy. The response is always the same and virtually unanimous — students agree that textbooks are not enjoyable to read. My follow-up question also receives agreement by the students, this time with all hands being raised: "How many of you think that textbooks like this are dry, boring, and filled with information that is hard to connect with, and therefore, hard to remember for tests?"

There is a reason for these responses — students are both honest and accurate. They also are appreciative of honesty on the part of the teacher when I agree with them. I always take the opportunity to admit that textbooks are not the most interesting things in the world. I then go into a reflection on how textbook materials and other text are used in colleges and in the work force of the 21st century. I do this to help them understand that there will be much more text (of various types) in their futures if they are to achieve life-long success.

I also explain to them that much of the reading they do beyond middle and high school years will be independent reading through which they will be responsible for learning subject matter that will *not* be covered in a classroom — that they will be required to learn the subject matter on their own and be responsible for being able to apply the knowledge in intelligent and useful ways if they want to succeed. Then I explain that there exist many strategies that can be employed by any reader to make reading easier and more interesting, even though it might involve reading a text that is "dry, boring, and filled with information that is hard to connect with." After this brief introduction, I begin the lesson that will allow them to experience just such a strategy. What I have done in this brief classroom conversation is one of several elements of motivation that help students overcome their avoidance of reading content area text.

Low Performing Middle and Secondary Level Readers and the Cycle of Failure

Low performing readers at the upper elementary and secondary levels are often caught in a cycle of failure that has been a part of their academic lives since they left the primary grades (Collins, 1996). Having been identified as "remedial" readers, they have often been pulled out of the content area classroom for skill-development programs that teach anything but real reading. The focus of many of these programs is on decoding of print to gain only literal interpretation by reading aloud or answering dull worksheet questions.

Once students are past the third grade, the reading picture goes from bad to worse for many students. If they have not acquired strong literacy skills by then, and they have little or no support at home, they are in trouble.

No longer are they in classrooms where the teacher is one who has been prepared as a reading instructor. Now they face science teachers, mathematics teachers, and social studies teachers, etc. Few, if any of these teachers view their roles as that of helping students to perform literacy skills. Content area teachers tend to see their jobs as being presenters of subject matter.

One result is that, as each new school year begins, these students are once more identified as lacking literacy skills. So they are again assigned to pull-out programs, and they fall further and further behind peers. This results in the "Matthew Effect" wherein "the rich get richer, and the poor get poorer" (Stanovich, 1986). Another result is that most low-performing readers do not develop a sense of reading as a language operation. Each and every low-performing reader has the ability to use language and uses it to communicate daily with family and friends. *But few low-performing secondary readers see the written word as a language operation.* They do not hear a voice on the page. They do not synthesize with what they already knew before reading the text. They do not question. In short, they do not do what they routinely do in their daily lives (and what is measured on state and national tests) — they do not *think* while they read!

Low-performing middle and secondary readers view text as a source of "the right answer" to satisfy the teacher. This view is reinforced by much of what passes as classroom activity focused on worksheets or end-of-chapter comprehension questions. It becomes obvious upon observing students assigned such tasks in the classroom. Most students will start in the middle of the reading or at the end, skimming back and forth through the text on a brief hunting expedition to find answers. Rarely, if ever, do they actually think about the subject matter or develop a sense of the logical presentation as the author has organized it.

What do many teachers do when they realize that their students are not reading for homework or class work? They often resort to "round robin" or "popcorn" reading — wherein students read new subject matter material aloud in the classroom — exactly the opposite of what they should be doing! The focus in such activities is almost exclusively on decoding the print rather than comprehending (Vacca, 2002). With language comes thought; with oral reading, what often comes is simply decoding of sounds (Opitz & Rasinski, 1998; Worthy, & Broaddus, 2002).

Thus, low performing readers have had negative experiences with reading and generally view reading as a process of getting the word right rather than an act of making sense of the material. They do not hear a voice on the page; they do not know they can skip words as long as they are maintaining meaning; they do not know that they must do different things with different kinds of materials (Collins, 1996). Most importantly, they are not receiving the help they need at this important juncture in their lives as readers.

The result is that most of these students avoid reading whenever possible. They are often embarrassed that, after reading, they cannot do more than share with the teacher a literal interpretation of what was read. (Unfortunately, a literal interpretation is often all that is asked for by the teacher.) When asked to think critically about subject matter, students are often confused. (How can a person think critically about something that was never understood to begin with?) So, students begin to develop avoidance behavior which often results in either acting out in class or the passive-aggressive behavior of not participating at all in classroom activities. The older they are in age, the more serious this behavior becomes. Seeing themselves as failures in reading, not having experienced support at home, and failing to perceive help coming in the classroom, they begin to see themselves as "non-readers." Often, they appear non-caring, lethargic, and non-compliant.

The Cycle of Pedagogical Failure

Teachers actually *contribute* to the above-mentioned student cycle of reading failure. Many teachers, seeing that students are not reading homework assignments, and seeing that students have trouble discussing what they were supposed to have read, begin to have low expectations for students as readers. This might lead to teachers refraining from assigning reading, and, instead, lecturing or "giving notes" to students. Or, recalling the way things were done in their own schooling, many teachers have students do dull worksheets provided by textbook publishers requiring little more than decoding skills, or they have students do round-robin or "popcorn reading" out loud in the classroom. Thus, students who have been identified as low-performing readers, as well as those who read closer to grade level, get a steady diet of reading at only the lowest level of literal decoding. When asked to discuss what they have read, or to perform higher order thinking over the subject matter, they often disappoint themselves and their teachers. So teachers keep it simple, and the pedagogical cycle of failure continues.

Breaking the Cycle of Failure

Middle level and secondary teachers can help the low achieving or low performing student break the cycle of failure. To do so, teachers must provide the opportunities in the classroom for students to revalue themselves as readers/thinkers. Students must acquire strategies that will result in real comprehension. They need to develop confidence in themselves as readers of complex and difficult materials. When students have been caught in the cycle of failure for most, if not all, years of their educational experience, they need the support of knowledgeable teachers who can help them develop strategies for processing text. What they need is instruction in the same strategies their teachers know and use when dealing with text (Collins, 1996).

The most important first step is helping students develop self-confidence as readers by helping them acquire the strategies they need to succeed in reading difficult text. For such acquisition to occur it is necessary to motivate them to read — even when the reading is not the most interesting reading.

Ammann and Mittelsteadt (1987) demonstrated that the cycle of failure could be broken through the use of relevant materials such as newspapers to motivate students to learn strategies for reading. The students in their research were helped to revalue themselves as readers. Secondary reading teachers should heed the results of this research.

On the other hand, content area teachers do not always have the luxury of using highly interesting outside materials in the teaching of their curricula. They must adhere to a fairly structured coverage of a basic core of content that often corresponds closely to the content of their textbook. Many bend over backwards to find other, more interesting materials to help their students connect to the content, but few are aware that they could, if prepared to do so, actually use their own textbooks to help students become strategic readers while learning the course content. The question, then, is how to motivate students to read "dry, boring, difficult text." The answer to that is the key to **MAX** Teaching and the key to ending the cycle of failure. It all begins in the Motivation phase of the lesson.

The Motivation Phase of the Lesson

Now let's look at the **M**otivation phase of the lesson to see how **MAX** Teaching actually addresses each of the five lines of research on motivation (Marzano, 2003). The first of three steps in **MAX** Teaching is motivating students to read. Let's look at what happens during this critically important phase of the class to see how, if properly done, the teacher helps students beyond any fears of possibly failing at the reading task, and, at the same time, establishes an affective environment that supports active participation.

To recall what was stated in chapter 3, in the motivation stage of the lesson, the teacher uses writing, discussion, and/or cooperative learning to

- find out what the students already know about the topic to be studied,
- assist students in connecting to and seeing the relevance of subject matter,
- provide for increased conceptual understanding for all students,
- introduce and model a literacy-related skill that the students will use to probe text and gather information for development of new understandings, and
- help students establish concrete purposes for actively probing the text.

Let us look at each of these ideas to see how they actually address student motivation to take on the difficult and complex task of reading for learning. Then, we will look at how the teacher can establish an appropriate emotional environment in which a variety of students can excel at constructing meaning from the printed word – reading.

Building Bridges to New Knowledge

A teacher who is using the MAX Teaching framework of instruction never starts a class without first finding out what students already know about what they are about to learn. In fact, the teacher most often has students recall this knowledge in some form of writing. Students might place a set of check marks on an anticipation guide to make predictions. They might do a three or four minute long "focused free write." Or students might just list several things that they know (or don't know) about the subject matter in the first step of a "PreP" activity (Langer, 1981). Whatever the specific activity involved, the teacher uses the concrete task of writing to get students committed to paper so that they can have something to share with others.

Writing is a very important step in the process. Think of the alternative – when a teacher simply asks the class, "What do you know about …?" – which often leads to a discussion between the teacher and one or two students in the class who feel confident in their prior knowledge either because they know they have more than average exposure to the content or because they are just more confident in themselves as successful students. Often students who are not "honor students" have important ideas to contribute to the discussion, but they are timid for various reasons about sharing their ideas. So they don't. Commitment in writing is one way to help average and lower level students beyond their reluctance to participate.

Teacher behavior during the gathering of prior knowledge is important. During this part of the motivation phase of the lesson, the teacher must be accepting of all student responses, finding what is right about each response. Students often have *mis*conceptions or *un*expected responses to share at this stage of the class. These, if treated properly by the teacher, can be as valuable to the learning process as those responses that the teacher expected. Teachers must be open to various interpretations and able to use unexpected responses to steer the discussion in the right direction. I always try to find what *is* correct about a less-than-appropriate response given by a student. It usually does not take a rocket scientist to figure out why a student shares an idea that relates in an inappropriate way to the discussion, but nevertheless can be used to add to the prior knowledge of the entire class (even if by recognition of why it does not relate directly to the topic).

When teachers are adept at using all student prior knowledge, both informed and misinformed, to connect students to the upcoming learning experience, they are motivating students to become active in the learning, a necessity for true comprehension of subject matter. Consider the misconceptions that were widely recognized as truth throughout periods of our history as the human race continually developed a sense of the realities we generally accept today. Such misconceptions as the notion that the sun and the stars rotated about the earth were mere stepping stones on the path to the understandings we have today about the solar system.

Once aware of the prior knowledge individually and collectively held by students, the teacher can begin to build bridges from that to the new knowledge that will come from the reading. Good teachers take prior knowledge and paraphrase it in terms that will relate to the coming learning experience. If done properly, by the end of the Motivation stage of class, students know much of what they are about to find out in the reading!

Building Prior Knowledge through Concept Development

Often, the prior knowledge of students is not adequate by itself to make the connections necessary for comprehension of the new subject matter. In such circumstances, the teacher can do many things to improve the connections for students. Previewing the text is one of the best, and I use it frequently. A systematic preview (Chapter 11) provides an opportunity to peruse the reading for a few minutes before actually reading the text. Most good readers do this routinely when confronting new text, but students often have not been exposed to it or mastered it.

Another way to build prior knowledge is to use video. I find that a five to seven minute long video to provide a visual image can be very helpful in providing background knowledge. A few seconds of a movie such as "The Patriot" can prepare students for a reading on the American Revolution. Three minutes of a volcano erupting on Monserrat in the Caribbean Sea from a National Geographic Explorer episode can help students to be ready to read about volcanoes. A 30-second clip from "The Weather Channel" can show students a moving satellite image of a low pressure system about which they will read in an earth science text. (If a picture is worth a thousand words, then a video must be worth millions.) By using video to prepare students for reading, the teacher is addressing visual modes of learning (Gardner, 1983, 1993) as a tool for enhancing comprehension of the coming reading.

Pre-learning concept checks (Chapter 32) take almost no time, and they can expose students to key vocabulary terms and allow the teacher to find out how much students know about the topic. These tend to help students develop a sense of responsibility for their own learning as well as give them a "heads up" on the central vocabulary terms of the reading even though they have not read it yet.

Mini-lectures help tremendously. Even though I do not advocate teacher lecture as a main source of learning — even most adults do not have the attention span to sit through long lectures — short, four-to-seven-minute mini-lectures, to build background knowledge for students, are well-received and can be just what students need to develop the sense of confidence in themselves to tackle a difficult reading.

There are many other background-building activities in the literature to help students prepare for reading. Some are listed in the teacher's edition of the textbook you use. You may create your own method for doing this important step in reducing the probability in any given student's mind that s/he will fail at the reading task that is to come.

A Focus on Skill Development

Reducing avoidance of failure is one part of the formula for motivation. The simultaneous and competing drive of striving for success is also enhanced during the Motivation phase of the class. By focusing on the Skill Acquisition Model (SAM), the teacher is helping students to recognize that, if they were to apply the skill of the day in other learning experiences, their learning would be easier and more thorough. Whether the skill is one of note taking, paraphrasing, summarizing, graphically representing, or otherwise reorganizing information, the emphasis on a life-long learning skill helps motivate students to want to learn.

Consider the alternative. What is it like for a struggling student to enter a classroom in which many or most of his/her peers are comparatively advanced in their understanding of the subject matter or in their ability to process the subject matter? What must it be like for a struggling learner to be told to accomplish a difficult task and not be shown a way to perform it? Much of the literacy-related work assigned to students in most classrooms fits into this category.

Many teachers, not aware of their abilities to help students develop advanced learning skills, feel that some students are not trying or are just lazy. They fail to realize that students do not all have the abilities to perform literacy-related tasks involving higher-order thinking. This often results in teachers reducing the curriculum to rote tasks involving worksheets or other basic decoding exercises.

Rather than assuming student skills or motivation are lacking, and therefore reducing the learning experience to a low-level exercise, teachers can provide challenging activities while providing the support for all students to be able to succeed at them. Teachers who are effective provide instruction in important learning skills, model the skills for students, and provide students with guided practice in the skills that are helping students develop as life-long learners. At the same time, they are helping students to more deeply learn their subject matter because of the level of processing that is afforded by more meaningful analysis, synthesis, and evaluation of the content.

Creating Concrete Purposes for Reading through Writing

Virtually every one of the strategies in Part II of this book requires students to use writing as a tool for gathering information for the eXtension phase of the class. With anticipation guides, the student makes note of the page, column, and paragraph where supporting information is found. With the Directed Reading-Thinking Activity (Chapter 15), the student writes answers in the "L" column of the "What-I-Know Sheet." Similarly, with the KWL sheet (Ogle, 1986), students record information learned in the "L" column. GIST (Chapter 18) requires students to gather information in the form of perceived main ideas. INSERT (Chapter 21) has students making marginal notes in the text. The only activities in which students do not gather written information while performing silent reading are those in which they are immediately responsible for recalling verbally after the book is closed — activities such as Paired Reading (Chapter 23) or Guided Reading Procedure (Chapter 19).

This is no coincidence. The fact that students know exactly what to do during the silent reading phase of the lesson has more than one benefit. The responsibility of writing reduces the sense of anxiety that students might have about the task of reading. Instead of reading for some abstract idea that might be in the teacher's mind, they are reading to gather information to bring to their group's discussion. Students are aware of the immediate, concrete reasons why they are reading, and they know, with the information that they are gathering, that they are up to the task.

A second benefit of having students gather written information during the reading phase of the class is one of classroom management. While the students are actively engaged in information gathering, the teacher can move about the classroom, looking over the shoulders of students as they are reading. This allows the teacher to see how well students are doing with the reading. It also allows the teacher to help either individual or whole groups of students in clarifying or reframing ideas, depending on what the teacher observes in terms of progress.

Many teachers think of writing as a tool for communicating ideas in paragraphs or essays as a product to be evaluated for a grade. Writing that is done during the silent reading activity in the Acquisition stage of the class is not for product, but rather for process. Students are using writing to prepare for higher order thinking that will result in discussion or further writing in the eXtension phase of the lesson. Thus, assigning, during the Motivation phase, a concrete, but meaningful, writing task related to gathering information during the Acquisition phase, gives way to deeper levels of confirmation during the Acquisition Phase of class instruction.

As you can see, by the time the student opens the text to read, s/he knows a good deal about what is about to be read, knows exactly what s/he is looking for in the text, feels good about how well s/he is doing at the task and in the class, and is aware that s/he is practicing a life skill in literacy that will lead to success in other situations long after the present class is over. This combination of factors is the reason that students exposed to reading through the MAX Teaching framework of instruction actually perform mature silent reading during the Acquisiton stage of the class in preparation for the final EXtension phase.

The Neuropsychology of Motivation: The Affective Domain

Throughout their day, students from kindergarten through high school dwell primarily in the affective domain. The term "affect" refers to a response to a stimulus that causes feelings or emotions. Feelings and emotions are important elements of virtually all that K-12 students do. The words affect, emotion, and feeling are often used interchangeably, but actually should connote slightly different things.

Feelings and emotions are essential elements of knowing and understanding. Only when a person feels strongly about something can s/he truly begin the process of cognition. Think back to a time when a book or text made you feel strong emotion. Can you think of one? Now, reach deep inside and think about why it made you feel that way. You may have remembered the time in "Charlotte's Web" when Charlotte the spider wrote one of her loving messages about Wilbur in an effort to save his life. Or, perhaps you recall a particularly passionate piece of poetry that moved you to tears. Think about why you can remember these things long after you have read them. Now, think about one of the most engaging and moving sections in your current textbook. Is it informational? — yes; is it needed? — yes; but, does it have the power to move students to be passionate about remembering it? — probably not. That is why, as teachers in content areas, we must engage our students' brains and emotions through other means.

Affect comes from the Latin "affectus," meaning to afflict or to touch. Affect could be defined as "a grouping of physical phenomena manifesting under the form of emotions, feelings, or passions, always followed by impressions of pleasure or pain, satisfaction or dissatisfaction, liking or disliking, joy or sorrow." (Cardoso, 2003). Teachers should be aware that what takes place in their classrooms will, in one way or another, create an affective response in students.

The word emotion comes from the Latin "emovere" which means to move or displace. It is used to describe those affective conditions that, due to their intensities, move us to some kind of action (Cardoso, 2003). These can cause physical and behavioral changes in a very short period of time.

Feelings, on the other hand, are affective states of lesser intensity and longer duration than emotions, but that have less influence on immediate behavior than emotions do. Love, fear, and hate are good examples of feelings, while passion, fright, and anger are examples of emotions. Either feeling or emotion may result from the affective context of a situation, and such feelings or emotions can either help or hinder the individual in the learning process. As we shall see, one part of the brain is primarily responsible for affective response, and that response can greatly influence how other parts of the brain function.

The Neurophysiology of Motivation: The Triune Brain

The human brain has evolved into three principle parts (MacLean, 1978), each of which handles different functions. (See Figure 4-1.) The most primitive is the brain stem, often referred to as the "reptilian brain," or the R-complex. This part of the brain is at the top of the spinal cord, and its functions are to deal with only the most basic of needs of life such as heart rate, respiration, or body temperature control. This part of the brain is extremely similar to the brains of reptiles and, thus, is given the name "reptile brain" or R-complex by some neurophysiologists. When important physical needs are present, the brain stem takes charge to see that the need is met.

The old mammalian brain (the limbic system) is a larger and newer portion of the brain located in the middle of the three brain parts, between the brain stem and the neocortex. The limbic system influences feelings and emotions by secreting limbic-system neurotransmitters that allow us to perceive feelings or emotion. The importance of the limbic system to the classroom experience is that it plays a great role in the learning process by determining whether or not the newest portion of the brain, the neocortex, will be able to fully function. Just as the reptilian brain takes over in matters of basic life support, the limbic system can take over from the higher levels of thinking possible in the neocortex if the emotional climate is threatening or stressful.

The neocortex — the newest and largest portion of the brain — deals with thinking abilities such as mathematical and verbal acuity and logical reasoning. It is composed of hundreds of billions of neurons that interact with each other and with the neurons of the other parts of the nervous system. This part of our brain is the most complex, and as a result, the slowest functioning part. The neurological make-up of the neocortex allows for learning to take place through associations that can number in the high trillions! It is the ultimate computer. The primary concern for educators ought to be that it be allowed to function to its fullest potential by eliminating the possibility of "downshifting" caused by the existence of threats. Downshifting is a well known phenomenon in which either the limbic system or the R-complex can "take over" from the neocortex when threat is perceived or important physical needs are not met (Hart, 1983). This reaction can prevent the neocortex from functioning at its fullest potential.

Figure 4-1

The Triune Brain

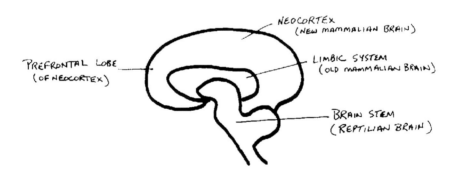

The Triune Brain: The three parts of the brain are shown here.

Sinatra (1986) points out that educators must be aware of the roles played by the R-complex and the limbic system in the learning process as being just as important as the role played by the neocortex. He states that "educators must realize that curriculum content cannot be approached solely by intellectual reasoning. The systems regulating feeling, emotions, and attentiveness are tied to the very learning of information" (p. 143). He further suggests that the teacher's attitude toward the reason for learning information, as well as the teacher's attitude toward the learners themselves, can be just as important in how well something is learned as anything else in the classroom.

The affective environment has everything to do with how well content is learned. Brain subsystems that support learning are activated in classrooms that are "brain compatible." Positive emotions lead to an ability to attend to the learning task, while negative emotions lead to the opposite. On the other hand, these brain subsystems can just as well hinder learning in a classroom that has an affective climate that produces feelings and emotions that are negative.

Let us consider an example: A student stays out in the hall to give a hug to his girlfriend every day, waiting until the last few seconds before rushing into the classroom just as the bell sounds to start class. He often enters right after the bell begins to sound, but before the bell has finished ringing. One day, he is confronted by the teacher who irritably says, "This is the third time this week, young man! I am going to have to assign you a detention." This leads to a confrontation in which the student claims to have been on time since the bell had not finished ringing by the time he entered, the teacher beginning to fill in a detention slip, and finally some inappropriate words whispered under breath, but heard by the teacher. One thing leads to another until the tension is thick enough to be cut with a knife. A simple detention turns into a referral to the office. The defeated student takes his seat, and the teacher begins class.

Downshifting has occurred. No matter what that teacher does in that class, that student (and perhaps many others indirectly affected by the exchange) will not be able to function at peak level in terms of processing complex thought. Any effort to help that student learn to factor trinomial expressions will probably fail simply because of the emotional state brought about by limbic system transmitters that prevent the neocortex from optimal functioning.

Teachers who are aware of the role of emotion in brain functioning can take advantage of that knowledge to create an environment in which the brain is allowed to function at its fullest potential. Teachers who are aware of the importance of the affective domain and its role in learning can create classrooms that facilitate learning. Such classrooms are characterized by important attributes. Slater (2002) lists four classroom characteristics as important for brain-compatible learning: challenge (with support), relevance, novelty, and a positive emotional climate (Slater, 2002). Marzano (2003) suggests feedback, engagement, opportunities to construct and work on long-term projects, and explicit instruction in the dynamics of motivation. Hart (1975) suggests the following as important characteristics of a brain-compatible learning environment:

1. making learning immediately important to students in order for them to make sense of the situation
2. giving students opportunities to talk about what they are learning to allow heightening of brain activity
3. providing a free environment in which students can move around and talk about the projects they are doing
4. allowing students time to build elaborate "programs" of thinking for storage and memory retrieval by the brain
5. limiting threats and pressures, which cause the neocortex to function poorly
6. stressing intuitive learning as much as step-by-step logic to allow creative thinking to occur (cited in Richardson and Morgan, 1994).

Teachers who are aware of brain function in the learning process and who wish to establish a positive affective environment in their classrooms in order to get students to take on the difficult tasks associated with mature silent reading should do the following in their classrooms:

- value all student responses
- use cooperative learning properly

- combine challenge with support
- establish the relevance of the subject matter by connecting it to what students already know
- make the learning concrete and immediately important
- measure success in multiple ways
- model expected behavior
- help students to focus on the big picture while attacking specific information
- be enthusiastic
- call on students by their first name or preferred name
- use a variety of classroom activities in order to have novelty and to apply appropriate strategies to different kinds of text

Motivation in the Acquisition and EXtension Phases of the Lesson

Looking back on the five lines of research on motivation discussed at the beginning of this chapter, we can see how each is addressed by the combination of MAX, SAM, and CL:

- Everything that takes place in the *MAX Teaching* classroom reduces the probability in the mind of the student that she will fail at the task, and indeed is explicitly directed at a life-long skill that will help the student in similar circumstance in the future (drive theory).
- Cooperative learning assures that students do not see their personal successes and failures as separate from and relative to all other students (self-worth theory). They see their efforts as "buffered" in a sense by the cooperation they have had in constructing meaning from the text.
- The opportunities for short-term success abound in the *MAX Teaching* classroom because of the nature of acceptance of responses by the teacher and because of the cooperative nature of the constructivist process modeled by the teacher and performed by groups of students (self-worth theory).
- The systematic practice of a learning framework to internalize a mental "program for learning" allows students to get beyond the day to day survival mentality of many classrooms to arrive at a mindset progressing toward self-actualization (attribution, self-system).
- The establishment of a positive affective environment in the classroom allows for the higher portion of the brain to function at its best due to the absence of threats (emotion).

Each of these theories on motivation is addressed in the other two phases of MAX Teaching as well. Students who learn this way acquire a sense of self confidence and self-worth because they internalize a sense of self-actualization not possible in a classroom in which they are dependent on the teacher for all knowledge. They begin to see that *it is what they themselves do that causes their success or failure in learning*. They begin to see the value of using the silent reading time to their own benefit. After all, the student is very likely to be successful in post-reading activities if s/he has been provided with the opportunity to read the text immediately before discussion occurs in class. (Unlike trying to read brand new subject matter at home for homework, in a **MAX Teaching** classroom, there is really little better to do during the Acquisition phase, since the student is present in class anyway, and has the time provided by the teacher to read.)

In addition, the student is in a low-risk opportunity to work in a personal way to process the text without regard for skill level or technique, or how much specific knowledge is actually being processed. I like to think of the Acquisition phase as the "all alone in a gymnasium with a basketball" phase of the lesson.

Consider a youngster who is not very good at basketball, but hangs around people who love to play, and are good at the game. Reluctant to look the fool on the basketball court, the person might refrain from getting into the game. But, given the chance to have an hour or so alone in the gym with a ball, that person might take the opportunity to try some new moves. S/he would probably take many practice shots with no one there to see the "air balls" when the shooter misses the rim, and no one there to see any falls that might occur in attempting elaborate moves toward the net. (The practicing shooter may not achieve the level desired in the time spent practicing it, but that person will not get any worse.) The next time there is an opportunity to enter the real game, the person who has had the time alone in the gym to improve will surprise the other players with newfound skills. Similarly, the risk of failure at the task of reading is reduced enormously through the opportunity to perform silent reading with concrete purposes — especially if the student is aware that cooperative discussion will occur afterward, in the eXtension phase of the class, to clarify understandings. Chapter 5 will address in much more detail what really happens in the Acquisition phase of the lesson.

In sum, Motivating students to read course-related materials in a mature and thoughtful way can occur in any classroom if the teacher is aware of the reasons why students are reluctant to read, and if the teacher knows how to overcome this reluctance. By applying the three steps of *MAX Teaching*, focusing on the embedding of skills instruction into the lesson through SAM, and incorporating cooperative learning into the process, teachers can take advantage of what we know about how the brain functions in learning and teachers can use that information to create an environment that assures success for all.

Chapter 5

Acquisition of LITERACY SKILLS IN CONTENT area CLASSROOMS

I hear and I forget. I see and I remember. I do and I understand.
        Confucius

The educational system in America expects students to learn, but all too often it does not teach students *how* to learn. This isn't likely to happen in other areas of life. We would never expect someone to play a piano concerto without his or her first learning how to read music, master the scales, and develop the necessary techniques required to perform. We would never expect someone to become a varsity baseball player without first helping that person acquire the skills of hitting, throwing, and catching. Yet schools frequently ask students to learn without helping them to acquire the strategies they need for learning. In most classrooms beyond the third grade, the only focus is on teaching the *content* of a subject area. This content-centered teaching works satisfactorily for those students I am calling autonomous learners (students who already know how to learn), but it does not work well for restricted learners (those students who lack the requisite skills for learning).

Autonomous vs. Restricted Learners

I am not using the terms *autonomous* and *restrictive* in a pejorative way, nor to indicate a judgment of students' innate abilities. Rather, I am speaking of the possession of learning strategies and skills—or the lack thereof. *Autonomous* learners know how to apply appropriate skills such as reading for understanding, studying, note taking, and organizing information. *Restricted learners,* on the other hand, either have not been shown those skills or have failed to learn them. Perhaps they were absent that day. (See Figure 5-1.)

The reasons why a student might be considered either a restricted learner or an autonomous learner vary. Family background, socioeconomic status, frequent absence, and other factors can contribute to a student's status as a restricted learner. Likewise, many factors may have contributed to a student's having acquired the skills of an autonomous learner who needs little additional help to process and retain knowledge. It is likely that the autonomous learner comes from a well educated family in which literacy and learning are valued and practiced in day to day life.

What frequently occurs as these differences in students' abilities become evident, is that schools identify the autonomous and restricted learners and place them in tracks of either remedial, average, or advanced coursework. Such tracking sometimes determines a person's ultimate academic fate early in life. When students of varying abilities enter the classroom, teachers often make unknowing decisions, selecting the few autonomous learners and teaching to them, and "writing off" the restricted learners as people who are lazy, unprepared, unmotivated, or otherwise not teachable. At times, the inverse occurs, and teachers teach to the lowest level of student, causing more prepared students to become bored and lose their motivation to learn.

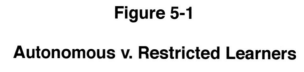

Figure 5-1

Autonomous v. Restricted Learners

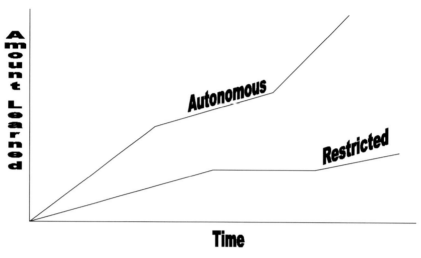

Figure 5-1 shows the learning curves of two students who might be in the same classroom. How does each student develop such a learning curve? What can teachers do in their classrooms to change a student's learning curve?

The central premise of this book is that any teacher can, in any classroom, create a learning environment in which *all* students are challenged and engaged in the process of learning subject matter at the same time that they are practicing and acquiring literacy skills. An understanding of how such skills are acquired may be aided by looking at two analogous situations – acquisition of language skills (first language as well as second) through "joining the language club" (Smith, 1988), and the acquisition of athletic skills through modern coaching techniques.

Acquisition in All Three Phases of MAX

As will be seen from the processes described in this chapter, acquisition is a most appropriate term to describe the process of developing learning skills through guided practice in a literacy-based classroom. Though the acronym "MAX" places the emphasis on acquisition occurring in the during-reading phase of MAX, it is important to note that acquisition is not limited to the middle phase of the lesson. The relatively invisible process of acquisition is happening any time students are imitating what strategic readers do all the time – setting purposes for reading, maintaining purposes and monitoring comprehension during reading, and extending beyond the text to process or reorganize information after reading.

Thus, like an athlete at a well-designed practice or a second language learner immersed in the country where the language is spoken, students are in the acquisition mode from the time they enter the classroom until they have finished their homework that night. If teachers gave students daily 50- to 90-minute practices in which to acquire new knowledge along with life-long learning skills, it would be difficult to avoid becoming a strategic learner.

What Are Literacy Skills And How Are They Acquired?

Literacy skills can be described as a broad, closely related and overlapping group of skills including reading, writing, speaking, listening, and thinking. The emphasis here is placed on *thinking*. (The other behaviors are all manifestations of thinking.) Developing literacy skills is as complex a process as learning a language (Krashen, 1996; McQuillan, 1998;, Shefelbine, 2001; Smith, 1988). Let us first look at the complexity of literacy and then at how literacy skills can be acquired. We begin with a consideration of reading and writing as being inseparable from thinking.

Reading is Thinking; Writing is Thinking

Contrary to much of the recent rhetoric over methods of teaching reading in the early years, reading is not just decoding print. Similarly, writing is not simply a process of putting words onto paper. If it were, we would be finished with teaching reading and writing by the third grade, since most students have mastered decoding sounds from print by that time. The United States is a leader in the industrialized world in reading by the fourth grade. Unfortunately, that is where our leadership ends. By eighth grade, American students lag when compared to most industrialized countries. Why is that? What should we be doing differently?

First, we need to realize that reading is far more than a basic skill (Schoenbach, Greenleaf, Cziko, & Hurwitz, 1999). The kind of reading that mature readers do is a complex process, much more so than even mature readers often recognize.

> Fluent readers are confident, competent, independent readers. They are readers who sample text, predict, confirm, and self correct quickly. They are readers who set their own purpose for reading, maintain meaning over an extended piece of discourse, and cope with more complex and less predictable texts. They also draw inferences and respond critically to an author's meaning (Whitehead, 1994, p. 24).

Whitehead's description suggests the complexity of the process. It involves being able to develop purpose for reading, even when the reading is something in which a person might not have inherent interest. It involves dealing with complexities of ideas, the wording of the particular text, and the reader's prior knowledge (Schoenbach et al., 1999). Reading involves problem solving — relating what the author is saying to other ideas and preconceptions that the reader may have or have been exposed to in the past. It involves attempting to get the main idea and hold that idea while perusing more information for detail, comparing, and fitting new information into the developing schemata of the reader, probing for consistencies and inconsistencies as one progresses.

Second, we need to keep in mind that reading is situationally bounded (Schoenbach et al., 1999). Being able to understand one type of text in no way guarantees the ability to comprehend a different type of text on another topic. A doctoral student will probably be able to comprehend a discussion of the relative merits of causal-comparative studies versus experimental studies better than someone who is finishing a bachelor's degree. An experienced auto mechanic will likely be able to read a description of how to rebuild a float-needle carburetor with greater understanding and ease than would a florist. On the other hand, the florist would probably be able to read with ease what would be quite difficult for the mechanic.

Characteristics of Proficient Readers

There are however, several characteristics that proficient readers do share. (Schoenbach et al.; 1999, Whitehead, 1994; Forget et al., 1996) Studies show that proficient readers are

- Strategy-oriented. They have a variety of techniques they might use to make sense of different types of text.
- Motivated. They desire to learn, and they use reading to do so.
- Purposeful. They know how to set purposes for the specific text they are reading.
- Metacognitive. They monitor their own understanding while they read, and they know what to do to "fix up" their comprehension when it fails (Brown, Bransford, Ferrara, & Campione, 1983).
- Engaged in making meaning. They use their own prior knowledge of subject matter to connect with the text, and they perform higher order thinking as they engage with the material they are reading. They analyze the author's ideas, they synthesize with what they already know, and they evaluate the relative merit of the author's arguments.

The operative word here is metacognition — thinking about thinking during reading — to enhance one's comprehension. What MAX Teaching is about is creating the opportunities in the classroom for students to practice metacognitive behavior both individually and cooperatively, and thus to have the opportunity to acquire the strategic awareness that is characteristic of proficient readers. The following sections will attempt to describe metacognitive behavior and to explain how students can acquire the ability to perform such behavior through practice in any content area classroom.

Acquisition of Metacognitive Strategies through Cooperative Construction

Constructivism is the philosophy, or belief, that learners construct their own knowledge through interactions with the text and with other persons. Constructivists recognize that experience and environment play a large role in how well the learner learns. They also recognize that language plays a critical role in acquisition of new knowledge. This language may be internal dialogue within the mind of the reader, or it may be external discussion among students in cooperative learning groups.

All reading involves construction of meaning. The reader combines prior knowledge with the ideas stated in the text to construct some new meaning. Done cooperatively, students in small groups consider the prior knowledge they have individually collected, and cooperatively construct, through discussion, and often debate, some group interpretation of the text.

Constructivist teachers, then, create opportunities for conversation both before and after the reading takes place, and they use what they observe in these conversations to orchestrate opportunities for students to succeed in acquiring information for use in thinking about subject matter. In other words, the constructivist teacher's role is to assist students as they create constructions of meaning from text and/or conversation. Much of what happens in the pre-reading Motivation phase of the class is really geared for the reflective conversations that will occur among students in the post-reading eXtension phase of the class.

What I am suggesting is that students in the eXtension phase of the class are Acquiring more than a clearer understanding of the content about which they have read. I would argue that, through reflective peer discussions, they acquire a sense of what it is like to be metacognitive in reading. Metacognition, or thinking about one's own thinking, is related to students' knowledge, awareness, and control of the processes by which they learn (Brown, 1987; Palinscar & Brown, 1984; Paris, Lipson, & Wixon, 1983; Paris, Wasik, & Turner, 1991; Paris, Wasik, & Van der Huizen, 1988). Recognizing, evaluating, and reconstructing ideas are characteristics of the metacognitive learner, and recognizing, evaluating, and reconstructing ideas are also the characteristics of the conversations students typically have in cooperative learning groups after reading in a classroom where the MAX Teaching framework is being used.

The Role of Cooperative Learning in Acquisition of Thinking Skills

When teachers are using the MAX framework in their classes, students are doing the thinking and the learning. Just as the teacher is the orchestrator of the process in the planning stage for the class, the teacher acts as the conductor of the symphony of thought that occurs during the learning experience. By being aware of the processes of metacognition, the teacher can facilitate "classroom metacognitive behavior." An example is when I frequently say to a class, "Today, we are going to practice what a strategic reader might do to make sense of this particular part of this chapter…we are going to do this as a class, but what we are practicing is how a good reader might make sense of this." By treating the learning experience this way, I am explicitly helping students to acquire metacognition skills.

Georghiades (2000) describes metacognition as a process of reflecting upon and taking action about one's learning. He further describes the metacognitive process and the resulting transfer and durability of learned concepts as follows:

"…by being reflective, revisiting the learning process, making comparisons between prior and current conceptions, and being aware of and analyzing difficulties, learners gradually maintain deeper understanding of the learned material. One can, therefore, safely make two assertions: first, it is more likely that the person who holds better understanding of a certain concept will be able to identify the use and purpose of this knowledge, to handle learned material in a different manner and to explore potential use of this material under a number of circumstances. Put differently, maintaining better understanding sets the bases for successful transfer. Secondly, better understanding means: (a) greater ability to utilize learned material, in order to meet the learner's needs, and (b) greater confidence regarding learned material. These outcomes can be related to longer durability of conceptions: (i) the more a newly learned… concept serves the needs of the learner, the longer it will last, and (ii) the learner who is confident about what he or she knows will have no reason to regress to the "safety" of any personal prior misconceptions. The links, therefore, drawn between metacognition on the one hand, and transfer and durability on the other hand, are, in my view, explicit…" (p. 128).

Though the work of Georghiades focused primarily on the transfer and durability of scientific concepts resulting from metacognitive awareness, my own experiences in teaching metacognition through constructivist classroom activities in various disciplines, as well as the work of others corroborate these findings to suggest the fact that transfer and durability of both content and skills result from this form of learning (Gallimore & Tharp, 1990; Schoenbach et al., 2001).

How Are Proficient Reading Skills Acquired?

Smith (1983, 1986, and 1988) argues that there is only one way that any individual can develop the complex skills that are involved in practicing literacy — that is to acquire them. These skills cannot be learned quickly and efficiently, and they cannot be taught in a timely manner! They must be acquired — just as a person acquires his or her first language (and possibly other languages later). As will be discussed later, it is useful to consider what Smith describes as the "club" to which a person might belong if s/he were to acquire complex skills such as those required to speak a language or to perform reading and writing successfully. But before exploring that concept, we first need to consider the role *writing* plays in the acquisition of reading skills.

Writing Is One Element

As Zinsser (1988) emphasizes, writing is thinking onto paper. We all know that there is a significant difference between the fuzzy thinking we may have about a topic and the precise thinking required to write about the same topic in a clear and concise way. Zinsser states that "Writing organizes and clarifies our thought. Writing is how we think our way into a subject and make it our own" (p. 16).

Writing about a subject in a content area allows students to process ideas through manipulating the vocabulary of the discipline they are learning about. Writing should be a part of each and every class every day. Yet teachers are afraid that it will take time, and students are reluctant to engage in what appears to be something that other people do but not something they feel capable of doing themselves. They feel as though they will be evaluated for everything they write, just as they may feel about their interpretations of reading. The act of writing becomes a measure of their worth, and they resist it. Thus writing is left to the language arts teacher, and students do not see the value of writing in their own learning.

In virtually every activity described in part two of this book, writing is an important component of the learning process. Chapter 8 focuses more on the role played by writing in the content-literacy-based classroom. In some cases, the writing is a graded evaluation tool; but in most, it is used simply to help students generate ideas, become engaged through concrete commitment, clarify their own thinking, or otherwise organize ideas in useful and meaningful ways.

How, then, do we get students to the point where they are able to practice reading and writing as a tool for thinking and learning? It begins with what reading and writing are all about — the use of language to communicate ideas — and it all begins very early in our lives when we first Acquire language.

Joining the Spoken Language Club

Consider the miraculous process that a child goes through in acquiring a language. The average child learns new vocabulary words at an astounding pace over the first several years of life. This amounts to thousands of words. In addition, the child learns the syntax of the language so that s/he can construct meaningful sentences and paragraphs (without ever knowing about topic sentences or supporting details). Some children know the differences between adjectives and adverbs even though they could not tell you what they are or how they work to modify nouns, verbs, or adjectives. How does this process occur?

Smith (1988) suggests that children develop these difficult and complex processes not so much by imitating other people as by "joining the club" of people with whom they identify. They join the "language club," just as an adult might join a bridge club, a golf club, a tennis club, or whatever other club there is. What happens when a person joins a club? What are the benefits of joining? How does one learn in a club? What are the results of membership in a club?

Benefits of Joining the Spoken Language Club

Smith (1988) notes that infants who join the language club gain several benefits:

- They see what spoken language does. They see the multiple purposes of language and they see the multiple ways in which "people like them" use it. No one tries to teach them abstract ideas such as verb, noun, subject predicate, and the like.
- Infants are admitted as junior members. There is no discrimination or attempt to exclude the new members, and they are not expected to act like veteran members. No one ever puts them down for making mistakes. Mistakes are expected to occur.
- Everyone in the club helps them to become experts. There is no formal instruction, but people help them try to say what they wish to communicate. Everything always makes sense. That is the goal – making sense.
- Infants are quickly admitted into a full range of club activities as long as the activities make sense to them. They are never asked to do nonsense.
- As members of the club, infants learn at a phenomenal rate – their vocabulary grows at the rate of over twenty words a day (Miller, 1977), and the syntax and grammar develops at a rate that is difficult to comprehend given no formal "education".

The acquisition of language never stops. Even as adults, we constantly find ourselves imitating people with whom we want to identify. We may unconsciously find ourselves saying something we heard from a movie actor or an athlete whom we admire. Language development never stops, and joining the language club is the way children acquire their language.

How the Spoken Language Club Differs from the Classroom

Smith (1988) suggests that learning through club membership has several characteristics quite different from what goes on in most classrooms:

- The learning is always meaningful – it always relates to what the learner is doing.
- If it is not immediately useful, it is ignored.
- Learning in the club is never an occasional or sporadic matter. If so, it would not relate to being meaningful, and it would be boring.
- Most of the learning that takes place is incidental – not intentional. The learning is a byproduct of trying to communicate rather than an attempt to learn. Smith calls this his "Can I have another donut?" theory of language acquisition. What we comprehend, we learn (Krashen & McQuillen, 1996).
- Adults unwittingly contribute to the development of the infant by assisting in communication. When the child reaches out her hand and says "wama" the adult rephrases in the form of a question "You want more?" thus contributing to the early development of the infant not really prepared for the language task at hand. In other words, the child is performing a task way ahead of her current development by unwittingly recruiting adults into the process.
- Children learn vicariously from what more experienced club members do.
- There is little or no risk for the novice club member. Just as in a bridge club or golf club, all other members do what they can to help a new member find his/her way around, and to perform well at what the

club is about. No one ever tells a club member that s/he has not progressed far enough yet and therefore cannot participate in club activities.

Thus, learning through the language club is meaningful, timely, interesting, incidental, ahead of schedule developmentally, based on modeling by more experienced members, and risk free. The resulting growth is phenomenal (Smith, 1988). To what extent does this set of characteristics describe our classrooms?

Consider, in this vein, the acquisition of a second language. I frequently ask teachers in staff-development sessions to raise their hand if they have ever studied a foreign language such as Spanish, French, or German. The usual response is that about 99% of teachers admit to having studied a second language. I then proceed to ask them how many of them are fluent in that language. A quite different response is given. Usually two or three teachers admit to being fluent in a second language. When I ask them how they developed their fluency, they inevitably respond that they were "immersed" in the language, either through living in another country, or through some other equally intense period of acquisition wherein they had to use the language in their day-to-day living. All the important aspects of joining a language club were present in their acquisition experiences. The question is, to what extent do our classrooms – even foreign language classrooms – create immersion experiences in the language of our respective disciplines?

Academic Language

Shefelbine (2002) has suggested that all "academic language" is the equivalent of a foreign language. Students do not normally have much day-to-day experience with the use of such terms as metamorphic, igneous, sedimentary, polynomial, ionic bonding, peristalsis, or any of thousands of terms used academically, but rarely in daily conversation (Shefelbine, 2002). Yet they might confront all of the above terms and hundreds more like them within a typical day in school. If students do not get the opportunities to acquire the vocabulary through meaningful use, they are doomed to short-term retention if any at all. Thus, it behooves teachers to create opportunities for students to manipulate the language — experiment with their understandings of terms — in order to *Acquire* them as their own.

Joining a Literacy Club

Smith(1988) points out that children become aware quite early in their lives about reading and writing and the purposes of those activities. They perceive environmental print in many varying contexts — notes on the refrigerator door, signs on stores, words on cereal boxes. One experimenter reportedly interviewed over 2000 young children to attempt to find one who could not read the word "McDonalds," and was unable to find one, although some said that the word spells 'hamburger' — not really an incorrect response (Smith, 1988). Thus, children very early join the "literacy club" The characteristics of the literacy club are very similar to those just described for the language club — the first club children join.

New members (of the literacy club) are assimilated into a world where written language is (1) meaningful — people pay attention to signs and labels and books because they make sense. The activities are also (2) useful — all the reading and writing that is done is done for a purpose. The learning is (3) continual and effortless — every encounter with print is an opportunity to add something to one's repertoire of useful knowledge. Much of the learning is also (4) incidental — practically every child in the world learns to recognize the word McDonalds, not in order to be able to recognize the word itself, but as a byproduct of getting a hamburger. Learning in the literacy club is almost invariably (5) collaborative — as other people, at your side or on the page, help you to understand what you want to understand or to express what you want to express. Such learning, I again believe, is frequently (6) vicarious — the author writes something and the reader learns. I call reading in this way reading like a writer. …. we can read as if we were writing what we read — and in effect the author writes for us. And finally, such learning opportunities in the literacy club are (7) no risk — a child striving to read or write something is helped and encouraged, not given a low grade and a program of exercises. Members of the literacy club are people who read and write, even the beginners, and the fact that one is not very competent yet is no reason for exclusion or ridicule. A newcomer is the same kind of person as the proficient club member, except that he or she hasn't yet had as much experience. It is the same in all normal sports and recreation clubs. (Smith, 1988, p. 11)

What can schools and teachers do to create a similarly supportive environment in the classroom? My argument, in this work, is that any teacher can create an environment in the classroom in which students are *immersed* in a literacy experience. In this environment, students will develop important understandings of the subject matter and at the same time, acquire the literacy skills they will need to be successful contributors to twenty-first century society.

Quality Coaching on the Athletic Field – Acquisition through Contact with the Ball

My development as a coach has considerably influenced my teaching. I have coached, either as an assistant or as a head coach, ice hockey, football, golf, and soccer. (What I am about to say concerning the similarities between coaching and quality teaching that facilitates skills development can be applied to virtually any sport. Pick your favorite sport and consider how what is described here applies to that sport. Soccer is described here.)

The vast majority of my coaching experience and greatest expertise is in soccer which I have coached at the recreational, select travel, varsity high school, and college levels for over twenty years. Some of the players whom I coached as youth now play professionally, and one has recently played for the United States National Team in international competition. What I learned at the United States Soccer Federation National Coaching School, and from other coaches (in various sports) with whom I worked over the years is, that the number of touches on the ball and the quality of the experiences in which the ball is touched make all the difference in the world as to how a team performs in competition.

Consider the following scenario of three teams with three different coaches all showing up at the practice fields at the same time for practices. Each coach has a practice area of roughly equal size and makeup as the other coaches. Each team is roughly of equal talent physically and has about the same time each week for practice, but their practices look quite different from one another.

As the players arrive at practice, Coach A awaits them with whistle and ball in hand. He has brought a ball in order to have the team engage in scrimmage — one half of the team against the other half. Coach B arrives at the field with a bag of 20 balls and a whistle. Coach C also has a bag of 20 balls and a whistle. Let us compare the practices as they take place:

Coach A. Coach A starts practice by getting the players stretched and then gets the scrimmage started. The coach throws out the ball and players begin to practice the game as they have been taught. The coach moves around yelling advice with regard to positional play and other game-related behaviors. Play frequently stops at the coach's whistle — to explain to the players how the coach perceives what has been happening and how to improve — and then continues again. This coach is very knowledgeable about the sport and has had a great deal of experience at the game in high school and college. The players respect the coach and listen to the advice given. During the course of the practice, each player gets to touch the ball 80 to 100 times, and spends an average of ten to twelve minutes in contact with the ball.

Coach B. Coach B runs practice differently than Coach A does. This team warms up and stretches with each player having a ball to use personally. The coach leads the team in fast-footwork drills to develop coordination and also stamina since the amount of work done is equal to running laps, except that each player is getting approximately 60 to 100 touches on the ball each minute of the warm-up. The coach then proceeds to introduce the skill and/or tactic of the day. Each practice, the coach begins by modeling a skill or tactic that the players will then use throughout the practice in order to become comfortable with their own abilities to perform it. After introducing the skill, the coach arranges for the players to work together in small-sided games that allow them to practice this tactic under various conditions of pressure — one against one, one against two, two against one, and so on. Again, the players are each getting many touches on the ball as they work to solve the problems that the coach has arranged for them in the small-sided games. Finally, the coach moves to a full scrimmage in which his players play full-field with one ball. Here, the coach acts a bit like Coach A, blowing the whistle to stop play to assist players in understanding their play and the consequences of their actions on the field. In this practice, each player has spent approximately 45 to 50 minutes actually touching the ball, and has touched the ball more than a thousand times.

The question is, which of these two teams will win in the game when they play each other on Saturday? More to the point, which team has the players who are more likely to have acquired the skills needed to be successful in the sport? Anyone who has coached seriously knows the answer to this question and to the first question. The team with more talent in individual ball skills will win 99.9% of the time.

Acquisition of Knowledge and Skills through Contact with the Concepts

The comparison of MAX Teaching to traditional teaching is analogous to the comparison of the two teams. Which students will perform better on standardized tests six months after being exposed to new subject matter — the students who were allowed to manipulate the ideas individually through reading and then through small-group discussion? Or the students who sat through a lecture or copied notes from a teacher who expounded on his/her knowledge of the subject matter?

Through MAX Teaching — and the combination of a literacy-based learning framework, cooperative learning, and a skill acquisition model — teachers provide all students with the opportunity to get many "touches" on the vocabulary and concepts of the subject matter about which they are learning. Rather than have few touches — dominated by the teacher — students are engaged routinely in individual and small-group interaction with ideas and with each other. The result is acquisition of both knowledge and skills.

Coach C. You are probably wondering what happened to the third coach. Coach C, as you recall, also had a bag of balls for the players to use at practice. The problem with Coach C is that he forgot to put air in the balls. Even though each of the players had a ball, the ball each player had did not act in any way like the one on Saturday will act because that one will be inflated properly. Coach C is like the teacher who relies on worksheets or end-of-chapter questions for students to learn new subject matter. Anyone can find the answers to the questions without ever reading, thinking, or understanding the text. Thus, students who "learn" new subject matter this way rarely remember it for any length of time. They do not really ever take ownership of the material. It does not become part of their schemata. Thus, it's the quality of the touches on the ball that counts. So too does the quality of contact with new subject matter in the classroom.

Classroom Coaching – Creating Literacy Clubs in Grades Four through Twelve

What can schools do to help post-primary-grade students improve their achievement in literacy skills while learning new subject matter? The systematic use of reading and writing to help students learn their subject matter is one answer. Any teacher has the ability to create a literacy club in his/her own classroom through MAX Teaching. Students who are placed in an environment in which they are allowed to pursue learning through the means of reading, writing, discussing in cooperative groups, and thus manipulating ideas to construct meaning are finding that learning does not have to be difficult or boring, but rather can be fluid and engaging. What do students in such an environment learn? They learn that, regardless of their skill level upon entering such an environment, they can succeed as learners. A collateral benefit is that, while students in content area classes read, write, and discuss in order to learn, they actually improve the thinking skills directly related to higher performance in reading and writing.

What About Students Who Are Performing Well Below Grade Level?

Reading involves construction of meaning. Modern views of reading suggest an active role played by the reader in using the "set of tracks" left by the author, relating that material to the reader's prior knowledge, and thereby constructing a message. The good news is that students who are reading below grade level, and who do not at a given time have the skills to read a piece of text independently, can read text several grade levels above their diagnosed reading grade level, given the support of competent peers and/or a facilitating teacher (Vygotsky, 1978; Dixon-Krauss, 1996) — especially as they work cooperatively to manipulate the ideas and themes of their course (Dixon-Krauss, 1996).

In addition, students who have previously been frustrated by their lack of literacy skills are able to develop appropriate skills and strategies. And in time, through the MAX Teaching method, those students acquire the ability to perform learning skills *autonomously*. Research suggests that scores on achievement tests are only one of the benefits of this form of pedagogy. Self-esteem, social skills, reduced ethnic and racial stereotyping, and comprehension of text all show gains as well (Johnson, Johnson, & Holubec, 1993; Slavin 1991; Stahl, 1992). Any team has players of varied abilities. During the course of a season, the best players tend to get better while the weakest players tend to close the gaps between them and the best players *if the coach has focused on skill development in practice.*

Making Reading Easy

The quote at the beginning of Chapter 3 is often misunderstood. Many people think that by suggesting a way to make reading easy, the idea is to "dumb down" texts. That's not at all what I'm talking about in this book. The way to make reading easy is to facilitate the process of reading difficult text.

The use of activities that actively engage students in classroom reading and writing helps develop the abilities of students in the upper grades to use reading and writing as tools for learning. Content area teachers can use numerous strategies in their classrooms to teach their subject matter while at the same time developing the learning abilities of their students. However, many subject area teachers are not aware of the benefits of using content area literacy activities to help students learn. In addition, most teachers assume that by the time students have gotten to high school, they will have attained the requisite literacy skills needed to succeed in learning from text. Teachers who treat students this way take for granted that students know something they in fact do not know. Teachers often assume that students know *how* to read, that they *will* use reading to learn, and that they should be *motivated* enough to do so.

When students who have not yet acquired the appropriate literacy skills are placed in situations where they are neither prepared nor motivated to read or write for the purpose of learning, their experience could be compared to that of athletes sent into a match to play without ever having been coached in the sport. For teachers to expect all students simply to read and learn from the material assigned to them is comparable to handing them musical instruments and asking them to play a song—even though they have never had lessons with the instruments!

Students who find themselves in such circumstances are likely to be doomed to failure. In some cases, schools may simply lower expectations to the point that little or no reading or meaningful writing is required to pass a course. Perhaps this would explain why 57% in a national sample of high school seniors recently tested on a measure of their knowledge of history scored "below basic" (*Cincinnati Enquirer*, May 19, 2002). Twelve years of worksheets, teacher lectures, and copying notes from an overhead projector leave students unprepared for either the university or for the 21st century work force.

It does not have to be this way. Any teacher can teach in such a way that students coming through her or his classroom not only learn more deeply the subject matter, but at the same time, acquire literacy skills — two for one!

Helping Students Learn How to Learn

There's an alternative to the all too common situation in which students find themselves without the requisite skills to succeed in academic work requiring literacy. That alternative involves helping students to become independent learners by teaching them *how* to learn through reading and writing while in the process of learning the subject matter of mathematics, science, vocational or other courses. This involves *embedding learning-strategies within the context of any content lesson*. Students are taught the *"how"* of learning while in the actual process of learning the content of their classes. In this alternative vision, reading, studying, and thinking skills are taught and modeled by all teachers. These skills do not comprise a separate course of study; they are part of every class.

Duke and Pearson (2002) list six comprehension strategies that they suggest ought to be taught to students to improve their reading abilities. They include tactics that should be used before, during, and after the reading. They are

- prediction,
- thinking aloud,
- understanding text structure,
- visually representing text,
- summarization, and
- questioning,

These, and the various ways to achieve them, are the principle strategies that can be acquired through practice in the activities in Part 2 of this book.

Guided practice in comprehension strategies on the part of students gradually enables all students to develop their own reading for learning skills. The process involves a gradual change from students' dependence on the teacher to students taking charge of their own learning. It is a process of gradually phasing out the teacher as a dispenser of knowledge, and phasing in the student as an active learner.

The goal of content-area reading instruction is to gradually transfer from the teacher to the student the responsibility for learning through reading. This transfer can be accomplished through engagement, modeling, guided practice, and reinforcement — in other words — through MAX Teaching. The process of content area literacy instruction consistently places students into situations in which they experience guided practice in strategic reading and writing.

A Skill Acquisition Model for Teaching Literacy Skills

It is important to note that the MAX framework of instruction parallels the complete learning process that any individual uses to learn something new. What I am advocating is that teachers use the framework in the classroom to provide an atmosphere of *guided practice* in which students, as a group, are continually exposed to the MAX model. The result is that *students internalize the correct learning process* and are able to apply it on their own outside the classroom and in their work in other classes or in the work environment.

If teachers use "embedded curriculum," they are paralleling the process of apprenticeship known for thousands of years in the trades. This technique, which can be used in the teaching of any strategy, involves embedding learning-strategy training within the context of any lesson. Students are taught how to learn in the process of actually learning the content of their classes. The teacher is not only a master of the content, but is also seen as the master learner, always modeling for students (apprentice learners) strategies they should use to become autonomous in their own learning.

Through embedded curriculum, reading, study, and thinking skills are taught and modeled in such a way as to gradually transfer ownership of the skills from teacher to students through the use of a skill acquisition model (Figure 3-2) that involves a three-step process to introduce, model, and provide practice in skills that accomplished learners often take for granted, but which can be acquired through overt instruction and guided practice (Forget, et al., 1996; Atwell, 1987; Duke and Pearson, 2002). The teacher acts in the role of the master learner; the student is the apprentice learner. Students are encouraged and enabled to practice good reading and writing procedures and carry out a complete thought process with each lesson. The result is the development of lifelong learners, able to process text in meaningful ways and to think critically about what they learn.

The teacher overtly teaches learning skills by practicing a *skill acquisition model* that follows these steps that correspond to the three steps of the MAX Teaching framework:

- Introduce and model the skill to be practiced in learning
- Provide guided practice in use of the skill
- Have students reflect on their success in learning because of their use of the skill.

Step 1 takes place in the **M**otivation stage of the lesson. Step 2 takes place in the **A**cquisition phase. Step 3 takes place in the e**X**tension stage of the lesson. Thus, the teacher facilitates the practice of a learning skill while students are probing new text. (Instruction in the *skill acquisition model* is written into each of the lessons in Part 2 of this book.)

Chapter 6

EXtension

We are what we repeatedly do. Excellence, then, is not an act, but a habit.
Aristotle

The essence of the EXtension phase of the lesson is that students are provided the opportunity to perform higher order thinking while rehearsing in meaningful ways what they have acquired in the first two phases of the class. Marzano (2003) refers to this process as "multiple exposure to and complex interactions with knowledge" (p. 112). (In chapter 5 on Acquisition, I referred to the coaching process in sport as setting up opportunities for students to have as many quality touches on the ball as possible in a practice. Multiple exposure and complex interaction refers to the academic version of a well-designed practice.) The outward manifestations of such behavior take the shape of discussion, debate, lab application, writing, reorganizing, rehearsal, or other similar activities that allow students to continue to process the ideas about what they have read in the text even after they have read it. At this point of the lesson, students have confronted new information, and they are ready to make sense of it.

Two Levels of EXtension

It is important to note that EXtension is occurring at two levels. First, in this post-reading phase of the lesson, students get to extend beyond the literal interpretation of what they have read. Through the application of conversation and other means such as writing or otherwise reorganizing the information they have encountered in the reading, students work together to construct meaning from the text.

Secondly, the act of Acquisition is also extended into the later part of the class and beyond. That is to say, the process of acquiring the complex skills of literacy continue as students interact with their peers, with the teacher, and with their own conceptions of both content and skill. Where students had the opportunity to acquire and practice metacognitive behavior individually during the silent reading part of the class, now they have the opportunity to extend the experience beyond the personal, to interact with peers to construct a refined sense of what the text said. Students thus continue to acquire new understandings of content, thinking skills, and metacognitive strategies simultaneously during the EXtension phase of the lesson.

This chapter will attempt to describe what occurs in the EXtension phase of class, how cooperative construction of meaning works to help students internalize the metacognitive strategies involved in reading and writing, and why taking students to higher levels of thinking in the third phase of class leads to greater understanding and longer retention of material. It is important to note that, even though the EXtension phase of class can and should continue into homework and even evaluation, the focus of this chapter is on what occurs in the classroom after the silent-reading phase of a MAX Teaching lesson.

Multiple Exposure and Complex Interactions

What would happen if every student in your class, each day, had read the homework assignment with the assistance of an adult, and then discussed the subject matter with two or three peers for 20 minutes on the way to your class? Would things in your classroom be different than what generally occurs there? It is sad to say, but the vast majority of teachers today have become inured to the idea that most students will not do course-related reading for homework, or, at best, will only do the simplest of "busy work" types of homework assignments. It is rarely expected that students will go home and thoroughly read eight to ten pages of new textbook material in preparation for classroom discussion the following day. (The assignment is still routinely given by teachers, but those teachers know that most students will not do it, and that they will have to teach the subject matter to the students in class the next day.)

Let's fantasize though. What if every student in your class were to come to class after having read the homework assignment with the assistance of an adult, and then discussed the subject matter with two or three peers for 20 minutes on the way to your class? The list from chapter two tells what could be expected. To review the list, I have included it below. However, I have highlighted several of the statements to focus on what, based on frequency of response, teachers obviously recognized as important goals. Study the bold phrases to see the pattern.

Overall Changes in the Classroom

Classrooms would be more productive.
Dynamic, lively discussions would take place.
Energy level of class improves.
Enrichment could occur.
Fewer disturbances would occur in class.
It would be more fun for teachers and students.
Lively discussions would occur.
There would be an increase in Socratic dialog.
There would be increased cooperation, give and take, improved social skills.
They (students and teachers) would love to come to class.
We would have an energized atmosphere.
You'd have some discipline.

Changes among Students

Active learning would be the norm.
Dropout rates would go down.
Focused thinking would occur.
Grades would go up.
Graduation rates would go up.
Higher achievement would occur.
HOTS (higher order thinking skills) would be possible.

Interest would go up.

More productivity would occur.

More students would experience success.

Prior knowledge would be improved.

Retention would improve.

Student interaction would increase.

Students would be analyzing, synthesizing, and applying information.

Students would be confident and competent.

Students would be engaged.

Students would be learning by talking about stuff.

Students would be more self-directed.

Students would be prepared more for discussion.

Students would gain mastery of material.

Students would have better understanding of concepts.

Students would have more success in learning.

Students would lead in the learning process.

Students would retain more.

They would all be on the same page.

They would be responsible for their own learning.

They would teach each other.

They'd actually learn.

They'd be prepared.

They'd learn the material.

We'd have interested students.

Changes among Teachers

Finally, we would get down to interesting new stuff.

I could go in different directions.

I could move more quickly.

I could reach more students.

Less class time would be wasted.

Less time spent would be spent on discipline.

Our job would be easier.

There would be less teacher frustration.

There would be time for hands-on activities.

We could build on what they know.

We could go from concrete to abstract thinking.

We could have an enriched curriculum.

You would not have to reteach things as much.

To what, if anything, do these bold-print statements refer, if not to multiple exposure and complex interactions? The implication from these bold-print teacher comments is that such behaviors happen all too rarely in most classrooms. Yet, the premise of this book is that these bold-print statements all refer to what *routinely* occurs in the E**X**tension phase of a content-literacy-based classroom in which MAX Teaching is being applied.

My contention, based on many years of classroom practice and also on an enormous and growing body of research (Dewey, 1933; Dixon-Krauss, 1996; Forget & Morgan, 1997; Georghiades, 2000; Marzano, 2003; Palinscar et. al, 1983; Schoenbach et al., 2001; Vacca, 2002) is that students who routinely interact with content area text in meaningful ways will

- better understand the subject matter,
- retain the information longer,
- acquire important literacy-related skills, and
- develop mental patterns of literacy-related behavior that will serve them throughout their lives.

The reason that these four results occur is that the students process the information through cooperative interaction that inevitably leads to higher order thinking, and, in such cooperative discussions, they have multiple opportunities to rehearse the subject area content in meaningful ways.

At the same time, students are collectively performing behavior that, when performed individually during the reading process, is known as metacognition (Brown, 1987; Flavell, 1976; Gunstone, 1994; Palinscar and Brown, 1983; Georghiades, 2000). Even though the silent reading (**A**cquisition) phase of class has ended by the time students are in the E**X**tension phase, students in the E**X**tension phase are *collectively* doing what a strategic reader does *individually* during the reading — thinking about one's own thinking regarding the reading — metacognition. Thus, the E**X**tension phase of the class is instrumental in not only helping students to process the subject matter and therefore to acquire new knowledge, but also in helping the students to acquire the skills of metacognition.

Higher Order Thinking – What Is It, and How Can You Help Students Perform It?

Higher order thinking … critical thinking … reflective thought … call it what you may, it is what you are doing right now. *Real reading is thinking.* Reading is not so much about decoding of words as it is the creation of meaning about those words. It is about taking the two elements of prior knowledge and text — the reader's prior conceptions and misconceptions about the topic, combined with the tracks left behind by the author in the form of words on paper — to construct personal meaning from the combination of the two.

As you are reading these words, you *analyze* the argument that I am making for the use of reading and writing in the classroom. You are thinking about how the ideas stated here *synthesize* with what you already know about classroom teaching. You wonder how some of the ideas might *apply* in the subject area that you teach. You *evaluate* my arguments, perhaps disagreeing or qualifying some of the things I say because of the specific type of student that you face in your class, or because of the content of your course. Perhaps you are thinking of how to *create* a classroom environment in your own subject area that uses the ideas contained herein. What you are doing is performing what most would call *higher order thinking skills* (HOTS).

The most widely known characterization of HOTS is to be found in Bloom's Taxonomy of Educational Objectives (Anderson & Krathwohl, 2001; Bloom, 1956; Marzano, 2001). The original taxonomy of objectives described six levels of thought, each increasingly complex in nature and interactive with the less complex levels below it. The six levels have been labeled variously as knowledge, comprehension, application, analysis, evaluation, and creativity (Anderson & Krathwohl, 2001), or as knowledge, comprehension, application, analysis, synthesis, evaluation (Bloom, 1956) or as describe, compare, associate, analyze, apply, and argue (Cowan & Cowan, 1980; Vaughan & Estes, 1986).

Recent works turn the six levels of thinking into a three-dimensional model. Anderson & Krathwohl (2001) expand the concept of taxonomy into a three-dimensional phenomenon by considering each of their six levels of thinking in light of the four additional dimensions of factual, conceptual, procedural, and metacognitive knowledge (p. 41). Likewise, Marzano (2001) proposes a new taxonomy based on increasing levels of conscious processing on the part of the learner. His taxonomy includes the important roles played by metacognition, motivation, and emotion in the process of learning, and proceeds through the six levels of retrieval, comprehension, analysis, knowledge utilization, metacognition, and self-system thinking.

Regardless of how the thinking process is analyzed or whether it is called higher order thinking, reflective thought, or critical thinking, the process generally describes the use of the various levels of thinking within these taxonomies. Such taxonomies have been instrumental in helping teachers to write objectives for student learning, and setting goals for student classroom achievement. The underlying assumption is that if students were to participate in thinking beyond the most rote levels with regard to subject matter, the likelihood is that students would process information in more meaningful and lasting ways.

Awareness of the role played by higher order thinking in helping students to both understand and retain information is not new. Dewey referred to the process as "reflective thinking," which he defined as "active, persistent, and careful consideration of any belief or supposed form of knowledge in the light of the grounds that support it and the further conclusion to which it tends" (Dewey, 1933). Such thinking cannot be divorced from the course content — in fact, thinking is a way of learning content (Raths, 1967). When HOTS are taught in isolation, students are only being prepared for tests of isolated skills. But when HOTS are applied in the learning of new subject matter, students actually *acquire* both the skills and the content, and thus, can transfer both to new learning situations as a result.

This means that teachers of content area subjects must create the conditions in their classrooms in which thinking about their subject matter can and will occur. It is much easier to teach students to memorize facts and then evaluate their recall with multiple choice tests, but a course that focuses on helping students think about subject matter will include analysis, application, synthesis, evaluation, and creativity on a routine basis in the classroom. Such a course will also create opportunities for metacognitive behavior and emotional satisfaction and involvement (Chapter 4).

The role that critical reading (Zintz and Maggart, 1984) can play in this process is the essence of MAX Teaching. When students are evaluating, drawing inferences, and arriving at conclusions about subject matter through the use of text in the classroom, they are getting the practice that they need to acquire those skills, and they are getting the added benefit that they are immediately applying this thinking to the content area. Thus, they think like a mathematician in mathematics class, or like a geographer in geography class, or like a scientist in science class. The fact is that they have a very important concrete prop in their hands to enable them to perform such thinking — the text. As has been stated in earlier chapters, students have the textbook open during the third phase of the class. They are able to refer to the text, make their own inferences about what it means, and use the vocabulary of the discipline in their conversations. For this to happen routinely, and for all students, it is important to employ cooperative learning in a very systematic way.

Marzano's (2001) expansion of the taxonomy into three dimensions by considering each of his six thinking levels in the three domains of information, mental procedures, and psychomotor processes is most useful in understanding MAX Teaching methods. Students in a MAX Teaching classroom are systematically engaged in HOTS in the three domains, partly as a result of how cooperative learning is used. As was discussed in chapter 5, students in a MAX Teaching classroom are involved in **A**cquisition of both content and metacognition skills by cooperatively constructing meaning through teacher-guided and cooperative application of metacognitive processes to learn new subject matter.

Effective Cooperative Learning for EXtension beyond the Text

How one sets up cooperative learning to create the environment in which students collectively perform the thinking that leads to metacognition is important. The essential elements of successful cooperative learning in a content literacy-based classroom are as follows:

- heterogeneous groups of student,
- a real problem to be solved, and
- a three-step process that assures engagement by all students.

Heterogeneity improves the probability that all students will experience success. Though some teachers may fear that lower-level students will become dependent on the more advanced students in such a grouping, I have found that such behavior does not occur if the other two essential elements are present in the classroom. It is only when students are not engaged in group-worthy tasks (Lotan, 2003) or when they are not systematically engaged through the three steps of cooperative learning (Forget et al., 1996, Richardson & Morgan, 2003) that students become dependent on their "more able" peers.

A real problem to be solved refers to the idea that when students are given meaningless tasks (such as many worksheets tend to be) to do in groups, they usually see such work as hardly worthy of their efforts. Such students realize that even if they perform the task, they will derive little real understanding from it. Thus, they often elect to shun the work for more important activities like writing a note to a boyfriend or doing the homework due next period rather than "waste" their time on the assigned work. Once one of the persons in the group is finished, the rest of the group can copy the answers. (I would argue that it is natural for a student to think this way. I might do the same thing in the same circumstance.)

If we want cooperative learning to work, we need to have activities for students that are group-worthy tasks (Lotan, 2003). Such tasks should be

- open-ended and require complex problem solving,
- provide students with multiple entry points to the task and multiple opportunities to show intellectual competence,
- deal with discipline-based, intellectually important content,
- require positive interdependence, and
- include clear criteria for the evaluation of the group's product (Lotan, 2003).

Virtually all of the activities in part two of this text provide opportunities for cooperative learning that has each of these characteristics. The size of the group may vary, and the process may as well, but the challenge in processing text in intellectually stimulating ways is offered through each of the activities.

A three-step process that encourages engagement can insure that the thinking that occurs in the EXtension phase of the class is performed by *all students* rather than by only a few. This system is characterized by three important steps (Forget et al., 1996; Richardson & Morgan, 2003). By including the three steps, teachers facilitate the involvement of otherwise reluctant students in a process that will allow for their acquisition of thinking skills related to reading. These steps are

- individual written commitment by each student before entering groups,
- an attempt at achieving small-group consensus with regard to interpreting the text after the reading, and
- teacher-mediated discussion in an attempt to achieve large-group consensus as a whole class as a concluding activity.

Each of these steps is discussed below.

1. Commitment: Unfortunately, teachers often put students into groups before the students have thought about the problem to an extent that they will have some contribution to the discussion. It is natural in such circumstances to defer to the more advanced student or to the more aggressive one. Knowledgeable teachers can reduce the probability of this occurring by *getting all students to write what they think before entering the group.* (This seems like such a simple concept, yet I constantly observe group-work activities that leave out this important step.) Students with something in writing which they have committed to paper are much more likely to have given some thought to the issue to be discussed, and they cannot hide from their commitment once they have brought the written evidence of it to the group. Based on this awareness, a teacher would instruct students to make predictions on an anticipation guide, for instance, *before* putting them into groups. They would then have some differences of opinion to discuss.

Think of the alternative. What if the teacher were to give the anticipation guide to the already-formed group? It would be perfectly normal for the students to look to see what each other is marking down, probably deferring to the "honor student" in the group. Meaningful discussion rarely happens in such circumstances because students have let someone else do the thinking for them. (During-reading activities in Part II of this book almost always require students to write as they are reading to gather information as they read in preparation for the post-reading discussion. Paired Reading is one exception.)

2. Consensus: Immediately after the reading, many of the activities in Part II ask for students to attempt to achieve a consensus in their small groups about what the text is saying. There are two reasons why this is an important intermediate step in the process. One is that students, in attempting to achieve agreement about how to interpret the text are really providing one another with one-on-one reading instruction (without any reading specialist in the classroom!). In sharing ideas as to how they are constructing meaning from the text, students are helping each other to practice the essence of reading – constructing meaning by combining prior knowledge with new information from the text to form some new meaning. When students are routinely placed in the environment wherein they can have such constructive dialogues, they acquire the skills and strategies of metacognitive behaviors that they will use throughout their lives.

The second reason why the attempt at small-group consensus is important is that it is often a social challenge for a student to address a whole class of 30 or so students. However, when the student has already "rehearsed" the argument in a small group, it is much easier to do so. Thus, the final whole-class discussion tends to be more animated, with more students willing and able to participate.

3. Mediation: Finally, if teachers really want to have cooperative learning work in their classrooms, they should allow it to come to a cooperative, whole-class conclusion, with the thinking taking place in the minds of the students, rather than coming from the teacher. I have found that, if the teacher is willing to act as a mediator/arbitrator of the student-owned discussion that takes place in the final attempt to come to a whole-class consensus on interpretation of the text, more students will be engaged in the discussion. Even those who do not participate actively find themselves listening intently to see how their peers resolve the problem presented by interpretation of the text.

One chief role of the teacher in the final classroom consensus-oriented discussion is to paraphrase frequently student ideas to help more students be able to participate because, as a result of the paraphrasing, students understand what is being argued. By continuously probing for detail and understanding, the teacher facilitates the construction process for all students. (There are times when the class cannot come to a consensus because of strong feelings or because of multiple interpretations each of which has some validity. In this case, I sometimes suggest that we temporarily drop the discussion in light of the time factor, suggesting that we may be able to agree on some consensus after we have more expertise in the subject. This is an honest way to save valuable classroom time, and it is better than resolution by "telling" the answer. Students are likely to stay tuned all the way to the end of the discussion the next time you have one if the teacher behaves in this manner. If the teacher, as "sage on stage," resolves each discussion, students will quickly learn that they needn't be engaged, but rather might just wait until "the answer" is given.)

In sum, the EXtension phase of the process allows students to collectively construct meaning from text, and permits students to perform cognitive and metacognitive skills through guided practice in the classroom. In addition, repeated practice in such meaningful processing of subject matter provides the opportunity for students to develop brain programs (Hart, 1983) that foster success in life-long learning skills. Thus, EXtension beyond the text leads to acquisition of both content and skills.

Chapter 7 will demonstrate the entire process of MAX Teaching by describing, step-by-step, a class in which the process is used to help students learn science. You will see how a teacher uses one classroom activity – the anticipation guide – to engage students and allow them to acquire skills through a combination of well structured guided practice (**MAX**), **cooperative construction of meaning**, and the focus on a skill through the **skill acquisition model** *while the students do most of the work.*

Chapter 7

Important Elements of a Reading/Writing to Learn Classroom

A teacher is one who makes himself progressively unnecessary.
Thomas Carruthers

In this chapter, we will visit a classroom in which reading, writing, cooperative learning, and skill development is occurring. We do this to analyze the elements of the reading/writing classroom to see how the various parts come together to form a whole experience in which students deeply learn subject matter through active engagement with text and with each other. The right side describes the class, and the left side annotates the three daily elements that make the class work to motivate students to participate actively in processing text:

- *MAX Teaching* – *M*otivation, *A*cquisition, and e*X*tension, before, during, and after the reading,
- **Skill Acquisition Model** – Introduction, Guided Practice, and Reflection on a Skill
- **Cooperative Learning** – Written Commitment, Attempt at Consensus, and Teacher Mediation

As you read how this class progresses, note how these three daily elements of MAX Teaching are woven together to create a total learning experience for the students present.

		Reading and Writing to Learn in a Science Classroom
1.	Heterogeneous groups for developmental support	1. This biology class begins with students taking their seats near other students with whom they have been grouped. The teacher frequently regroups the students heterogeneously based on their reading abilities, assuring that each group is compose of students of varying abilities. (However, the students are not aware of this since the groups always appear randomly assigned.)
2.	Routine preparation for homework even before class discussion begins	2. Students begin the class even before the teacher tells them to, by copying into their two-column notes from the chalkboard the three listed knowledge objectives for the day. They are accustomed to starting each class this way, and no communication is necessary

	(See Chapter 3 & Chapter 9, FAQ 7)		on the part of the teacher. Today's objectives are about classification of living things.
3.	Motivation through threat-free awareness of vocabulary and need to find out	3.	The topic of the day is how scientists classify living things. The teacher points to a list of terms on the chalkboard, including phylum, kingdom, order, species, and others. He asks students if they know any of the words they see written there. One or two students tell what they think one or two of the words mean. The teacher says to the class that by the time they are done with today's reading, they should be much more familiar with the terms and how scientists use the words to classify all living things.
4.	Step One of the Skill Acquisition Model – Introduction of skill	3.	The teacher explains to the students, "What strategic readers do when they read non-fiction text such as this section of your textbook that we are about to read is that they make predictions about what the text will say. They make such predictions based on their prior knowledge. Then, when they go into the text, it really does not matter whether they find out that their predictions were true or not.
5.	Modeling of skill	5.	"I did it just this morning when I picked up the newspaper and looked at this article about the President. I predicted it would tell about how he felt about what he said in his speech, how his cabinet members would comment on it, and other predictions. Because I made the predictions, it was easier for me to read the article. While I was reading, if I found that a prediction had been correct, I just felt pretty good about myself and my prior knowledge. When I found something about which I had predicted incorrectly, I said to myself, 'Wow, I didn't know that!' My point is that it is not so important whether you are right or wrong in your predictions – the fact is that *the reading becomes easier to do because you know what you are looking for in the text!* "Anyone can make reading easier by making predictions about what they are about to read. The result of having made the predictions helps them to stay engaged in the text because they are looking for verification of their beliefs. You will see that making predictions will help you to read this section from our book. Today, I am helping you in this process because I have already made some predictions for you, on this anticipation guide." (The teacher passes out, one to each student, a single sheet of paper which he calls an anticipation guide [Figure 7-1]. The teacher also places a transparency of the anticipation guide on the overhead projector and projects it onto the screen in front of the classroom for the purpose of modeling how to mark it up.)

6. First step of cooperative learning – each student individually commits in writing to what s/he believes

6. The teacher continues, "All you need to do is, before you even look at the textbook, place a check mark next to the statements you think are probably true, based on what you have already learned in this course or other courses as well as things you have seen in books, at museums, on TV, or in movies, etc. Leave the spaces next to the other statements blank. Don't be worried at this time about whether or not you are correct. Remember that you are just practicing the habit of predicting prior to reading. You will see that by having made predictions, the reading will make more sense to you and be easier to comprehend. The fact is that some of these statements will prove to be correct, some will prove to be incorrect, and some will be arguable. That is, some of you may interpret a statement to be true, and have evidence to prove it, while others in the room will have evidence that seems to disprove it. We will have to resolve those issues at that time."

Figure 7-1

Anticipation Guide for *Classifying Living Things*

Name_____   Date_____

Before reading: In the space to the left of each statement, place a check mark (✔) if you agree or think the statement is true.

During or after reading: Add new check marks or cross through those about which you have changed your mind. Keep in mind that this is not like the traditional "worksheet." You may have to put on your thinking-caps and "read between the lines." Use the space under each statement to note the page, column, and paragraph(s) where you are finding information to support your thinking.

_____1. Dogs, cats, elephants, and humans are alike.

_____2. Scientists know exactly how many different types of plants and animals exist on this planet.

_____3. When scientists classify things, they are putting them in groups of things that are alike.

_____4. Elephants, fleas, people, and fish are all members of the same phylum and the same kingdom.

_____5. Elephants, fleas, people, and fish are all members of the same phylum and the same kingdom, but not of the same class or of the same species.

_____6. If two living things are members of the same species, that means that they are also members of the same genus and members of the same family, and members of the same kingdom.

_____7. Not everyone in this room right now is a member of the same order.

_____8. The first person who classified living organisms did it by how things appeared, but now, we use other features too.

		Students are then given a few minutes to read and commit to the statements on the anticipation guide. However students are told not to open their books yet. They are also informed that they should make their own predictions – without glancing at the predictions of their classmates.
7.	Building of background knowledge occurs through reading the statements the teacher has created to focus on important ideas, and through small-group discussions – social construction of meaning begins	7. Then the students are asked to discuss their predictions with the others in their assigned cooperative group in order to compare reasoning and to help build each others' background knowledge before engaging in reading. The teacher moves about the room to monitor the discussions, many of which are quite animated because of the nature of the statements and the students' various perceptions and misperceptions.
8.	Clear concrete purpose is established – students will write notations about evidence they find. They will write this on the concrete prop provided by the anticipation guide itself.	8. The teacher then gets the students' attention in order to describe how they should gather evidence in the reading and how they ought to note underneath each of the statements on the anticipation guide where they have found evidence. He points out to students that this activity is very different from a typical worksheet such as students often see in school. He says, "In fact, this activity is the opposite of a worksheet in many ways. Let me describe why I say that. First, you might have noticed that there are *no questions on it* – only statements – hypothetical truths that you are going to try to prove or disprove by referring to the text. I eavesdropped on some of your discussions, and you have some interesting differences of opinion on the validity of some of the statements. That's good. I also want to point out some of the other differences between this activity and a worksheet. Usually worksheets have questions that are worded exactly the way they are worded in the text." (At this, many students nod their heads in agreement.) "In addition, with a typical worksheet, you can find the answer in exactly one place in the text." (More affirmative nodding occurs.) "In fact, with the typical worksheet, you never really have to read! You just go on a hunting expedition for key words around which you might find the answers. You can start in the middle, at the end or the beginning – it doesn't matter – because you are just looking for the right answer to fill in the blank on the worksheet. This anticipation guide is different."
9.	Scaffold provided by clarifying purpose – interpretive reading	9. "First, you will not find anything in the text worded exactly like the statements on the anticipation guide. So you will have to read interpretively. In addition, in order to prove any of the statements on the anticipation guide either true or false, you may have to cite

	two or three different ideas from two or more paragraphs to prove your case. In fact, I am asking you to act like attorneys – to gather as much evidence as you can for your interpretation so that, after the reading, you will be able to present your interpretation to the others in your cooperative learning group, and you will be able to defend your interpretation by reference to the text."
10. Modeling of the evidence-gathering task expected during reading	10. To explain the process of gathering evidence, the teacher uses a large-print version of the overhead transparency of the same anticipation guide that thestudents each have. On this, he models how students might take notes in the spaces under each of the statements. Students are reminded to note the page, column, and paragraph that they are interpreting so that later, they might be able to cite that portion of the text to help prove whether an anticipation guide statement is verifiable or not.
11. Teacher makes clear the expected behavior – establishing the environment for serious individual reading	11. The last instruction to the students before they begin silently reading to gather information to verify their individual predictions is to "perform the reading without distracting either themselves or others" while reading the section of the chapter on classification of living things. The teacher also reminds them that if they run across any term or concept that they do not understand, that they should raise a hand so he can move in to resolve the confusion and whisper the meaning to the student.
12. Step two of Skill Acquisition Model – guided practice for acquisition of new knowledge and meta-cognition skills	12. The classroom settles down as students quietly concentrate, engaged in reading to find out whether their predictions were correct or not. There is virtual silence for about fifteen minutes as students pore over the text.
13. Teacher supports comprehension and practices authentic assessment	13. The teacher quietly moves around the room to monitor student work with the anticipation guides. He carries a textbook, and he is modeling the search for evidence by frequently writing on his copy of the anticipation guide. The teacher occasionally stops to answer a question or to whisper an encouragement to a student, but he is very cautious to avoid any overt distractions during the reading time.
14. Step two of cooperative learning – attempt at consensus	14. After about fifteen minutes, many of the students are stirring, anticipating the next step in the procedure – to meet again in their groups to attempt to come to a consensus as to which of the anticipation guide statements should be checked, and which

	should not. The teacher instructs them to do just that, reminding the students that to come to consensus is different than attempting to find a majority. He does this to be sure that all voices are heard, and that all students are active in the process. He points out to them that if all members of the group are in agreement about a given statement, they need not discuss that one statement. They only need to discuss those about which at least one person in the group disagrees with others. He reminds them of the need to convince their group members based on evidence that they have found in the text and which they are interpreting based on their prior knowledge.
15. Teacher facilitates interactive discussion	15. Once again, the teacher moves around the room to monitor and assist in this process. In addition, the teacher reminds students that they must "act like attorneys, presenting evidence from the text to support their claims." Occasionally the teacher stops to join in the discussion about a statement with a given group. However, he is careful not to "tell the answer" to them. He listens to their reasoning and acts like a coach in helping them to clarify their thoughts. At times, he reminds them of related things they have learned in other chapters earlier in the course to assist in their synthesis of ideas.
16. Students use academic language to make their cases for interpretation. Higher order thinking occurs as students analyze, synthesize, and apply new knowledge in order to argue their cases.	16. This time, the room is loud with students often pointing a finger at the text and arguing vociferously over such statements as "Dogs, cats, elephants, and humans *are* alike!" (Some students are focused on how they are alike, while others are focused on the differences.) Many such arguments occur in the small groups as students clarify their interpretation of the text and of the new vocabulary that they have learned. By arguing this way, students are bringing higher order thinking into the discussion since they must use synthesis, analysis, application, and evaluation thinking to make their points.
17. Step three of cooperative learning – teacher mediates large-group discussion	17. The teacher locates the group that has first achieved consensus, and he writes down which statements the group feels should be checked after reading and discussion. He notes these on the transparency of the anticipation guide he has on the overhead projector. The next phase of the learning experience occurs when the teacher turns on the overhead projector and calls the attention of all the students in order to go to the next step of the process toward understanding how animals are classified – attempt to achieve a classroom consensus.

18. Teacher behaves as a mediator or arbitrator of student-owned discussion	18. Now the students, who all have had practice in small group discussions, sort out their differences over the few statements about which all the class had not yet achieved consensus.
	This process takes a few more minutes, with students obviously relishing the ability to present their interpretations of the evidence they have found in their textbooks, and which they have just practiced discussing in their small groups. The discussion is orderly and mature, and all students seem interested in the outcome. The teacher is careful to facilitate the discussion between the groups who disagree with each other. The teacher does not wish to "tell" the answers. Rather, he wants students to experience the process of making sense of the text through their own discussions. He knows that real reading instruction is occurring when this happens – even though there is no reading specialist in the classroom! By discussing the reading with peers, first in small groups, and then in the whole class, students are acquiring the ability to construct meaning from text, which is what reading is. This teacher also knows that he does not have a monopoly on the "right answers" with regard to the anticipation guide statements. In the class that was in the classroom before the present one, students all agreed that, on number 7, indeed "everyone in this room is a member of the same order," and the item should not be checked. This class will decide differently!
19. Purposeful oral reading develops fluency	19. In the present class, one group has decided to check statement 7, and believes that they can defend that it should be checked. Rather than put them down, the teacher first asks the group that did not check the statement where they found their evidence. They immediately cite the page, column, and paragraph where they found the information suggesting that all humans are of the same order. The teacher is not satisfied, and asks them to "read the part that says it, and tell us how you are interpreting the text." All students in the classroom are focused on the page, column, and paragraph that is being cited by the student speaking for her group as she reads from the text and then tells her interpretation of what she just read.
20. New interpretation leads to challenge in constructing meaning –	20. Once the student has presented her evidence, the teacher then turns to the group that has checked the item, asking them if the information that was just cited by the girl's reading has convinced them that the statement should not be checked. Rising to the challenge, the statement checker spokesperson says, "It depends on what is meant by the word 'everyone.' We didn't read it the same

	way. We are suggesting that there are billions of microorganisms in our own intestines, and that they are of a different order than the humans in the classroom right now. In addition, there are probably thousands of insects in the carpet and in the walls of this classroom. They also are of a different order than we are. If you include all of these things as part of 'everyone,' then shouldn't we check statement number seven? No further questions, your honor!"
21. Students acquire ability to thoughtfully interpret in creative ways.	21. Suddenly, the class has been taken to a new level of thinking. Nothing that the teacher did or said has led to this. The students themselves, relishing the ability to find ways of interpreting text, and willing to argue their points, have allowed for recognition of a minor shortcoming in the thinking of all students. Instead of simply finding answers in the text, the students in this class have had the opportunity to question their own thinking as a result of this one group's actions. As a result, all students have taken a step closer to acquiring their own inquisitiveness about vocabulary and its possible interpretations. The teacher, at this point, goes to the overhead transparency to facilitate consensus regarding number seven. He points out that both groups have made valid arguments, and that to come to some consensus, perhaps the statement on the anticipation guide should be altered to account for the differences in interpretation. He proposes to change the word "everyone" to the words "every human." He asks if all students would agree with this amendment to the anticipation guide. When they agree, he asks all students to make sure they make the same amendment on their own copy, and to check that of those of the other group members.
22. Acquisition of skill	22. Through this process, all students have come closer to becoming discriminating readers. Students have acquired the ability to critique their own thinking through the discussion that occurred. This way of thinking does not end in this class today. It carries over into future readings wherein students who have participated in the process today are prone to think skeptically the next time they read – in any classroom. They have acquired an important skill.
23. Step three of the Skill Acquisition Model – Reflecting on the use of the skill	23. Once the discussion has ended, the teacher says to the class, "By a show of hands, how many of you felt that, by using the predictions that you made on this anticipation guide before reading, you found the reading easier to comprehend than if you had just been

	assigned to read it for homework or given a worksheet to do with the reading?" Virtually all students raise their hands to signify that they recognize the value of prediction in engaging one's self in reading text.
24. Homework that is reflection on what they have read in class with the assistance of their peers and the facilitation of the teacher.	24. The class is near the end, and students are reminded that they must go back through the reading as a homework assignment to complete their notes based on the objectives that were on the chalkboard at the start of the class, and which each student has copied into his/her notebook. Now that students (many of whom read two or more grade levels below the ninth grade) have read, analyzed, and thoughtfully discussed the text in class with the help of the teacher and their peers, they are easily capable of rereading it on their own at home. This teacher finds that most students do his homework assignments, and they also perform well on his tests.
25. Students acquire a positive attitude toward reading for learning	25. Students usually like the science classes of this teacher. They say, "We always get to *think* in his class. It's more interesting." The teacher, on the other hand, is used to letting the students learn through techniques that encourage them to set their own purposes for reading and then pursue the acquisition of knowledge from text, and reflect on it through discussion or writing. He is able to see the students develop their own understandings of the subject matter. At the same time he knows that active pursuit of these understandings will help the students retain the information they acquired because of the way they acquired it. He also knows that upon leaving his classroom, students will have practiced, and thus acquired, a learning skill that they will be able to use in any other subject area class or on the job. This teacher is proud to be a teacher who facilitates use of literacy skills to learn new subject matter, and he is comfortable that his students will perform well on the state's tests at the end of the year because his students have processed the subject matter through higher-order thinking, and are thus more likely to recall important concepts than students who have only heard the concepts through the words of the teacher or have searched for right answers on hundreds of worksheets throughout the year. He also knows that his students have acquired the skills of reading interpretively, a skill that is an important component of most all state tests, and a skill that will help them in all future learning experiences whether they go on to higher education or become members of the work force of the 21st century.

Duke and Pearson (2002) list the following behaviors to characterize what strategic secondary level readers do when reading:

- Good readers are active readers.
- From the outset, they have clear goals in mind for their reading. They constantly evaluate whether the text, and their reading of it, is meeting their goals.
- Good readers typically look over the text before they read, noting such things as the structure of the text and text sections that might be most relevant to their reading goals.
- As they read, good readers frequently make predictions about what is to come.
- They read selectively, continually making decisions about their reading – what to read carefully, what to read quickly, what not to read, what to reread, and so on.
- Good readers construct, revise, and question the meanings they make as they read.
- Good readers try to determine the meaning of unfamiliar words and concepts in the text, and they deal with inconsistencies or gaps as needed.
- They draw from, compare, and integrate their prior knowledge with material in the text.
- They think about the authors of the text, their style, beliefs, intentions, historical milieu, and so on.
- They monitor their understanding of the text, making adjustments in their reading as necessary.
- They evaluate the text's quality and value and react to the text in a range of ways, both intellectually and emotionally.
- Good readers read different kinds of text differently.
- When reading narrative, good readers attend closely to the setting and characters.
- When reading expository text, these readers frequently construct and revise summaries of what they have read.
- For good readers, text processing occurs not only during reading as we have traditionally defined it, but also during short breaks taken during reading, even after the reading itself has commenced, even after the reading has ceased.
- Comprehension is a consuming, continuous, and complex activity, but one that, for good readers, is both satisfying and productive.

Think how the anticipation guide in the science class provoked students into virtually all of the behaviors that Duke and Pearson (2002) list. Everything that has happened in the above classroom can happen routinely in any content area or career/technical classroom. High levels of engagement, thoughtful, purposeful reading, and intelligent discussion by all students are the routine behaviors in a content literacy classroom.

Though the above described science class used an anticipation guide as a reading strategy, it just as well could have been a preview of the reading, paired reading, and a focused free write, followed by two-column note taking for homework. Or the teacher could have had the students create graphic representations of the text they read. Without even being aware of it, each of the students in this classroom has moved closer to acquisition of several things: new knowledge, a reading strategy (predicting), self confidence as a reader and thinker, and a sense that learning and classrooms can be engaging and interesting.

Duke and Pearson also list five effective comprehension strategies that all strategic readers employ. Their list of effective comprehension strategies includes:

- prediction
- think-aloud
    i.   story structure
    ii. informational text structure
- visual representations of text
- summarization
- questions/questioning

(Each of the strategies described in part 2 of this book involves one or more of the items on this list.) Regardless of which classroom reading/writing activity the teacher decides to use, the classroom follows the same format of weaving together the three steps of the MAX Teaching framework of instruction, the three steps of the skill acquisition model, and the use of cooperative learning to create an environment in which students interact with peers, self, teacher, and text to actively construct meaning about important subject matter. If teachers were to do this 130 to 150 times throughout the school year, the vast majority of students would acquire a sense of facility with literacy skills. They would be less dependent on teachers, and more autonomous in their abilities to handle any new learning experiences.

Chapter 8

The Roles Played by Writing in a Literacy-Based Classroom

Ideas won't keep; something must be done about them.
Alfred North Whitehead

It is inappropriate to separate the processes of writing and reading since they are quite interrelated in a classroom in which students are active in constructing meaning about subject matter. Such a distinction is almost as unseemly as separating speaking from listening. Almost all of the reading strategies in this book involve some form of writing before, during, or after reading, and most involve writing in all three phases of the lesson.

Two Types of Writing

Certainly, the process of cooperative learning is enhanced when, *before* coming together in groups, each member of a cooperative learning team has a written contribution with which to begin a discussion. Using writing to gather information *during* reading lends purpose to the reading process. Writing is always a tool for extending beyond the text *after* reading, since writing helps students slow their thinking long enough to reflect on details that might support their understandings of what they have learned.

In other words, writing is an important tool in the content-literacy-based classroom. Such writing may be formal writing such as paragraphs or essays that will be graded for content, format, grammar, and usage, or it may be informal writing to be used to enhance the learning process.

Certainly *formal writing* is an important component of quality course work at any level of schooling in most subject areas. Essays, term papers, and other presentations can be used to assess students' understandings of subject matter. However, writing as an assessment tool is not the only focus of this chapter. Rather, this chapter focuses as much on the varied ways that *informal writing* might be used to enhance understanding of subject matter before, during, and after the learning experience as well as how it might be used to assess student mastery of content.

Informal Writing to Learn New Subject Matter

Writing can be used in all stages of the lesson framework — before, during, and after reading. Writing is a tactile-kinesthetic and concrete way to engage students in the learning. Some of the many purposes for using writing to learn are:

- Focusing students' attention on subject matter
- Engaging students actively with subject matter
- Arousing students' curiosity about subject matter
- Helping students discover disparate elements in subject matter
- Helping students connect subject matter with their own lives
- Helping students to construct meaning from text
- Helping students to practice higher order thinking through association, analysis, and synthesis
- Diagnosing students' learning successes and problems
- Preparing students for subject matter discussions

Figure 8-1

Writing Activities for Learning New Subject Matter

Reason for Writing:	Suggested Teacher Instructions:
1. Discover what one does or does not know	Write down what you already know about ... (PreP, Free-Write)
2. Assemble information by taking notes or making notes about subject matter	Write two-column notes about the following objectives... Take reading notes on your draft of a graphic representation ... Summarize text in the left column of a page divided into equal -size columns, and then write your reaction in the r ight column...
3. Predict what will happen next in the text	Write what you think will happen next in the story...(fiction) Write what you think the next section of text will tell us...(non -fiction)
4. Paraphrase, translate, or rephrase text	Summarize in your own words ... (GIST, No -Research Papers, Math translation , 2-Column Notes, PQRST, Free W rite, etc.)
5. Associate images, events, ideas, or personal experiences with subject matter	What do you think of when you see the word ...?
6. Define concepts or ideas about subject matter	In your own words, define ...
7. Create problems to be solved with subject matter	Make up a word problem that reflects a real -life situation in which the solver would have to use the formula for finding ...

Several activities that I use frequently to get students to manipulate ideas through the concrete activity of writing are described below, in this chapter. However, done properly, almost all of the **MAX Teaching** classroom activities described in Part II involve some writing. Figure 8-1 suggests some ways teachers might use some of the strategies in this book to engage students in writing for learning.

The type of writing that is used in most of these activities is informal writing that is not to be graded, but is used to assist students in becoming engaged in the learning. Informal writing can be found at any of the three stages of the lesson, and often involves as little as writing a word or two to be shared with others, or even writing only a check mark next to a statement with which the student agrees. Other times this informal writing is in the form of a paragraph or a graphic representation. Such informal writing can help students set purposes for subsequent reading, gather information during reading, or reorganize information after the reading has occurred.

Focused Free Writing — A Pre-Learning or Post-Learning Activity

Free Writing (Chapter 16) is one way to get students to determine what they already know about a topic. It is useful as a pre-reading activity when students are asked to focus on the subject they will be studying. It can also be used at any point in the lesson when the teacher recognizes that an idea has been introduced about which the students may have varying opinions or with which they may have had experience — or related knowledge. At that point, the teacher can stop and ask students to focus on a question, idea, or statement and respond in writing for several minutes. By getting students to commit in writing to what they are thinking, the teacher can observe progress, and also assure more participation than if s/he simply poses an open question to the class for oral discussion. (Without student writing, such discussion often tends to be dominated by a few confident students.)

Such writing can be followed by further discussion or reading to clarify students' conceptions. This can also be valuable if a class discussion is lagging and students need to get their thinking back on track. Free Writing can also be used as a culminating activity to help students reflect on what they have learned. When used in this way, students have the opportunity to synthesize the concepts they have learned in the class. At the same time, it provides an informal, but useful assessment device for the teacher. After collecting focused free writes, the teacher can scan them for understandings and misunderstandings. Normally, these should not be graded. (Regular use of non-graded reflective writing teaches the student the value of reflecting in writing, slowing down the thinking to be able to synthesize all the various components of the lesson. Eliminating the threat of a grade for this allows the student to focus on the thinking involved rather than mechanics, grammar, etc.)

The procedure is simple. State the topic, question, or statement on which you wish students to focus. Students write for a specified length of time, without stopping. The idea is for them to keep writing and thinking about the topic. If they come to a point where they can't think of anything more to say, they should still keep writing, even if they just repeat the last phrase or sentence until another thought comes. Most often, it will come.

This procedure is very effective at motivating students to write. Instead of calling it a "paragraph," which often has negative connotations to students reluctant to engage in the writing process, a "free write" sounds like something easy to do, especially when the teacher limits the time to four or five minutes. By thus minimizing the nature of the task, the teacher is making writing more palatable to many students.

Math Translation

Math translation (Figure 8-2) is a tool that helps students to use the concrete tool of writing to actively construct meaning from mathematical formulas and mathematical problems performed in numerals and symbols. One difficulty that many students have in mathematics classes is that they tend to minimize the nature of the mathematical "language" that is used to convey ideas. They often do not take the time to realize all the meaning that is conveyed through symbols. One way to combat this, while also getting some insight into how well students understand what is being performed mathematically, is to get students to practice math translation, the rewriting in prose of what they perceive in symbolic form. This process is described in detail in Chapter 17.

Figure 8-2

Student Example of Math Translation of a Solution to an Equation

$2x + 3 = 17$ $2x + 3 = 17$ $\underline{\quad -3 \quad -3}$ $2x \quad = 14$ $\dfrac{2x}{2} = \dfrac{14}{2}$ $x = 7$	A two-step equation is given. Two operations are involved. One is addition, and the other is multiplication. To get the variable all by itself on one side of the equation, you first use the inverse operation of addition (subtraction) by taking three away from both sides of the equation. Now the variable is almost all alone on the left side, but it is still multiplied by two. So, you again use an inverse operation (division this time) to get the variable by itself. Anything you do to one side, you have to do to the other side as well, so you divide both sides by two. The equation is then solved because you have an x on one side and a seven on the other side. That is the answer.

Formal Writing

Most formal writing in content area classes is used to assess student learning. Essays and paragraph answers on tests can help the teacher to determine if the students understood important concepts about course work. Other essays and papers are also used to assess student understanding and to help students synthesize important concepts related to the course. My experience with using writing in this way is that, *if you expect it, they will do it, but you may have to show them how.*

Many teachers tell me that their students will not write on tests. When given an essay question, the students respond with a "one-liner" if they respond at all. For students to be successful in organized writing, they should receive modeling from the teacher, be provided with a rubric that allows them, in advance, to know what is expected, and they should be scaffolded into the process.

Every test that I gave in my own classes was composed of 50% objective questions and 50% writing responses. This was true in every subject but mathematics, whether I was teaching 7th grade or 12th grade or anything in between. Every test had a major, multi-paragraph essay that was worth 25 to 30 points, and every test had several shorter "paragraph answer" questions. (Notice they are not called "short answer" questions. If you have "short answer" questions on your test, that is what you will get — short answers — often less than a sentence).

On the other hand, if you have spelled out ahead of time that paragraph answers must include a main idea sentence and several supporting detail sentences — *and you have modeled the process in class* — then students will write beautiful paragraph answers on their tests. Let students know that they are not so much answering questions as "showing off" how much they know.

Similarly, a multi-paragraph essay, if expected, will be what you get, if you have prepared them to write it. This takes some preparation and modeling, but students will be able to perform this task if you get them ready to do so. As in many of the skills I expect students to learn throughout the year, I model the process for them, gradually scaffolding them into performing independently as the year progresses.

The first essay, on the first test of the year, is one that we all work together as a class to plan ahead of time, usually the day before the test. I like to pose the essay question that will be on the test, have students fact storm the answer, and then work on the chalkboard or on an overhead projector to model use of a graphic representation that will create a holistic picture of a complete response. This often takes the better part of a class (and reviews the essential learning experience of the unit). Once we have finished the graphic representation, I often model composing the opening paragraph. Then, when they receive the test the next day, the same question is on the test, and so is the graphic representation that we worked together to create. Students are thus empowered to write from the graphic based on the discussion of the prior day's class.

As the year progresses, I gradually wean the students from dependence on my assistance in preparation of the essay. Later in the year, I often give a few points of extra credit to those students who create a graphic representation as they prepare their essay response on the test. Thus, as in much of the instruction in the literacy-based classroom, the teacher gradually fades out of the picture as students develop as autonomous performers of complex literacy skills.

No-Research Papers

This is a technique that demands of students many of the skills of writing a major term paper, but it eliminates many of the problems associated with research papers. It is imperative that all students have the opportunity to write research papers.

The ability to select a topic of interest, examine many various resources for information, synthesize information, plan a well thought out paper, and develop the skills associated with citing sources are all important abilities that ought to be practiced by all students. Few would dispute that the act of synthesizing various materials in a cohesive, well-prepared essay is important in developing complex programs of thought that help students improve the way they think about all new learning. What if we were to offer the opportunity to do this while, at the same time, eliminating one or two of the obstacles in the process?

No-Research Papers are essays or term papers that demand careful analysis and synthesis of large amounts of information, without the hassles of deciding upon a topic, making trips to libraries, or citing sources. That's because the major source of information is the textbook!

Textbooks are valuable tools. Though the textbook should not be the only information source in a class, the textbook is an often-neglected or misused tool for learning. The fact is that most of the content being measured by standardized tests is to be found in textbooks. The basic themes of a course and the vocabulary of the discipline are to be found there. The problem is that, even though many of the questions on standardized tests require interpretive reading, most students are not being exposed to thoughtful interpretation of text.

No-Research Papers are a way to get students to reflect on "the big picture" of the course they are taking. Regardless of the course you teach, certain fundamental ideas are usually very important to understanding the important themes that run throughout your course and your textbook. In geography these would be the five themes of geography. In mathematics, the big themes might relate to solving problems and writing equations. In a science course, the big ideas might relate to scientific method, the dynamics of life, etc. What are the big themes of your course? Where are they described in your textbook?

I first discovered the concept of the No-Research Paper when I was teaching United States and Virginia Government several years ago. I realized after helping students learn the first four chapters of the textbook that few students had a complete grasp of what the U. S. government was all about. To many students, a chapter on the British roots of the U. S. government was just that. Few saw that it also related to the constitution that we eventually created in 1787. The same could be said for the chapter about the approximately 200 years of the American colonial experience, and the chapter on the period from 1776 until 1787, when Americans lived under a government that was too weak to defend itself, and had little power to deal with other problems that arose.

In order to get my students to truly understand the constitution that our forefathers created, it seemed to me that students ought to synthesize what they had learned in the first three chapters of the text with what they were finding out about the basic principles of the U. S. Constitution in chapter four. My solution was to assign a "seven-to-ten-page, typed, double-spaced paper" on the topic, "Why We Have the Constitution We Have."

By assigning such a paper over a month's time, I immediately accomplished two important goals. First, I put my students into a manageable but complex task that I knew would help them to synthesize the basic ideas fundamental to understanding the rest of my course. Secondly, I allowed them to practice the process of writing a lengthy work (the first for many of them) with the use of a rubric to emulate.

The process took slightly more than a month to do. We had already read the first three chapters when the assignment was given. A great deal of support was provided in the form of modeling of the use of graphic representations to analyze and synthesize. A rubric was provided for students. A peer-review process was established, and timetables were set to monitor progress. Some of the work was done in the classroom; however the majority of the project was on the students' own time (homework).

The benefits of a No-Research Paper are enormous. First, by eliminating the need to hunt for information in the library, etc., two great obstacles are automatically overcome; the need for a topical decision, and finding the time to do research. On the other hand, a similarly complex level of thinking is required in the process of deciding what to include in the paper, what not to include, and how to restate the essential understandings of the course in one's own words. Instead of gathering 100 pages of notes on a topic, each student is already in possession of 100 pages of subject matter, all of which s/he has read and discussed in class. The focus in a No-Research Paper, then, is developing deeper understanding through analysis and synthesis.

Since my first experiences with this form of student writing, I have been greatly reinforced in my original beliefs that students would benefit from the process. A paper on the five themes of geography, scientific method and how it applies in earth science, tools for problem solving in algebra, the merits of various genre in literature, or any other topic, can lead students to practice of higher order thinking skills while they are solidifying their understanding of the most important concepts of your course. At the same time, students are experiencing success in articulating a well-thought-out argument, presented in writing.

No-Research Papers can be of various lengths. They need not cover several chapters. One chapter or even a section of a chapter can be processed in this manner. The teacher may also provide other materials that augment the text. Clearly, any time we help our students reflect through writing on the major themes of our disciplines, we are helping them in more ways than one.

Teaching Students How to Write Well

Any time teachers can get students to articulate content-related ideas in writing, they are helping students to understand their subject matter. Teachers can use the writing process to help students construct meaning in learning. By stressing the process of writing a quality paragraph that has a central idea and then supports that idea by elaborating through supporting details, the teacher is helping students to learn subject matter.

Consider how little time is required for a teacher to recognize, when the lesson has been completed and there are seven or eight minutes remaining in the class period, that a sound conclusion to the lesson might be having each of the students write a single paragraph that states the main objective that was learned in the class, followed by two or three statements of elaborating details. A teacher who uses this time in such a way is helping students to more deeply process the content while helping them to acquire the skills of writing well.

The same may be said of multi-paragraph essays, and ultimately longer works. In any case, the teacher will need to model the expected behavior the first few times the writing tasks are originated. But, gradually, students will see themselves as people able to individually articulate ideas in your subject area — an important step in mastering the content of your course.

Hunt for Main Ideas

This reading strategy (described more in Chapter 20) is a reverse way to teach the writing process. Instead of writing, students are encouraged to take apart the writing of others. Again, the textbook may provide the vehicle for this activity, but it can be any text the teacher elects to use. Students can make light-pencil marks in the margin of the text while they are reading — these are placed next to what the student perceives to be the main idea sentence of each paragraph. By placing students into this task, the teacher is helping students read strategically, monitoring their own comprehension of the text. By following the cooperative learning paradigm described in earlier chapters — individual written commitment, followed by small-group discussion, and then whole-class discussion — students compare their varying perceptions of what the main idea of each paragraph was. The result of this discussion is most often a deeper understanding of content. The two skills that are unconsciously acquired are the ability to read in a metacognitive way and the ability to write well.

One caveat — many textbooks leave something to be desired. In some paragraphs, for instance, there may not be a main idea. At times, a paragraph may just include two to three sentences supporting an idea already stated elsewhere. It does not hurt to have students discover these things. Often, students can see why it is so important to write well as a result of discussions about such text.

To What Audience Should a Student Write?

It has been my experience that many students write to the teacher when they write a paragraph or essay on a test. In other words, they assume that the teacher already knows the subject matter, and that they just have to skirt the topic to let the teacher know that they know something about the answer. Writing in this way is the opposite of quality writing. A solution that helps to overcome this assumption is to tell students to "…Always write as if you are explaining this idea to a friend of yours who really needs to understand the concept, but has no prior knowledge about it… Write as if your friend missed class the day the subject matter was learned, and you must get the idea across to the friend. Explain each idea fully, and be sure to provide many clear examples that elaborate on your ideas. In other words — show off how much you know." By writing this way, students are asked to analyze what they have studied and to synthesize the various components. Thus, writing becomes a tool to enable higher order thinking skills.

Chapter 9

Frequently Asked Questions

Not everything that is faced can be changed, but nothing can be changed until it is faced.
James Baldwin

Fourteen years of working with teachers in workshops, at the college of education, and in my own school has provided me with a list of important questions, the answers to which I hope I provide below. No matter where I am, these same questions occur. That is because each of the questions deals with important concerns that all teachers deal with on a day-to-day basis. They are the same questions that I had when I first began to teach using content-literacy based classroom activities. My responses follow these 16 questions:

1. **Where will I find time to do these activities? I have a curriculum to cover.**
2. **Many of my students can't read. How could this work with them?**
3. **I'm not a reading teacher. Why should I do this? What are the reading and English teachers doing?**
4. **I have to prepare for standardized tests.**
5. **How often should I use reading or writing for learning in my classroom?**
6. **How often should I use a particular reading or writing activity? Could I select one or two of my favorites and use them over and over?**
7. **What about homework? If you do all the reading in class, don't you believe in homework?**
8. **What evidence exists to show that content-literacy-based instruction works?**
9. **If content literacy instruction works so well, why don't more teachers use it?**
10. **What about mathematics? My mathematics book doesn't have much reading in it.**
11. **If lecture & worksheets worked for students in my generation, why shouldn't they work today?**
12. **My textbook is .. (less than adequate). Why should I use an outdated and/or inaccurate text?**
13. **What about teaching vocabulary?**
14. **My students are not motivated. What about students who refuse to participate?**
15. **Why is round-robin or popcorn reading not an appropriate way to help students learn new subject matter?**
16. **What about work sheets? You seem to think them to be a waste of time. Why do textbook publishers make them, then?**

FAQ 1. Where will I find time to do these activities? I have a curriculum to cover.

This question is the most often asked in the workshops that I perform for teachers. The pressure to cover a prescribed curriculum is stronger today than ever before as a result of the accountability movement at both the national and state levels. Accountability means end-of-course tests that all students must take, and the resulting scores reflect on students, teachers, schools, and communities. Many of the tests are "gateway" tests which determine whether a student will progress from one grade to another or whether a student will graduate. Thus, teachers everywhere perceive the need to attempt to cover as much as they can of the prescribed curriculum for their course. So where does a teacher find the time to have students read in the classroom? There are three parts to the answer.

The first part of my response to that is that in all the years in which I used content area reading in my classes on virtually a daily basis — as the principle method of facilitating learning of new material — I always covered as much or more of the prescribed curriculum as any other teacher in my school teaching the same course and using the same text. Most often I covered more than other teachers.

Secondly, my students do not passively learn from lecture or worksheets, but rather, find themselves in a year-long conversation about the essential themes of the course, whether the course is in mathematics, science or social studies. Through active engagement in the subject matter, they develop understandings that allowed them to retain the information longer than a student who copies notes from an overhead projector or from the teacher's lecture without true understanding.

Thirdly, students who learn through active engagement with text accompanied by the routine opportunity to interact with others about making sense of that text learn how to read. They acquire the metacognitive skills that will serve them throughout a lifetime of learning from text and other sources. When compared to other students on a test of metacognitive strategy awareness, ninth grade students exposed to nine months of content literacy instruction significantly outperformed their peers exposed to a more traditional curriculum, even outperforming the majority of twelfth grade students tested (Forget, 1991, 1997).

Compare the traditional classroom to a content literacy classroom. In the traditional classroom, the teacher has assigned an eight-page reading from the text for homework with the section review questions as part of the assignment. The next day, three students out of 30 have done the reading. So, the teacher can carry on a wonderful four-way conversation, with most of the students in the classroom wondering about what they are talking about. The teacher then spends most of the class period explaining the concepts to the rest of the class since most did not read the assignment. Dedicated teachers have been behaving this way for years. I know I did before I started using MAX Teaching in my classes. I truly wanted my students to understand important concepts about my curriculum. Thus, I had to describe, provide examples, and generally develop the conceptual understandings of my course through teacher-led discussions that took up most of the period. For most students, a shallow understanding is the most that can be expected from such a curriculum.

Consider the content literacy alternative. No more time is spent learning important concepts through daily reading and interactive student discussion than through lecture and teacher-led discussion. The big difference though is that students who learn this way are actively processing important course concepts and developing deeper understandings that will lead to higher order thinking and greater retention. Instead of the three students who did their homework discussing with the teacher, all students can be active in the discussion because they have all read the text which they still have open on their desks. They can use the vocabulary of the discipline in attempting to make sense of complex ideas, and they help each other do it.

Daily use of reading and writing to learn new subject matter thus takes no more time than other more traditional methods. There is one big difference though. Students who learn through content area literacy techniques also acquire the ability to learn from text. Students who learn in the traditional classroom just get exposed to the concepts of the course. They do not receive the same opportunities to develop the skills associated with processing difficult text — a skill they will need throughout their lives.

FAQ 2. Many of my students can't read. How could this work with them?

There are two parts to this answer. The first is that your students *can* read. The vast majority of students who made it as far as the fourth grade can read. They know letter-sound relationships. They may hate reading. They may avoid reading every chance they get. But they can read. Try this — give the sports section of the paper to a "non-reader" the day after he missed a televised game played by his favorite team. You will see reading occur. Better yet, try MAX Teaching.

My experience in many different classrooms in many different subject areas is that, done properly, students will readily become engaged in reading if the MAX Teaching process is used. The combination of enhancing prior knowledge, cooperative learning, focus on a skill to make the reading easier, and a concrete task to perform during the reading all help to get reluctant readers past their fears. Once the process is started in a classroom, and students have had successes over a period of days, even the reluctant readers forget that they did not like to read. Year after year, this has been my experience with "non-readers."

When I was teaching twelfth-grade U.S. and Virginia Government one year, I had a student who overcame his dyslexia through months of guided practice in reading in my classroom. This particular student had an IEP that had him meeting every day with his resource teacher during the last class of the day so that she could read all of his homework assignments to him for all his courses. She would ask him all the questions at the end of the chapter or whatever other homework assignment had been given in each of the courses, and he would respond so that she could write down his answers for him. By March of the school year, she approached me to ask what I had done with him since he no longer needed her. My response was that I had done nothing other than take him, along with his peers in the classroom, through the three steps of MAX Teaching on a daily basis. He learned to read in a twelfth grade social studies classroom! This young man would have gone through the rest of his life thinking that he could not read. This is just one extreme case. Countless other reluctant readers have discovered, over the years, in my classroom, that they can read better than they ever dreamed they could.

There are several reasons why some students avoid reading, and they have been discussed in chapter 4 on motivation. These include avoidance of failure, lack of background knowledge needed to understand the reading, misconceptions in interpretation based on incorrect prior knowledge, and lack of skill. Each of these is systematically dealt with each day in the MAX teaching process. Most students that consider themselves non-readers fit into the category of students who are not motivated to read. There are many factors that are built into the MAX Teaching system of instruction that would help these students get past their reluctance.

The second part of the answer to how to deal with poor or reluctant readers is that there are many scaffolds that you can use to create a successful reading experience for these students. One is that you can utilize one of the strategies in this book with the additional step of your reading part of the text aloud to the students. Though I abhor round-robin reading or "popcorn" reading done by students in the classroom, I am an advocate of using some reading aloud by the teacher, especially near the beginning of the school year. A teacher reading aloud can read with fluency, modeling that the text is language as in conversation. By reading some text aloud, the teacher can stop to facilitate small-group or class discussion of the topic from time to time. It is very important when the teacher reads aloud that students follow along in their text at the same time. This is an activity that improves fluency for the students. (They must not be allowed to "kick back" or put their heads on the desk when the teacher reads.)

Even if the teacher adds the scaffold of reading aloud to the class, students should be weaned from this as soon as possible. This can be done within a single class period if the reading is interesting enough and the motivation is there. Often, with special education students, such weaning may take a longer period of time. Nevertheless, it should be the goal of the teacher to develop independent readers as soon as is practical.

FAQ 3. I'm not a reading teacher. Why should I do this? What are the reading and English teachers doing?

I am not asking any teacher to become a reading teacher. I only ask that you consider using well-researched reading and writing strategies in your classroom to help students more deeply learn your subject matter. The collateral benefit will be that they improve their reading skills. Teachers all know how important the reading of text was in their own educations. None of us would be here if we had not depended on text. Certainly, college lectures would never have sufficed in preparing us in our discipline.

More than half of all students who go to college today do not finish their freshman year. I would argue that the principal reason for this is that they do not have a clue about how to be strategic in their learning, especially learning that takes place through expository text. Even students who love to read novels often struggle with the dry, boring, difficult text that they confront in middle school through college. This is especially true in college where students are suddenly accountable for reading massive quantities of text the subject of which will not be covered in classroom lectures. What are teachers doing to share the strategies for approaching text that they have developed for themselves over the years? MAX Teaching is a way to routinely put students through guided practice in exactly the strategies that experienced readers use all the time. The teacher, then is the master learner, while the students are treated as apprentice learners when it comes to how to handle text. In this sense, all you are doing is sharing your knowledge of skills with the students.

Equally as important, though, is the fact that students who read to learn in the MAX Teaching format learn the subject matter better because of the hands-on nature of the knowledge base in the classroom. Everyone is on the same page — literally as well as figuratively. All students become acquainted with the vocabulary of the discipline, and they use it routinely in class discussion to construct meaning from the text. Not only is it true to suggest that we cannot leave the teaching of reading to the language arts teachers, but students need to acquire the literacy that is unique to your discipline.

FAQ 4. I have to prepare for standardized tests.

The best preparation for standardized tests is to have students who truly understand the content of your course, and who are able to read well to make inferences and perform higher order thinking about the subject matter. Students who have a steady diet of such activity in the content literacy based classroom thrive on the kinds of questions that are on most standardized tests. Those who have had a steady diet of worksheets, copying notes from overhead projectors, and teacher lecture do not.

FAQ 5. How often should I use reading or writing for learning in my classroom?

Content-literacy based instruction is not a once-a-week or a once-a-month way of helping students learn. By immersing students in the use of text and cooperative construction of meaning to learn new subject matter, teachers are providing opportunities for students to sink their teeth into subject matter. Rather than some ethereal teacher-dominated discussion of content well-known to the teacher but very abstract to most of the students in the room, students in this paradigm are the ones who do the thinking and discussing. They are empowered to do so by the concrete nature of the text that they have in their hands, and by the activities that the teacher has organized to see that they succeed at both the learning of the content and at the use of text to learn.

This can be a major paradigm shift for many teachers who have become used to being the "sage on stage" for most of their teaching careers. On the other hand, new ways of doing things should not be shunned by teachers. Imagine if pilots or surgeons shunned new ways of doing their work. Any professional should be not only willing to change, but anxious to embrace changes that are well researched and shown to be effective. My experience working with teachers from all over the country is that when they are willing to try this format for teaching over a brief period of several weeks, jumping in with both feet, they never look back. They quickly find that they are having greater success with more students than ever before. No teacher wants anything other than success for all of his/her students. Once these methods are tried, and you see the success of your own students, you will join the crowd too.

However, you will see that it does not work as well if you make it a once-in-a-while activity in your class. Students deserve to be engaged in learning on a daily basis. They respond well when the opportunity presents itself, and they rebel against boring, busy work. The good news is that, once you have tried the activities in Part II, you will see that most of them take little or no planning time on your part. They do take energy in the classroom. You can't sit at your desk and enter grades in your book while students are busy with a worksheet. Instead, you will find yourself actively supporting their successes in individual and group work during the classes. The trade off is that you will find yourself with more free time out of the classroom.

The answer to the question, then, is just about every day. Picture your students entering your classroom every day, knowing that they are going to be actively engaged in meaningful processing of your subject matter, and that their thinking and their interpretations are important to the conversation that takes place in your classroom. That is the way content-literacy based learning works, but only if it is the routine, not a once-in-a-while way of learning.

FAQ 6. How often should I use a particular reading or writing activity? Could I select one or two of my favorites and use them over and over?

There are two important reasons why teachers should not limit themselves to the use of just a few of the activities, but rather should use several different reading and writing strategies in their classes. First, novelty is an important component of a brain-compatible classroom (Slater, 2002). Secondly, and perhaps more important, each of the activities in Part II get at slightly different underlying skills than the other activities do. Anticipation guides help students to use predicting as a tool for setting purposes for reading; KWL activities use questioning; paired reading focuses on paraphrasing during reading as a tool to enhance metacognition; and so on... each activity focuses on particular skills and works better with different structures of text or different purposes in learning. Thus, teachers who use a multitude of classroom content-literacy-based activities find that their students develop more varied skills, and are more likely to participate in the classroom because class does not get stale through repeating the same activities over and over.

FAQ 7. What about homework? If you do all the reading in class, don't you believe in homework?

Yes, I believe in nightly homework. Only, my homework looks different from the traditional homework assignments that have been handed out over the years in most schools. Typically, the assignment is something like "read chapter 3, section 2 for tomorrow's discussion, and do the section review questions that follow." In the vast majority of public school classrooms, a significant percentage of students read at least two or more grade levels below the level of the text that has been assigned to them. This percentage often exceeds 70% of students! If that is the case, why would a teacher assure the failure of these students by assigning them a reading that will, at best, be frustrating to them?

Consider, on the other hand, a situation in which these students read the text in class, with the assistance of their peers and the facilitation of their teacher to assist them in constructing meaning from the text. Then, they are sent home to *reread the text* that they have read in class, *making notes* that they will subsequently be able to use to study for the test. This homework assignment is described in Chapter 12. It is a homework assignment that I have used successfully over twelve years of teaching in many different subjects, and I have found that, gradually, almost all students will develop the habits of doing homework through this assignment.

Homework that is too difficult for students, or homework that requires students to merely "find answers" without having to read carefully to see the logical presentation made by the authors, but rather to "hunt for answers" is a waste of students' valuable time. They know it. That is why so few do their homework. It makes so little sense that they might as well copy someone else's homework. When students do homework that is a form of *reflection* on what they have learned in class, they are learning a life skill, and they are much more likely to remember the content months later on the state test.

Teachers who assign the traditional "chapter 3, section 2" assignment are used to the fact that even if students do show up with the questions answered, often, they still do not understand the essential concepts of the lesson. Those teachers spend the majority of their classes "teaching" what the students might have learned the night before in their text. In a content-literacy-based classroom, the learning takes place first — in class, through reading — and students more deeply imprint their learning through a second reading for homework.

FAQ 8. What evidence exists to show that content-literacy-based instruction works?

MAX Teaching is a product of an enormous body of research compiled during the 20th century by cognitive researchers such as Piaget, Bruner, Vygotsky, Bloom, and many others. What we know is that students develop (acquire) abilities and knowledge through the processes of construction of meaning, a life-long process. Awareness of these processes and how they can be stimulated should inform teachers of what works in the classroom. We know that what *has* been occurring in more traditional classrooms worked well in schools of the 19th century when the major goals of education were fairly limited to producing citizens with the most basic of skills to perform in a world very different from the one in which we live today. In today's world, knowing how to learn is more important than what is learned. Certainly a core body of knowledge is imperative in a thriving democracy, and this way of teaching in no way diminishes that awareness. On the other hand, MAX Teaching allows for students to acquire that body of knowledge at the same time that they are acquiring life-long learning skills.

Evidence of the successes of using content area reading and writing as a principal method of instruction comes in many forms (Dixon-Krauss, 1996; Forget, 1991; Forget & Morgan, 1997; Forget, Lyle, Reinhart-Clark, & Spear, 2003; Greenleaf, et al., 2001; Vacca, 2002; Zingraff-Newton, 1995), each of which will be further discussed below. The results include:

- higher achievement test scores,
- greater metacognitive strategy awareness,
- the ability to read materials that are several years higher than measured student reading grade level,
- improvement in measured student reading grade level,

- improved student attitude toward reading,
- improved learning of subject matter as measured by tests,
- greater percentage of students passing classes,
- lower dropout rates, and
- better attendance rates.

Some of the above-mentioned outcomes clearly influence some of the other results. Students who are having greater success in class as a result of the fact that their teachers are helping them to successfully use reading and writing as tools for learning would likely have an improved attitude toward reading and writing. Greater amounts of reading and writing lead to higher achievement test scores. Improved grades on tests lead to lower dropout rates and higher passing rates. The fact that students are empowered to read materials that are technically above the students' measured reading grade level leads to improvement in reading grade level. And so on... The point to be made is that significant differences have been shown in all of the above measures when comparing groups of students who were exposed to content literacy instruction with comparable groups who were not so treated.

Achievement Tests: Marzano, et al. (2001) report data on meta-analyses of studies of the effects of nine categories of classroom activities that work to improve student achievement (Marzano, Pickering, & Pollock, 2001). Their work indicates that percentile gains of students in the subject studies range from +22 to +45 when treated with these categories of instruction compared to students in control groups. This work suggests that significant achievement gains can result from classroom activities that include: identifying similarities and differences, summarizing and note taking, reinforcing effort and providing recognition, homework and practice, non-linguistic representation, cooperative learning, setting objectives and providing feedback, generating and testing hypotheses, and use of questions, cues, and advanced organizers. Each of these categories of behavior is included in one or more of the various classroom activities in Part II of this work. Marzano, Pickering, & Pollock (2001) show the results; this book shows how to get the results in your classroom.

It is the rare school that gets an entire faculty to commit to using content-literacy-based instruction in the classroom. However, it does occur. In one study conducted by a Georgia middle school whose entire faculty has been developed to use content literacy instruction in all content areas, tests of students' cognitive abilities were measured before the school year began. The school's mean scores on the cognitive abilities test place the school right at the median of all the 16 middle schools in its district each year. Yet, on tests of language arts, social studies, science, and math at the end of the year, the school consistently comes in first or second in the district. The only significant difference in how students are developed through the year is the form of instruction used to help them learn new subject matter. This school believes that content literacy instruction is making the difference for them, and they continue to support the development of their new and returning teachers as teachers who employ content-literacy-based instruction in their classrooms (Forget, et al., 2003).

Metacognitive Strategy Awareness: In three studies conducted with high school students, subjects were measured with a test of metacognitive strategy awareness to ascertain if they would report strategic ways to prepare themselves for reading before reading, maintain purposes during reading to enhance comprehension, and contemplate what they had read after the reading. The groups included social studies, language arts, and mathematics classes, each being compared to control classes not receiving similar content-literacy-based instruction. In each of the three studies, the group means were significantly different for the two groups even though the students had taken the same courses with the same objectives and textbooks. Students in the content-literacy-based classes showed significantly greater awareness of strategies to enhance their own comprehension when reading (Forget, 1991; Forget & Morgan, 1997; Zingraff-Newton, 1995).

Reading Difficult Materials: Evidence that students can read materials that are four or more grade levels above their diagnosed reading grade level is based on the Vygotskyan notion that "any student can do today, with the assistance of competent peers and/or a facilitating teacher, what s/he will be able to do alone tomorrow" (Dixon-Krauss, 1996). Teachers who properly apply the Motivation activities of building sufficient background knowledge, focusing on a skill to make the reading easier, assigning a concrete enough task to perform during reading, and allow for cooperative peer discussions to occur both before and after the reading among groups of heterogeneously grouped students will find that "reading grade level" means little. Students can perform well beyond their "diagnosed" reading levels if they are motivated to do so.

Improvement in Student Reading Grade Level: Countless teachers using reading and writing across the curriculum are finding that their students improve rapidly in their abilities to take on new text in learning situations. One group of practicing teachers in a program for ninth grade urban students has shown an average gain of two years in the diagnosed reading grade level of their students over a six month period (Greenleaf, et al., 2001).

Certainly this relates to the fact that students, as reported above, can read materials that are at a level that is above their measured level. This is analogous to an athletic team "playing up" by competing against teams that are superior to them at a given time. Such competition has the tendency, if coached properly, to improve the team such that when they play teams at their own level, they find the task easier than if they had been limited to that competition all along.

Other Indicators of Student Success: Students learn subject matter in deeper, more meaningful ways when they manipulate the concrete prop of text facilitated by a knowledgeable teacher in a content literacy classroom. In addition, they are acquiring the life-long skills needed to perform in an information age (Vacca, 2003). Multiple anecdotal indicators from teachers all over the country who begin to use content literacy instruction in their classrooms suggest that the typical gain in student test scores is anywhere from 10-25 points on average, using tests that teachers had been administering for years on the same subject matter (Forget, et al., 2003). In addition, largely because of the levels of engagement students experience in content-literacy-based classrooms, attendance rates and dropout rates improve significantly. In one comparison group measure of ninth grade students, the attendance rate for the year for the content literacy class was five percentage points higher than for other ninth grade students in the same school, and the failure rate (not being promoted to the tenth grade) was seven percent for the content literacy group compared to 21% for other ninth graders in the school (Forget & Morgan, 1997).

Attitude toward Reading: Finally, student attitude toward reading in general was compared between groups of students who had received six months of content-literacy-based instruction in one social studies class and groups of students who had not received the same treatment. This study also showed significant differences in the attitudes of students toward reading (Forget, 1991).

More research is called for on the effects of whole-school content-literacy-based instruction on student achievement, attitude toward reading, and other measures. One problem in gathering such data is that whole schools rarely work as a team, implementing content-literacy-based instruction. It is much more common, even in schools where content literacy staff development has occurred, for the vast majority of teachers to go back to doing what they have always done. Yet, a body of knowledge on the effects of content-literacy-based instruction is being accumulated, and it shows that significant growth can occur for students who are given the opportunity to learn through facilitated cooperative construction of meaning derived from text in classrooms using content-literacy-based instruction methods.

FAQ 9. If content literacy instruction works so well, why don't more teachers use it?

Despite the fact that content area reading has been in the literature since the beginning of the 20th century, the number of school-wide reports on success from its use is small. Nevertheless, there is a growing body of research showing that the use of a content area reading framework of instruction has proven effective in helping students to master content material as well as to improve their ability to read (Alvermann & Phelps, 1998; Estes & Vaughn, 1985; Herber, 1978; Manzo & Manzo 1997; Richardson and Morgan, 1994; Tierney, 1995; Vacca & Vacca, 1996).

Classroom readers should be actively engaged in the search for meaning, and should be able to use multiple strategies, including self-questioning, self-monitoring, organizing information, and interacting with peers in order to construct meaning from text. Indeed, many researchers believe that it is the cognitive processing that is induced in the strategic reader rather than the strategy itself that is responsible for promoting active reading (Dole, Duffy, Roehler, & Pearson, 1991; Pearson & Fielding, 1991).

Yet this active engagement in constructing meaning is precisely what is left out of reading instruction in most school settings. Instead of engaging students in setting their own purposes for active reading and thinking, most students are sorted into those groups that need remediation and those that do not. Rather than creating for students an environment that would help them to develop their language skills and learn to pursue knowledge on their own through text, they are fed a constant barrage of worksheet drills that encourage them to decode print without ever interpreting or thinking (Bartoli, 1995; Richardson & Morgan, 1997; Stack, 1995).

The principal reason for the dearth of evidence on school-wide improvement through the use of content literacy skills across the curriculum is that it is unusual for a school, or even for a significant number of teachers within a single school to embrace the pedagogy. Secondly, teachers who do embrace the pedagogy often alter it to fit what they have already been doing, often watering it down to the point of being ineffective. Either they use the techniques once in a while, or they choose one or two of the classroom techniques that seem to fit their teaching style and limit themselves to those activities only, even though the activities they have chosen are the least constructivist of content literacy activities. For instance, the use of Cornell Note Taking is the one strategy reported by more teachers that have been staff developed in content literacy activities than any other strategy. One reason that teachers favor Cornell Notes is that the technique fits into the "transmission model" (Draper, 2002) of teaching to which they are accustomed.

The reasons for teacher reluctance to use content area literacy instruction as a tool to help students learn new subject matter are many. In a recent study, Manzo & Manzo (1997) asked three related questions as the central themes of a study of teacher practices in content area reading instruction: Do teachers know and are they inclined to use available teaching methods found in most college textbooks on content area reading instruction? If they have knowledge of such teaching methods, why do they not use them? What do teachers think would induce them to become more frequent and strategic users of published teaching methods? (Manzo & Manzo, 1997).

Eighty-five practicing teachers, primarily from urban Midwestern schools were surveyed. Applying factor analysis to the data, the researchers found that when asked why they do not use published methods, teacher responses centered around 13 factors, an unusually large number and a strong indication of the complexity of the dynamics and crosscurrents within this inventory of responses. These factors include (in the order of the strength of the correlations found) the following:

1. The strategies seemed incompatible with teaching/learning styles.
2. There was little incentive to use the strategies.

3. Fear of change.
4. The strategies might lead to class management problems.
5. Strategies would place new strains on teacher energy.
6. Feelings of need for technical support to employ the strategies.
7. Strategies imposed on teacher's coping and management style.
8. Lack of confidence.
9. Feelings of being overwhelmed.
10. Feelings that the strategies do not align with the classroom situation and demands.
11. Feelings of isolation.
12. Being told how to teach is ego deflating.
13. The classroom situation is beyond teaching methods solutions (Manzo & Manzo, 1997).

In a second series of responses to the question "What would it take for teachers to employ the published teaching strategies?" six factors emerged. The teachers indicated that for them to make such changes it would require

1. Greater incentives to perform the strategies in the classroom, largely in the form of relief from current burdens & technical support in mastering the methods;
2. Constructive feedback, consultation, and more planning time;
3. More careful training and an opportunity to adapt methods to personal style and fit;
4. Demonstrations and more time to incorporate;
5. Greater participation and control over objectives and methods, as well as greater appreciation and commiseration along the way;
6. Earlier and better training in strategy options and reinforcement from students for using them.

Manzo & Manzo (1997) summarized their interpretations by suggesting that more "practice-oriented" training in these basic methods in professional education programs is needed. They also found that teachers are reportedly not using the strategies because of insecurities about knowledge, training, and competence in their use. They found that more and better training should reduce the effects of uncertainties teachers have. Finally, they found that teachers would be more inclined to use the published strategies if there were more support from supervisors, better prompts during teaching, more technical assistance in mastering the methods, and more opportunity to corroborate with other teachers in the endeavor (Manzo & Manzo, 1997). It is hoped that the lessons in Part II of this book will help teachers to overcome some of the insecurities about knowledge, training, and competence due to the detailed nature of the lessons provided there.

FAQ 10. What about mathematics? My mathematics book doesn't have much reading in it.

This is a misconception. Mathematics books have as much as or more reading than any other textbook. The difference is that the reading is not in the same form. The symbols are different. Students must read text like $2x + 3 = 17$. Such text includes many ideas, including the fact that this is a two-step equation that involves the operations of multiplication and addition, and that the variable is multiplied by 2, and the product of that multiplication is augmented by the addition of 3, such that the total is equal to 17.

Reading is thinking. Reading is metacognitive and strategic. Reading mathematics is no different in terms of those two processes. In fact, the National Council of Teachers of Mathematics (NCTM) has stated that mathematics programs from prekindergarten through grade 12 should enable all students to

- organize and consolidate their mathematical thinking through communication;
- communicate their mathematical thinking coherently and clearly to peers, teachers, and others;
- analyze and evaluate the mathematical thinking and strategies of others;
- use the language of mathematics to express ideas precisely (NCTM, 2000).

Obviously, this list suggests that students should be working together to construct meaning about mathematical concepts, read and write mathematics, and think mathematically. All too many mathematics programs are focused on the imitation of algorithms rather than the actual understanding of the mathematics involved. My argument, borne out in years of doing it in the classroom, is that by reading, writing, speaking, listening, and thinking about mathematics individually and cooperatively, students better learn to think like mathematicians.

FAQ 11. If lecture & worksheets worked for students in my generation, why shouldn't they work today?

They never really worked for your generation either! You learned *despite* lecture and worksheets! The vast majority of teachers who look back on their own educations may remember the worksheet, but, if they think about the few teachers who really influenced their growth, chances are that they were teachers (or parents) who used anything but worksheets. They engaged you in the process of learning. They piqued your interest. They gave you hands-on activities. You learned from projects that had you researching and thinking through deep conceptual problems and analyses.

The fact is that, in a former era, before the information age in which the amount of knowledge doubles about once every six months, such activities might have seemed appropriate for students of the time. More important today is the ability to process knowledge or apparent knowledge, and the ability to decipher which is which.

FAQ 12. My textbook is … (less than adequate). Why should I use an outdated and/or inaccurate text?

I would be the first to recognize the limits of textbooks. I taught geography in the 1998-99 school year with a book that still had maps of Czechoslovakia and the Soviet Union, both of which had dissolved years earlier. So what? That is what gave me the opportunity to share several significant social studies concepts with students regarding the changing nature of maps and political systems.

The textbook has the unique ability to be a foundation from which the conversation can start. Yes, we would all like to have updated textbooks each year. However, reality is that school systems purchase textbooks once in a while, often six or more years apart. Therefore, inadequate, and outdated text is the norm rather than the exception. That is why we have newspapers and internet. I love to have students discover the disparities between what their textbook says and reality. It can only teach them to be active processors of information, always skeptical of what they read.

Use the textbook as a starting point so that students can get the basics from a fairly reliable source. Once they have the basics, use other text or sources to have them refine their understandings. The fact is that even an obsolete text in most subject areas has a basic body of knowledge that has not changed much over the last several years. By rejecting the text, and making students rely on you as their principal source of knowledge, you rob them of the fundamental tool that exists in an organized text, and you make them dependent on you for their learning. I would rather have them get the basics from a less-than-complete source and then provide opportunities to discover new knowledge as it develops or presents itself from a variety of sources (including me). It is much more valuable to have students versed in the basics before expanding to state-of-the-art.

FAQ 13. What about teaching vocabulary?

The use of classroom time to have students look up words before confronting them in reading is less than appropriate. Students need to learn the strategies that you and I use to make sense of new vocabulary words we find. Vocabulary learning should emphasize having students take increasing responsibility for their own learning. If we are to help students become strategic readers — readers who have strategies for making meaning from print and who know how, when, and why to use comprehension strategies — we must give them opportunities to examine their own processes of making meaning as well as guiding their study of vocabulary. The teacher should first model a vocabulary strategy, then guide student application of the strategy, and then have the students use the strategy on their own. The use of small groups can facilitate this process.

Vocabulary should be learned in context. Looking up and memorizing words out of context is less useful in taking ownership of the terms. On the other hand, confronting the terms in context helps students to see that they can apply the life skills of contextual analysis and structural analysis on their own. Such skills require some modeling, but are important enough that all teachers should teach them. Some other vocabulary-related teaching strategies are

1. Introduce major concepts with which students are not familiar by giving them a synonym or related word/concept with which they are familiar. Have them brainstorm all words and ideas that come to mind. Use these ideas to build a bridge to the understanding of the new related concept and vocabulary that you wish to develop.

2. Model the development of a graphic representation of text with the students during several lessons. When you feel that they understand how this graphic helps show relationships among vocabulary/ concepts, help students take ownership of this strategy by giving them the vocabulary words and having them construct such a graphic in small groups after reading the material. Later you might ask them to identify the important vocabulary in an assignment as they read. They might then construct graphic representations in their small groups and present each one to the class, explaining why they organized them in the ways they did. Variety in organization can be a springboard for a good discussion of the material. This would be a good example of gradually releasing responsibility to students so they make this note-taking and study skill strategy their own.

3. Use examples from your textbook to show students how the author has provided context clues to help them understand important technical terms. Refer routinely during your lessons to sentences or paragraphs that contain such clues to meaning. Have students read these, explain the meaning of the term, and tell how they used context to help them.

4. Show students how to look into new words for familiar elements that might assist them in predicting the possible meanings of new words. Let students explain how they have applied this skill to lesson words.

5. Have students use new words in a context that is related to their own experiences. For example — My father often has nocturnal meetings that keep him from helping me with my homework after dinner. My family is very democratic when we share ideas about vacations and vote on where to go.

There are many other ways to help students more deeply learn new vocabulary, but *the most effective meth-*

ods involve learning in the context of print. In other words, the teaching of vocabulary terms in the context in which they are found, making sense of them through manipulating them individually and in small groups, provides opportunities for students to learn deeper meanings and to retain the meanings longer (Brozo, 2003).

FAQ 14. My students are not motivated. What about students who refuse to participate?

When a student refuses to participate, there may be several reasons, among them an inability to read at the level of the text provided, lack of explanation as to why the strategy is being employed, and rebellion against the idea of actually having to think — being placed in a situation different from the pure decoding that is required in answering the questions at the end of the chapter or on a textbook-published worksheet. These can be overcome by using MAX, cooperative learning, and the Skill Acquisition Model.

Students whose reading ability is significantly below that of the text often fear failure in reading. If the teacher asks a student to participate in prediction, that student may see the activity as some sort of quiz or test of understanding. S/he may feel s/he is being put on the spot — asked to show his/her level of ignorance. If the student has difficulty in most school activities, and has been a somewhat passive spectator up to the point at which the teacher introduces student-centered activities, s/he may feel threatened by being exposed. The resulting behavior might be rejection of the activity. As in any coaching situation, the teacher needs to exhibit a sense of empathy for this — we all have been there in one sense or another, at some point in our lives. The response should be a combination of ignoring the behavior and support for success in future situations.

Many times, usually near the beginning of the year, I have had one or two students who would put their heads on the desk when it was time to read. I would gently nudge them and whisper to them that they too could do the reading and that the task at hand was easy. I might remind them of where to start in the text and of what we were looking for in the text. If that did not work, I might choose to ignore the behavior on this occasion, choosing to deal with it at another time (probably the next day). When the same student sees the level of engagement of other students in the discussions that follow the reading, s/he may see that the activity is really quite non-threatening, and quite engaging.

I usually begin the school year with the most engaging activities — ones that are easy to participate in because of their concreteness or because of their facility. I often use an anticipation guide first because it is so easy to become committed to ideas that have already been stated as hypothetical truths. The next day, I might use "Stump the Teacher" which involves no commitment on the part of the student before the reading, no unexpected "quizzing" by the teacher, and even allows the students to see the teacher get one or two wrong!

Cooperative learning should also contribute to any one student's feelings of security in the classroom. Most of the activities have students meet after reading to construct meaning as a group, and it is the *group* report that is compared to other groups' findings. Thus, the low performing student is, in a sense, a member of a "family" whose job it is to solve a problem (interpretation of the text) and help each other in doing so. If the classroom is run on the basis of cooperative construction of meaning to process text in this manner, the problem will go away.

Another possible reason why a student might not participate is that the teacher did not sufficiently explain why the activity is being used. This is where the skill acquisition model comes into play. In each of the step-by-step lesson formats provided in Part II of this book, the instructions provide for explanation to the students of why the activity is being used in the particular learning situation. For anticipation guides, for instance, the instructions in chapter 10 of this book quite explicitly describe what to say to students to let them know why we use anticipation guides. Most often, this will help students get past their timidity.

The final possible answer is that some students really come to school for all the wrong reasons — it's a cool place to hang out. "My friends are there." Since they have had no more serious challenge than looking up vocabulary words, doing worksheets, listening (or not listening) politely to lectures, and answering the questions at the end of the chapter, they have become used to not being challenged at all intellectually. The first time that they are so challenged, some students rebel. But, as in the solution to the first problem, they usually get caught up in the enthusiasm of the rest of the class who are responding to the brain-compatible way they are learning. It is a fact that the brain evolved to take on massive input and to accept the challenge to make sense of that input — to make meaning. Most students will respond positively to the opportunity. Those who have been robbed of the opportunity thus far in their careers will come on board eventually. Be patient, and use a combination of MAX Teaching, cooperative learning, and the Skill Acquisition Model.

The one thing I would not do is pull rank and resort to discipline measures until all else fails. Sometimes, faith in people is more powerful than power. Choose to ignore for a time, while gently encouraging. Find what the student is doing well and comment on that. Ignore what is not going so well. This is a tool of good coaches. When a player messes up in practice, s/he immediately looks to see if the coach saw it. As a coach, I often make it a point to look the other way when the error occurs, even though I may have seen it. People need the opportunity to take risks and fail at trying difficult new things without being called on it. When I see the same player later try the same thing and succeed, I make sure the person knows I saw it, and I reinforce it. We can do the same thing in the content literacy classroom with reluctant readers.

FAQ 15. Why is round-robin or popcorn reading not an appropriate way to help students learn new subject matter?

There is an established body of research (Opitz and Rasinski, 1998; Rasinski and Hoffman, 2003; Worthy and Broaddus, 2002) on why having students read aloud can be actually counterproductive in the learning process:

1. It most often focuses on decoding print rather than making meaning from print.
2. It embarrasses lower-level readers; even if the teacher allows volunteers to read, the implicit understanding is that some students cannot read.
3. Reading out loud occurs at a rate of 125 words per minute at best, while the average fifth grade student reads at the rate of 230 words per minute reading silently.
4. It is distracting to hear students stumble over words that are new to them, and thus, it makes it difficult to listen.
5. Many students do not listen unless their turn is coming up, and once over, they go back to daydreaming or whatever else they wish to do.
6. The tests that are used to measure their reading achievement are taken silently.

If, as a teacher, you decide that it will help students to hear the text read out loud, ***YOU should do the reading aloud to the students!*** You can turn the text into *language* rather than poorly-decoded nonsense. (Your students use language all day long every day with their family and friends, but many low-performing readers do not see the printed word as language. Stumbling over poorly pronounced words does not help.)

It is important that when you do the reading, every student follows along silently in his or her own text. Do not allow students to put their heads on their desk to "relax" while they listen. It is also important that you follow the three steps of MAX as well. Once you have motivated students so that they have enough background knowledge to become engaged in the text, and they have clear purposes for reading, you can read aloud to them, pausing at times to have them reflect on what has been read. Thus, you are still going through the steps of **M**otivation, **A**cquisition, and **EX**tension, only you are altering the silent reading part to include their hearing your reading aloud to them.

For instance, if I am doing an anticipation guide, and I am reading the chapter aloud to students, I might read five to seven paragraphs and then pause to ask students, "Are we able to prove or disprove any of the statements on the anticipation guide from what we just read?" Usually students will point out that we are indeed able to do so. At this time, I ask the student to tell which statement, tell whether it should be "checked" or not, and where in the text she has found proof of her interpretation. *It is at this point that I have a student read a paragraph or two to defend her interpretation.* This is a different form of reading aloud — to defend a belief — and this form of reading should be encouraged. The focus is not on decoding, but rather, on defending a notion, something altogether different.

Even in special needs classes, I try to get students into silent purposeful reading as soon as possible. This might mean that I read the first several pages of the story or textbook reading, pausing frequently for student discussion, and letting them read the last page or so silently once they are "hooked" on the reading. Sometimes, I will wean them from dependence on me a few weeks from the beginning of the school year, and sometimes I do it right away. At times, it might be months for special needs students. It depends on the students in my classes as to how quickly I make the transition to independent silent reading, but I do so as soon as I feel they are ready for it. The message is clear — we read to make meaning, not to hear words pronounced.

In conclusion, Acquisition is different from learning. It takes place in a natural way, with little or no effort, in an environment where its primary function is to make sense. The person involved in Acquisition may not even be aware of what is being Acquired. S/he is only aware that meaning is being derived from the circumstance. This phenomenon can work with students of all ability levels, and it can work across a wide and complex group of literacy-related skills. Students exposed to this form of teaching Acquire both content and skills — two for the price of one — no extra charge!

FAQ 16. What about worksheets? You seem to think them to be a waste of time. Why do textbook publishers make them, then?

WORKSHEETS ARE NOT MEANT TO BE THE PRINCIPAL LEARNING TOOL FOR NEW SUBJECT MATTER!! There *is* a place for worksheets, but it is not the place that a great number of teachers recognize. Worksheets are one way to focus on key vocabulary and concepts *once the concepts have been learned*. They are a method of review — one way to assure multiple exposure. They do not foster the kind of thinking and reading that we have been discussing in the earlier chapters of this book. They focus on everything that is wrong about teaching and about reading.

There are two problems with worksheets — the level of reading and thinking needed to perform with a worksheet, and the way they are used in the classroom. Most of the published worksheets ask questions that are pretty much limited to the literal level of interpretation. Any student who walks into a classroom and is told by a teacher to do a worksheet is very unlikely to ever read the text. The student will never see the logical argument that is presented by the author of the text. If you watch students who are assigned to do worksheets, they almost invariably begin somewhere in the middle of the reading, scanning for key terms that will allow them to find the answers *without reading!*

Secondly, too many teachers substitute worksheets for teaching and learning! In schools across the country, teachers have stacks of worksheets on their desk for students to do. Once a student has finished one sheet, it is time to grab another, and the process goes on.

Most worksheets are not made to *teach* new subject matter to students. They are one way to *practice* what one has learned. Thus, an appropriate way to use a worksheet is to have students hypothesize the answers, discuss with their peers, and then go back through the text to see if they are correct. In other words, a worksheet can be one form of "multiple exposure and complex interaction" for students who use them. To use worksheets this way, teachers should have students first read the text, in class, through one of the thoughtful processes of content-literacy instruction described in Part II of this text. Then, students should be led through the three-step process of cooperative learning recommended in this book — individual written commitment, small-group discussion, and then, complex interaction — this time, facilitated by the worksheet and the text. In other words, the worksheet is not used as the principal learning tool, but rather as one more way of getting students to interact over the subject matter, extending beyond the text.

The pattern might look something like this:

- Students read through the MAX Teaching framework.
- Teacher gives worksheet with all textbooks closed.
- Students work individually to "check" their knowledge.
- Small-group discussions occur to compare individual student responses.
- Students go back into the text to verify answers. (This could be for homework.)

Incidentally, the worksheet, when used in this way, can be an excellent homework assignment when students do not have a textbook that they may take home with them. It is a crime that the situation sometimes exists — students' not having access to books to take home — but it is a reality in some school districts or in some schools. In most of these situations, the teacher has a class set of texts for use only in the classroom. If this is the case, then use the text in a meaningful way to help students learn new subject matter as described herein, but then use worksheets as a homework activity patterned after the process described above. Don't grade them, but rather, have students use them to extend beyond the text outside of the classroom. If they have done a reasonable job of reading the text in class, most of the worksheet will be doable. If some answers cannot be recalled, they can be dealt with in the cooperative learning groups with or without the text in the first few minutes of class the next day.

Part II

MAX TEACHING:

generic lesson plans for content-literacy-based classroom instruction

Preface to Part II

The activities described in this second portion of the book are generic lesson plans that are based on many years of experience using them in classrooms across the curriculum. Each chapter describes a different classroom activity. Every classroom procedure described herein can be used in any subject area classroom to help students develop a deep understanding of the content, and to acquire important literacy skills at the same time.

Each activity is presented in the same format:

- A note on which phase(s) of the **MAX Teaching** lesson framework to which the activity pertains. (Sometimes, you will want to do one activity in the **M**otivation phase of class and follow it with one or more activities in the **A**cquisition and e**X**tension phases. You will quickly see how they "mix & match" to provide a complete learning experience.)
- a brief introduction of the activity and why it works to help students acquire both content and skills
- explanation of how to make any related materials
- a "quick overview" of the lesson
- detailed step-by-step instructions to perform the activity in a classroom
- extra scaffolds you may wish to use with disadvantaged students.

I am aware that teachers are often asked to write detailed lesson plans and submit them to a supervising administrator, often for a week or two in advance. Usually, these lessons should include the step-by-step description of classroom procedures the teacher plans to use.

The detailed, yet generic, lessons included in this section of this book are suitable for copying and attaching to a lesson plan so that you do not need to write out each lesson in detail each time you plan a lesson. I recommend that you include a format that follows to some extent the format in Appendix 1. This is a format I used over the last 15 years of my teaching using reading and writing to help students learn subject matter in my classrooms. Certainly, this can be adapted to a somewhat different format if your school requires it. However, it does include the essential elements of a complete lesson, including objectives, materials, key vocabulary, and the three steps of **M**otivation, **A**cquisition, and e**X**tension. Of course, e**X**tension should include homework and assessment.

The lesson descriptions are based on years of my own classroom experiences in using the activities in all subject areas and with all levels of students. Each one includes the essential steps to perform the learning through **MAX**, the use of cooperative learning, and the steps of the Skill Acquisition Model (SAM). These three components are woven into the description of the activity so that you do not accidentally leave a part out of the lesson and so that they flow smoothly to help students acquire content and skills.

Each detailed lesson format is enclosed in a grid, and each step of the lesson is numbered so that you can follow a sequence that will facilitate student engagement and prevent you from accidentally leaving out an important element. If you copy the lesson format into your lesson plan, you can have it on your desk while the class is progressing, and you will be able to make reference to it throughout the class.

Many of the lessons are written at the introductory level. That is to say, they are meant to be used the first few times you do them with students. After that, you will find that with most of the lessons, you will need to refer to the written lessons less and less as you are more experienced with the activities. You will find that you will only need to glance at the "quick overview of the lesson" before you use it in class.

My advice to you is to use every one of the activities in Part II to help students develop as learners of your subject matter and as literate life-long learners. Use reading and writing for learning as the central way of acquiring new knowledge in your classroom. Even when your class is viewing a video, going on a field trip, or listening to a guest lecturer, you should assure their meaningful engagement in the learning process by incorporating MAX Teaching and the accompanying classroom activities as a framework for the learning.

I also advise you, once you have acquired a facility with this way of teaching, to go outside of these activities and find more of them with which you might experiment. There are many published content area reading textbooks filled with brief descriptions of classroom activities that help students learn. Once you have internalized the sense that students can better learn through their own active processing of new information, you will want to try other ways of accomplishing this type of learning in your classroom. Journals such as *The Reading Teacher, The Journal of Adolescent and Adult Literacy*, and many other publications that are probably already in your school's professional library are excellent sources of new and engaging ways to use reading and writing to help students learn.

My goal in this book is to provide teachers with enough detail about how to use a select few of what I consider to be very effective means of using reading and writing in the classroom for the purpose of learning. It is my hope that I have provided enough detail so that you feel you can do this for your students without the anxiety that you might do it incorrectly or that you might be leaving out something important.

By the same token, please feel free to make your own adaptations to the lessons as they are presented. I have tried to represent each of the procedures as I have developed or adapted it through years of employing it in various subject areas. Trust me. I have learned the lessons I have learned by doing them the wrong way as well as the right way. These lesson plans are a reflection of all of those experiences.

The most important final piece of advice I can give you about these lessons is the same advice I have always given my teams just before a game, whether it was the first game of the season or the final championship of the league — *Have fun!* You will see that by using these classroom activites to help students learn, you will have more of that than you ever did before in the classroom. So will your students.

Chapter 10

Anticipation Guides

When you give us worksheets to do, it's, like, an insult to our intelligence…when we get to discuss like this, it's more interesting because we get to argue about what we think.

Cosmetology student reflecting on a class that used an anticipation guide for reading and thinking.

Motivation ✓

Acquisition ✓

e**X**tension ✓

Of all the classroom activities in this book, Anticipation Guide (Herber, 1970; Readance, Bean & Baldwin, 1981) is my favorite. I have used it in every discipline, and the results have been phenomenal. Partly because of the concrete nature of the guide itself, and partly because students love to argue, it inevitably ends up with all students in the class involved in meaningful discussion about the subject matter. A well-made anticipation guide creates a bit of ambiguity and uncertainty in the classroom. Yet, students have something in their hands that they can use to process the text in a concrete way.

This chapter describes how to make anticipation guides that will provoke thoughtful reading and discussion, and provides you with a detailed version of a generic lesson that will allow you to get the most from the procedure. My recommendation is to make the anticipation guide using the recommendations below, and then have the later part of this chapter on your desk, during the lesson so that you don't leave out any of the important steps in the process. The steps of the process, described in table format near the end of the chapter, are based on years of using this activity in classrooms of all different disciplines, with all different types of students.

Using Anticipation Guides to Motivate Students

This strategy can be used to guide students through all three phases of the MAX teaching framework. It provides Motivation to readers by asking them to react to a series of statements that are related to the content of the reading materials and also to the students' prior knowledge. Because students are able to react to these statements, they anticipate or predict what the material will be about. Once a student has committed to the statements, s/he will have created a meaningful purpose for <u>A</u>cquisition of new knowledge. Purposeful reading leads to improved comprehension and, thus, acquisition of an important comprehension skill. Finally, teacher-mediated student discussions allow for students to experience e<u>X</u>tension beyond the text. As students work to iron out any differences in interpretation by attempting to come to consensus on construction of the author's meaning, students manipulate ideas in such a way as to experience higher order thinking about the subject being learned. This is the point at which application, analysis, synthesis, and evaluation level thinking takes place. The result is better understanding and higher retention of subject matter.

How to Construct Effective Anticipation Guides

1. Assess the material for major concepts to be learned. I like to have closure within one class if possible, so I usually choose to cover one section of a normal textbook or a corresponding length of text — about 6-8 pages — in a 45 to 60 minute class. For a 90-minute class, I like to do two sections of text, or about twice as much (except near the beginning of the year because it might be too much to ask of students to read 12-15 pages if they are not used to it). What I like to do is read through the text with this thought in my mind — If these students were really good readers, able to infer the really important concepts from this piece of work, what would those concepts be? Then, I simply state those concepts on the anticipation guide. Sometimes the concepts are those I know to be important because of my expertise in the field. Sometimes they are what the state curriculum says must be learned (even though not stated directly in the text).

2. Write statements based on the concepts. (Depending on the material and the age of students, the number of statements may vary from three to ten or more.) Statements that are likely to engage students in reading and discussion reflect the following seven characteristics:

   * **Each statement concerns an important concept of the lesson.** You should limit the number of statements to the quantity of important concepts that must be learned. For young students, 3-5 statements may suffice. For advanced placement seniors, 14-15 statements might be required to get at the key ideas.

   * **Every statement rephrases what the text says.** There are two reasons for this and they are explained below.

   * **All statements are plausible.** Don't waste students' time with inane ideas.

   * **One or two statements include ideas that are intuitively appealing to students, but which will prove to be incorrect upon reading the text.** All statements should be believable rather than outlandish in nature, but some should create an "Aha!" effect once students actually get into the reading.

   * **Some statements should be written in such a way as to force students to interpret large segments of text such as a paragraph or two, perhaps even from different pages.** This prevents the exercise from turning into a simple "decoding exercise" as in many worksheets. Students are encouraged to maintain meaning over longer pieces of text rather than to just "find the answer." Even though a student might find some evidence relating to a statement, s/he is likely to continue to carry that thought, continuing to seek more evidence that might either negate or at least qualify the original information found. To make statements this way, I usually seek information further in the chapter that relates to a statement, and I just go back and add qualifying terms or phrases to statements that I have already made on the anticipation guide. thus, students who find information near the beginning of the reading that seems to corroborate a statement, later in the reading,

find information that either negates or, at least, limits their original interpretation. This provokes mature, thoughtful, and skeptical reading.

- **Some statements are worded in such a way as to provoke critical thinking about the key concepts.** Rather than true/false statements, they are either controversial or somewhat vague or interpretational in nature. Such statements can be made by using vague qualifiers such as "many" or "most" or by using value-laden terms that will cause disagreements. Based on either the students' prior knowledge or on the material being presented, students might disagree with one another and provide some valid evidence for either side of the argument, both before and after the reading. Teachers should relish such arguments. Arguing is the highest level of most taxonomies of thinking, and when students are arguing over interpretation of the text, they are developing deeper understandings and longer-lasting concepts of the content of your course.

- **Some statements may not have a correct answer — it is a good idea to include some statements to which even the *teacher* does not have an answer.** These can stimulate great discussion leading to deeper understanding of the subject matter. A good example of this sort of statement is a statement that compares and contrasts the elements of an entity or the steps in a process. For example, "*Of the five steps in this lab, one of them is clearly more important than the other four.*" is the kind of statement that provokes students into carefully processing each of the steps of the lab, and allows them to argue about which one they perceive to be the critical step. In the end, each student usually has a pretty good picture of the entire lab process that you wanted them to learn.

In sum, these seven characteristics of quality anticipation guides all contribute to creating an experience that engages students in intelligently processing the text. It is not important that each of the statements has all of these seven characteristics, but it is important that every statement on the anticipation guide have the first three characteristics: important ideas, wording that is different from the wording in the text, and plausibility. (Two of these are described in a bit more detail below.) At least one of each of the other statements on the guide should have each of the other four important characteristics listed above. In addition, one of the first three statements on an anticipation guide should be something to which students will find some exception near the beginning of the text they are to read. This makes them skeptical about the rest of the statements, and skepticism makes them careful readers.

Rephrasing the Text

This first characteristic is the most important. It is important to use different terminology than the text uses for two reasons. The first is that we need to get away from the "worksheet mentality" of approaching text as a place to "find answers to questions" rather than as a resource to read to make sense of reality. Students need to have the opportunity to read interpretively from text. Students who are used to worksheets rarely ever really read anything in textbooks. They simply go on short "hunting trips" to find answers. They never see the logical argument presented by the author. They start in the middle of the reading, or often near the end of the reading, skimming and scanning for bold print or other clues that will direct them to a place where "the answer" will be found. Once they have "bagged" the answer, they can forget that idea and progress to the next question. This approach to text is part of the reason that most students who start college do not finish their freshman year, and why 57% of high school seniors scored below basic on the 2000 NAEP History Test. Eleven and a half years of teacher lecture, worksheets, and end-of-chapter comprehension questions have led to what can only be considered an inappropriate outcome in a democracy that purports to be a world leader.

The second reason for rephrasing the text is that many students in most classrooms read at a level that is significantly below the level of the text that has been assigned to them. In light of this problem, the teacher can phrase the statements in such a way as to make important ideas from the text understandable even though the text might be less so. The teacher is thereby setting students up for success in interpreting the text by scaffolding their ability to interpret difficult reading. Students who otherwise might be frustrated with a reading can work their way through difficult text and say to themselves, "I *think* that this is what the book is saying. At least this is how I am interpreting it."

By approaching text in such a way, students are actually acquiring the ability to read materials that are closer to their grade levels or even higher than grade level, even though they would not be able to do so if the teacher had just assigned the reading to be done at home or away from the classroom.

Plausibility

Each of the statements on an anticipation guide should be believable. It is inappropriate to insult their intelligence by having middle grades or high school students relate to statements such as "*The largest bodies of water in the world are called continents.*" On the other hand, a statement like, "*The largest bodies of water on earth are called oceans, and it is fairly easy to look at a map or globe to tell where one begins and another ends.*" Such a statement gets students to focus on an important truth, but leaves room for discussion and interpretation of the text and of maps. In other words, it makes them think.

Answer Key?

My contention is that the teacher who has made a quality anticipation guide should never walk into the classroom with an answer key. The reason for this is that there should always be room for interpretation of the statements on the anticipation guide and for interpretation of the text. I cannot list all of the times when I thought I knew which statements should be checked or not checked, but was proven wrong by logic that I had not anticipated or logic that was based on a valid interpretation that I had not anticipated. (This actually makes it easier to make anticipation guides. You do not have to know the answers! You get to read and think along with the students.)

Classroom Procedures for Anticipation Guides

Lifelong learning skill(s) to be discussed with students and practiced during the process:
- Using prediction as a means of developing purposes for engaging in reading
- Constructing meaning and reading critically to clarify interpretation of text

Materials:
- Anticipation guides — one per student,
- Textbook or other reading,
- Transparency of anticipation guide

Quick Overview of lesson:
- Predict
- Discuss — small groups
- Silent reading, seeking evidence for interpretations
- Discuss — small groups
- Discuss — whole class

Anticipation Guide Procedure:

1. Introduce the content of the lesson by posing a hypothetical question, reading a quotation, previewing the text, showing a five-minute video, or some other brief interest-capturing idea to which students can react through discussion or writing.

2. Introduce the skill of prediction. Explain to students that strategic readers most often make predictions about what they will find in the text that they are preparing to read. Explain that it is not so important whether their predictions are right or wrong, but rather that, by predicting, they engage themselves in the reading, thus making the reading easier and more interesting. If they find out that their prediction was correct, they feel good about it. If they find out that their prediction was not correct, they can react with surprise at what they actually did find in the text.

3. Model use of the skill of predicting. You might wish to describe how strategic readers predict what they are going to discover in a text by just scanning it first for clues. (I like to use the newspaper from this morning. By doing so, I am modeling that I read the paper. I usually choose the headline article if I think most students will know a bit about the topic. Sometimes I use the sports page. It really does not matter as much as how you model it.) Discuss how predicting what you were about to read helped you to focus on the reading. Tell them one or two of the predictions you made that were correct and one or two that you made that were wrong. Let them know that you felt pretty good about yourself when you discovered that your prediction was right. Explain that when your prediction was wrong, you said to yourself, "Wow! I didn't know that!" Explain to students that it does not matter whether you are right or wrong in your predictions. By having made predictions, you make the reading easier to do because while reading, you know what you are looking for.

4. Explain to students that, for today's reading, we are going to use an anticipation guide to help us make the predictions so we can practice what strategic readers do. Tell them that the prediction guide has many statements on it, and that some of the statements will have evidence in the textbook that supports them, some will have evidence that negates them, and some may have evidence that is conflicting, and about which students will probably argue.

5. Tell students to read each of the statements on the anticipation guide you have given them and to place a check mark (✓) in the space next to each statement that they think, based on their prior knowledge, will probably be supported in the reading. Tell them to do this on their own, without looking at any of their neighbors' papers. Tell them not to worry about being right or wrong at this point. Remind them that they are just making predictions, and that once they get into the reading, they will be able to change their minds about any of the statements if they feel they should. Move around the room to see that students are committing to some of the statements.

6. Tell students to discuss, in their cooperative groups, the predictions that they have made. Ask them to share their logic with one another at this point. Explain that one student's prior knowledge may help the others in the group to understand the concepts that are to be encountered. The books remain closed at this point. Move around the room to monitor their discussions and answer any questions they may have. (An alternative to this small-group discussion is a teacher-led class discussion, especially near the beginning of the year or when students have very limited prior knowledge. However, I try to avoid this or get away from it as soon as possible since students do better if the discussion is truly student-centered rather than teacher-led.)

7. Students should break off the discussions and begin individual silent reading at this time. (Use Information In Appendix 8 the first time you use an anticipation guide with students.) Remind them that they should keep the prediction guide on the desk for reference while they read, and that they ought to use inferential thinking while they read. Tell them that they must interpret what they are reading in order to determine whether a prediction-guide statement should be checked or not, and that they must be able to refer to specific parts of the text to verify their beliefs. It is good to have students list page-column-paragraph notations under the statements they wish to verify or refute. (Their notations might look something like this: 251-2-4, meaning that information to support or negate a particular statement can be found on page 251, column two, paragraph four.) Again, move around the room to monitor progress and support students in their work. It is also good at this point to read silently along with the students, with the goal in mind that you may later need to model some of the thinking that goes into making inferences.

8. When most students have finished reading, tell them to get back into their small groups to discuss again the prediction guide, only now their job changes to attempting to come to a consensus within their groups about whether a statement should be checked or not. Here, they compare their various interpretations of what they have read, referring to evidence in the text to support those interpretations. Again, move around the room to assist in this process, making sure that students are referring to the text to support their opinions. Allow several minutes for the discussions to occur.

9. When at least one group has come to a consensus on the prediction-guide statements, use their decisions to conduct a whole-class discussion to attempt to achieve a classroom consensus. Make sure that students are able to support their beliefs either through direct reference to the text or through their interpretation of specific text. It is very important during this phase of the lesson that the teacher act as a mediator or arbitrator, avoiding telling students answers. Intellectual ownership must be in the minds of the students as they collectively construct meaning from the text. Near the beginning of the year, some teacher modeling of inferential reading might be necessary, but students will quickly take ownership of the process, and they will surprise you with their thoroughness of analysis.

10. Ask students to report on their use of the skill of predicting. Say — did the process of predicting what you were going to read before reading, and discussing it with your peers help you in concentrating on the reading, and in comprehending the reading? Did it help you focus and stay focused while you were reading? (Students inevitably realize at this point that, by practicing predicting before reading, they were engaged in the reading, leading to heightened comprehension.)

11. Take the opportunity to review and reinforce the use of the skill of predicting. Point out to students that they can use the skill in any reading that they do in any subject area to engage themselves, make the reading more interesting by setting a purpose for reading, and by keeping that purpose in mind during the reading.

12. Continue reflection through a free-write, homework, a quiz, etc.

Extra Scaffolds

There are two principal scaffolds for using anticipation guides with very low performing readers. The first is to read the anticipation guide statements to the students aloud, pausing at each one to facilitate a discussion of each of the statements and its relative merit. When you read the statements aloud to the students, conduct a discussion about each one. An alternative is to have students discuss the statement in small groups. Either way can work well.

The second scaffold is for the teacher, once students have made their predictions, to read out loud to the students from the text. When I read out loud to the students, I pause after six or seven paragraphs to ask students if they can, at this time, prove or disprove any of the statements on the anticipation guide. Usually one or two students will defend or negate one or more of the statements at this time. If they do so, I insist that they explain where they found the information in the text. They must read the citation aloud to attempt to convince the others in the class as to whether or not the statement is true.

Even if I elect to use the extra scaffold of reading aloud to my students, I wean them from this as soon as is feasible. This might be by the end of the first time we use an anticipation guide, or it might be several weeks into the school year. It varies with the students in question. As soon as possible, students need to have the opportunity to read silently to construct personal meaning from text. It is up to the teacher to decide when that time is appropriate.

Chapter 11

Previewing Non-fiction text

The best teacher is the one who suggests rather than dogmatizes, and inspires his listener with the wish to teach himself.

Edward Bulwer-Lytton

Motivation ✓

Acquisition

E**X**tension

Previewing the text is something that I learned at the age of 40. The surprising thing is that no person had ever suggested to me, at any level of my educational career, that any and every reading would be easier to understand if I took the time to carefully peruse the text beforehand, in a systematic and thorough way. Fifteen years of previewing experience later, I not only know the value of previewing before reading, but I have taught the process to thousands of teachers and students around the country. *I never read anything without previewing it now.* And, I probably use it as a pre-reading activity more than any other pre-reading strategy in my arsenal of activities. I may use it as much as three times a week.

If you have not been previewing, you should try it right away. Stop reading this chapter, and preview the rest of the chapter using the steps listed below. You will see that the reading makes so much more sense to you than if you had not done so. The word, "preview" is something that is part of the vernacular of all children these days. They all have seen previews of TV shows and of movies. The term connotes something positive to modern students. Students never protest the idea of doing a preview.

What students do not realize is that they are actually *reading* the section of the chapter that they are previewing. If you were to ask a group of students to "read this section of the chapter twice—once rapidly, and once more, carefully," they would think you were crazy. On the other hand, if you suggest that "we are going to *PREVIEW* the section of the chapter before we read it," students feel as though they can handle that. However, *a preview is a cursory first reading of the text.* It allows students to see the structure of the text, capture most of the main ideas, and become acquainted with new vocabulary and its relationship to the main ideas of the reading. If motivating students is done by helping students to overcome their anxieties about having success with text, then previewing can be one of the most important motivators at your disposal.

Usually, I only preview with students the section of the chapter that we are about to read that day in class. The process of previewing can become burdensome if you spend too much time on it. On occasion, I might preview a whole chapter, or even a unit. However, the time it takes to preview is about 5-7 minutes for a single section of a chapter. The larger the previewed section, the more time you will spend, and the greater the likelihood that some students will lose interest. So, my suggestion is to preview what you plan to read in class that day. (On the other hand, once each year, I preview the whole textbook with the students. Each textbook has its own unique characteristics, and doing a textbook overview can greatly enhance student's success throughout the school year with that text.)

As you will see below, the process is led by the teacher from the front of the classroom. It is very important that the teacher lead the process many times before weaning students from relying on the teacher's direction in the process. Previewing, if done properly, tremendously enhances student ability to read the text. Students will acquire a sense of the value of previewing if they have had enough experience with it. On the other hand, if they have not had enough experience, they do not appropriately value it, and thus, will do a shoddy job of previewing if you release them to do the previewing before they are ready.

I like to lead the preview from the front of the classroom at least 20-25 times before I ask students to do it on their own. Even then, I suggest that I feel that they are ready to do it autonomously, but that I am going to watch them do it. Then I proceed to allow them some time to preview while I walk around the room, quietly reminding people to be sure to look at the section review questions or to be sure to read the caption underneath the pictures before taking a look at the pictures. Eventually, by about mid-year, I have complete confidence in my students as competent previewers of text, and then I can go into the classroom and say to them, "Alright, you have 4 minutes to preview pages 461-470," and they will all do a careful job because they have acquired a real sense of the value of the process.

One way to get students to realize the value of previewing is an informal research project that we conducted in the classroom each year. It involved allowing one half of the class to preview while the other half of the class rested with their heads on their desks, followed by a limited time to read the section of the chapter, and then having a quiz on the subject matter. This was always followed the next day by repeating the experiment with the two sides exchanging roles. In every case, there were significantly higher scores for the students who got to preview the text before reading. This sort of informal research can help your students to see the value of the process as a life-long learning skill.

Previewing

Lifelong Learning Skill(s) to be Practiced During Learning:

- Using a quick overview of a textual reading to help recall prior knowledge and to build prior knowledge.
- Improving comprehension through prior recognition of text structure.

Quick Overview of the Lesson:

Lead students through a scan and/or discussion of:
- title
- introduction
- subtitles
- bold-print & italicized words
- pictures (includes reading captions)
- charts
- maps
- graphs
- summary
- review questions

Detailed version of lesson:

1. Introduce the content of the reading by posing a hypothetical question, reading a quotation, previewing the text, or some other interest-capturing idea to which students can react through brief discussion.

2. Introduce the skill of previewing by asking students how many of them, by a show of hands, love reading textbooks. (The vast majority will not raise their hands.) Let them know that their response is normal–that most people find textbooks, if not boring, at least tedious–but necessary! You might discuss the role of textbooks in college.

3. Now ask students, "By a show of hands, how many of you would like to have textbooks become a great deal *easier* to read, to connect with, and be able to remember more information for tests. Most usually will admit to these desires.

4. Explain to students that most people who are strategic about their approach to reading textbooks use a practice called previewing.

5. List for students the elements of the complete preview (listed above in the Quick Overview).

6. Hold your own book so that students can see what you are pointing to as you lead them through a preview of the text. Scan the room to see that they have their own textbooks open to the correct page so that they can follow along as you lead the preview. Tell students that they should follow along in their own books and that if they are not sure what you are discussing at any given moment, they can look at your hand to see the page and area to which you are pointing.

7. Begin with the title. Read it aloud, asking students to think about what they already know about the topic. You may wish to ask a student to share his/her knowledge (but this is not necessary).

8. Read the introduction out loud to the students. Most books do not name the introduction, but it is the first paragraph or two before the first subtitle in most books. Tell students to read along silently while you read it aloud. (This greatly enhances the probability of student success with the reading since, on average, student listening grade level is two years higher than reading grade level. Since the introduction normally covers essential concepts important to understanding the rest of the reading, The teacher's reading aloud from the introduction is a real help to students, especially the lower performing readers in the class.)

9. Read the first major subtitle aloud. You may want to focus on the overall text structure at this point by scanning the article for all subtitles of the same size and color. (Most often, this will demonstrate to students the overall structure. There may be three or four subsections so labeled. Even though there may be sub-subsections, this will allow students to see the big picture in terms of the format the authors have used.) At this point, I usually attempt to paraphrase what the reading is about, restating the three or four subtitles in terms the students will understand.

10. Continue to work through the article seeking bold print words, italicized words, studying pictures, charts, maps, graphs, etc. Each time you confront a picture, chart, map, graph, etc., say to students, "Read the caption under this image. I am going to call on someone to tell me what we can learn from this, or I may ask why you think the authors or publishers chose to include this image in this section of the chapter." Then use a few moments of wait time to allow students to study the image. (Scan the room to see that all students do so.) **It is very important at this point to be very tolerant of responses. Be careful not to expect too much since the students are only previewing. They have not learned the material yet. The important thing is that they are all engaged in attempting to make sense of the images.** My usual response to what a student says when I ask regarding a picture or map, etc. is, "Could be; we are not sure. We are just *previewing*. We are not meant to be experts on this just yet." I then proceed with little fanfare to the next image or part of the preview process, repeating the process of gently probing students for their understandings of what they are seeing in the preview.

11. Work through the rest of the preview in a similar manner, constantly scanning to see that all students are following along. Once finished, students are ready to proceed into some activity that will help them set purposes for a careful reading. Because they have previewed, the reading will come more easily to each of the students than if they had attempted to read without having done so. (After leading 15 or 20 such previews, you may "wean" students from your leading them, and allow them to preview on their own. My experiences lead me to know that if you do so too soon, many will not have learned the complete procedure well enough to appreciate its value. If you have done enough of them, even the poorest readers in the class will have internalized the value of the process, and s/he will have a life-long learning skill.)

12. Follow a preview with Paired Reading, GIST, INSERT, KWL, What-I-Know Sheet, PQRST+, Re-Quest, Hunt for Main Ideas, or any other purposeful reading strategy.

13. Later, after the reading has been completed, remember to ask students to report on their use of the skill of previewing. Ask, "By a show of hands, how many of you realize now that, by previewing—looking at all the important terms and pictures, etc. before reading—your comprehension actually improved as a result of doing the preview?" Take the time to reinforce the skill as something they can do in any class, in any reading.

Extra Scaffolds

Previewing is a scaffold. It is an appropriate activity for students at all levels. With lower level readers, you may wish to lead the process from the front of the classroom several more times before weaning students from you guidance than you might do with a more advanced group. All students will eventually internalize (acquire) the value of a careful preview as an important tool to aid in comprehension.

Chapter 12

Cornell note taking (2-column notes)

Education ... has produced a vast population able to read but unable to distinguish what is worth reading.
G. M. Trevelyan

Motivation

Acquisition ✓

EXtension ✓

The Cornell method of notetaking (Morgan, Forget, & Antinarella, 1996; Pauk, 2001) is a study skills strategy that can be taught and utilized in all content areas. It is a strategy that can be used with reading text or listening to a lecture. It is also a note-taking method that is *required* of students in many, if not most, law schools and medical schools — a fact that speaks well for its effectiveness as a tool for retention of great quantities of information.

Good notes are the product of strategic reading or listening. The Cornell method helps students organize information in a useful format, rank the importance of various elements contained in the reading and systematically study the information that has been evaluated and organized. The student recognizes a main idea and contributing points from which this theme is generated. The student then can judge how much detail to record in light of the assigned or expected outcome of the reading. In this way, the student gains control and becomes more efficient in the learning process.

By necessity, this note-taking system moves the student from a passive reader/listener to one actively involved with comprehension. It is this linkage to thinking and comprehension that results in long-term learning. The strategy helps the student become a better learner by acquiring metacognition skills. The student understands that the notes are a skeletal representation that must be dealt with correctly to keep the whole picture in correct context.

Good note taking forces interaction with the learning experience, leading to acquisition of the ability to be metacognitive in learning situations. Studies show that students consider note taking to be an essential learning skill for success in secondary school and college. Other research with students indicates that a good set of notes is very significant in academic success. Most importantly for middle and high school teachers is that Cornell notes can be a very productive nightly homework assignment. This will be discussed below.

Understanding the System

Cornell (or 2-column) note taking is a system that divides a page of loose leaf paper differently than the way it comes from the store. Most loose leaf paper has a red margin about one to one and a half inches from the left edge of the paper. In 2-column note taking, the note taker ignores that margin and draws a new margin about 1¼ inches to the right of the original margin, dividing the paper into 1/3 and 2/3 sized sections. Then, the note taker ignores the red margin, writing all the way to the left edge of the paper. The only thing that goes on the left side of the paper is a main idea. So there is a good deal of space on the left side of the paper between main ideas (all the easier to spot the key points). On the right (2/3) side go all the details relating to the main idea. These are the details that are to be recalled. The system is described in more detail below.

Figure 12-1

Format of Cornell Notes:	
Objectives 9/5	1. Describe the format of two-column notes 2. Explain how to use them to study
Format	Main idea goes on the left side of the notes. Details that relate to the main idea go on this side of the page. Typically there are anywhere from two to six or seven main ideas on each page of looseleaf paper. The process is repeated for each of the main ideas about which the student is taking notes.
Studying	This is useful as a study tool since the student can cover the right side of the page or Fold th page over to try to recall the details relating to the main idea.

The First step: Preparing the System

1. Use a large, loose-leaf notebook. The loose-leaf feature enables you to insert additional handouts, maps, study guides, and assignment sheets in chronological order.
2. The key to the system is to draw a vertical line about 2 ½ to 3 inches from the left edge of each sheet of paper (usually about 1¼ inch from the red margin if you have one). This column on the left is the recall column. Only key words or main ideas will be written in the column to the left of the new line, and if a red margin exists, the red margin is ignored. (Most college bookstores, these days, sell paper that has already been divided for two-column note taking, with pages divided into 1/3 on the left of the margin line and 2/3 on the right of the margin line. It is sometimes called "Law Board Paper.")
3. If the main idea is obvious, such as in a textbook reading well marked with subtitles, you might place the subtitle in the left (1/3 page) column. Then, after reading the subsection of text, jot the important details that relate to that main idea in the right (2/3 page) side. This condenses textbook readings into easy-to-review notes, and it makes locating information very easy later on.
4. In a lecture class, take notes on the right (2/3) side of the page only. Later, while studying, it is a great help to spread out the pages to see the pattern of the lecture or reading. Later, when reviewing notes, label the sections of the notes with key terms and reminders on the left side of the line.
5. Before each new class, take a few minutes to look over the notes on yesterday's reading or from yesterday's class lecture, so that you can connect the ideas from yesterday's class with those you are about to learn.

The Second Step: During the Reading (or Lecture)

1. Place the date at the top of the page. Indicate the source from which your notes will be taken — lecture, chapter title, supplementary reading source, etc. If the teacher writes the day's objectives on the chalkboard, it is advisable to copy those down at the top of the page. (See figure 12-2.)
2. Record your notes in simple paragraph form or other style that works for you. You may wish to use terse phrases that show important relationships but are not complete sentences.
3. Skip lines to show the end of one idea and the start of another.
4. Using abbreviations will give you extra time to listen (in a lecture format) and more economical use of space on the page. Avoid, however, using too many abbreviations or you might have trouble deciphering the notes a month or two later.
5. Write legibly. You can do so if you discipline yourself. Later, when you review, legible handwriting will let you concentrate on ideas and facts rather than on figuring out your scribbling. Doing your notes properly the first time also saves time in rewriting or typing them — this is not a form of review; it is a waste of your valuable time.

The Third Step: After the Reading (or Lecture)

1. If it is a lecture about which you have taken notes, consolidate your notes during the first free time after the class.
   a. Read through your notes
   b. Make any scribbles more legible

    c. Fill in any spaces purposely left blank

    d. Emerge with an overview of the reading or lecture

    e. Underline or box in key vocabulary terms

2. Using the main-idea column on the left side of the page, jot in key words and key phrases that will stand as cues for the ideas and facts on the right. In making these jottings, you will have reread all the ideas, rethought them in your own words, and reflected on them as you tried to think of a brief summarizing phrase or key word. In doing so, you will have organized and structured the ideas both in your notebook and in your mind.

3. Now cover up the right (2/3) side of the page, exposing only the jottings in the main idea column. Using the jottings as cues to help you recall, recite aloud the facts and details as fully as you can in your own words and with as much appreciation of the meaning as you can. Then uncover the right-side notes and verify if you have recalled the essential details. This form of rehearsal greatly enhances retention of facts and concepts.

4. You may wish to compare your two-column notes with another student in your class. Use this opportunity to add details to your notes and to discuss with your peer how s/he perceived the main ideas and the important details that related to those ideas. Quiz each other.

5. To add to the quality of your notetaking during reading, try the **PQRST+** reading/note-taking system.

A Nightly Homework Assignment

Two-column notes make the perfect homework assignment in any subject area class that is employing content literacy strategies, and I have used this as a nightly assignment in my classes for over fifteen years. It is not necessarily the only assignment students might have on a given night, but it is an assignment that students can do — *and it is an assignment that they will do!*

Once the teacher has introduced the system to students, modeling how to make the notes and also how to use them as a tool for studying, students will begin to use them on their own. (Compare the assignment of making two-column notes to the traditional homework assignment of reading a segment of a chapter for the next day's discussion in class. Most students do not complete that assignment — not because they are lazy, but because they are reading two or more grade levels below the level of the text, and they are frustrated by the assignment. When students have already completed the reading in the classroom with the assistance of the teacher, and they have discussed the subject matter with their peers, it is a completely different task to go back through the reading in order to make some notes that will later become useful in recalling the important ideas from the reading.) Two-column notes are a logical way to extend beyond the text in the form of reorganizing for review.

Cornell note taking is the nightly homework assignment for my students. Once they are used to it (It takes a few weeks.), most students get into the habit of making the notes even before they leave the school building. They often make the notes in the cafeteria, working with friends, while they eat lunch. As one additional part of eXtension, taking two-column notes allows for students to review important concepts while the ideas are fresh in their minds. Figure 12-2 shows how students begin to prepare for homework at the beginning of class each day.

Figure 12-2

Setting Up for 2-Column Notes for Homework

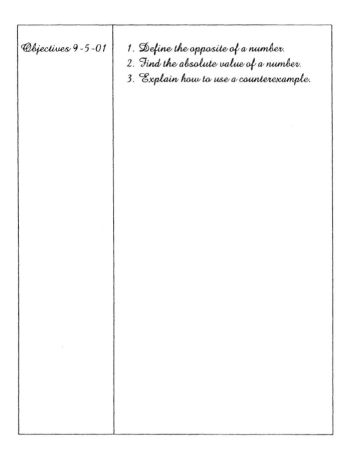

As in the example in figure 12-2, the date and the major objectives of the class are noted each day at the top of the notes. (I always have the day's objectives written in a space on the chalkboard reserved exclusively for that purpose.) The first thing students do when they enter the classroom is to get out a piece of paper on which they will set up their notes, drawing a line about an inch or so to the right of the red margin on their paper, and then they copy the objectives from the chalkboard. This is the daily "bell ringer" or "sponge" activity in my class. It is routine, and all students do it, and it only takes a minute or two. When they are finished, it often looks like the model in the above figure 12-2. The interesting thing is that, by the time the class has ended, all that most students have in their notes is just this — the objectives of the day.

Classroom activities that day most likely included a complete **MAX Teaching** lesson in three steps such as a preview of the text, paired reading, and a focused free-write by the time the bell to end class sounded. During the class, students would have been busy interacting with the text and with each other, yet no notes would have been taken in class. Each of my students, over the last 15 years of my teaching career, has known what to do for homework that night — create notes from the same readings we used in class to learn the content of the lesson.

Compare the making of 2-column notes as a homework assignment with the more traditional assignment of having students read brand new subject matter at home in preparation for the following day's discussion in class. In many public school classrooms, at least 60% of students are reading below the level of the textbook that has been assigned them. In many cases, the student is reading several grade levels below the level of the text. Sending such students home to read new text is setting them up for failure.

On the other hand, students who have knowledgeable teachers who use content reading strategies in their classrooms have the distinct advantage of reading with the facilitation of their peers and the teacher to make sense of difficult text. Assigning them to go home and *reread* what they already have read in the classroom is very different from the assignment of reading brand new text alone. This is a doable assignment, and students will do it!

When teachers routinely assign brand new readings to students to be done away from the classroom, they do so knowing that most students will not come in the next day prepared to discuss the readings. So they end up using as much time in the classroom, on the second day, explaining the subject matter about which students should have read at home as they would have used in having the students read it in class to begin with! The big difference is not in time spent in learning — it is in how the learning takes place. In the more traditional paradigm, students learn from the teacher, developing a dependence on others for acquisition of new knowledge. In the content-literacy paradigm, the students learn from reading, with the teacher as a facilitator for the process. Thus, they also acquire the skills needed to become independent life-long learners.

Teaching Two-Column Note Taking and Study Procedure

Teachers should not "give notes" to students. Teachers should teach the life skill of making notes. When students copy a teacher's notes from an overhead projector or from the chalkboard, all they are doing is decoding print at the most literal level. There does not need to be any real understanding of the content to accomplish such a task. (In fact, even when teachers take the time to lecture about the notes while students are copying them, students tend to be so focused on getting the notes before the teacher changes to the next page that they do not have the luxury of actually thinking about or understanding the lecture. They race to copy from one set of notes to another, and hope to figure out a way to memorize them later so they might pass a test on the subject matter. Such behavior is the opposite of real literacy — using the written and spoken word to understand and contemplate.

Nevertheless, near the beginning of the year, some classroom time must be spent in teaching the system to students. I have had great success with using the activities described below. I like to introduce the note taking system with notes that have already been formatted by me so that students don't have a great deal of process to think about at first. However, I quickly wean them from my assistance, expecting the notes to be made as homework each night within the first two or three weeks of school.

When students begin to take responsibility for their nightly notes, you will find that the quality of notes varies. This is to be expected. The making of notes is a life skill and needs to be developed. My experience is that the vast majority of students become quite accomplished at the process within the first nine weeks of school. By the end of the year, all students have acquired the method, and most will use it the rest of their lives.

Lifelong Learning Skill(s) to be Practiced During Making and Studying:

- Identifying main ideas
- Taking terse but useful notes
- Rehearsing as a memory-enhancing tool

Materials:

- Two-column notes, partially completed, structured for the specific reading that students would perform. *
- Plain transparency on which you have drawn a red margin to look like a normal piece of loose leaf paper
- Transparency of the structured two-column notes
- Textbook or other reading

*(The first few times you introduce this note taking system you may wish to prepare structured notes that are based on the main ideas of the reading about to be done. You may wish to use the subtitles of the textbook reading as main idea items for the left side of the notes. It is important to make some changes in the vocabulary used in the text. This does two things. It allows for easier comprehension if the words you choose are more characteristic of student language, and it forces students to "translate" or think about what they are reading. At any rate, it prevents the exercise from being a simple decoding exercise.)

Quick Overview of Lesson:

1. Explain the format for taking 2-column notes
2. Provide structured, but only partially completed, notes for students
3. Students read text to complete notes
4. Allow time in class for study of notes — two days in a row
5. Quiz on second day after studying
6. Stress value of systematic study of well-taken notes
7. Model the process from time to time for several weeks, persistently reminding of the responsibility of note taking by the students

---

Detailed version of teaching 2-column note taking:

1. Introduce the content of the reading by posing a hypothetical question, reading a quotation, previewing the text, or some other interest-capturing idea to which students can react through writing and/or discussion. A PreP strategy or preview of the reading might suffice.

2. Ask each student to get out a clean piece of paper, and once they have done so, let them know that they are about to do a three-minute focused free-write. (See Focused Free Write description in this manual.) Following the procedures of Focused Free Write, inform students that the focus of this short writing will be "How I take notes." Allow three minutes for this to occur. Afterward, have several students volunteer to read aloud what they wrote. If few or no students volunteer, collect all the free-writes. Be sure each student has a name on it before passing it in. (This can become a part of a student portfolio showing progress from the beginning of the year.) Read several of these free writes aloud to the class, but do so anonymously.

3. Place the transparency of a blank sheet of loose leaf paper on the overhead projector and project it onto the screen, asking students — does this look like the paper that your parents bought for you at Wal-Mart before the school year began?
    They will, of course, agree.

4. Mention to them that, for note taking purposes in this class, this year, you will be ignoring the red margin. Model for them by drawing a new margin about 1¼ inch to the right of the red margin that was on the transparency. Explain that most law students and medical students are asked to use the method you are about to introduce because they have to learn and remember so much. Explain that, now that you are ignoring the red margin, you will be writing all the way to the left edge of the paper, but that the only things that will go on the left 1/3 of the page will be main ideas. Write the words "Main Idea" on the left side of the transparency.

5. On the right-hand (2/3) side of the transparency, write the word "details" and fill in much of the space on the right side with lines showing how much space would probably be taken up in writing the details.

6. Then introduce the skill of taking quality notes — on the job or at the university. Let them know that quality notes are not too detailed, but containing terse reminders of key ideas.

7. Let students know that you have prepared structured notes for them to use as an introduction to two-column notes. Use an overhead projection of the formatted notes you have provided them, Such as the ones in Figure 22-1. Or have them formatted on the chalkboard if you do not have an overhead projector in your classroom.

8. Tell students that they should read along silently while you read aloud the first subsection of the reading for which you have formatted the notes. Read aloud. After the reading, have each student fill out his/her own version, and then allow students to compare with one another in small groups, making any adjustments they wish to their own notes. Then, using a transparency, allow them to compare to the notes you have taken.

9. Once this modeling is finished, ask if everyone has a clear understanding of how the process works and is ready to try it alone. Explain any instructions that are not understood, and clear up any misconceptions of the task at hand. Explain that each student should read to accomplish the task without the help of anyone else.

10. Provide guided practice in reading to find the best responses to fill in the blanks on the formatted notes. Move around the room to facilitate the process, coaching students who are having difficulty.

11. Allow students to compare notes after all students have finished gathering the information from the reading.

12. Remind students of the value of folding the page over to study these notes, focusing on the main idea as a reminder of the details on the right side. Show them the inverse of that — using the details to try to remember the main idea from the left side.

13. You may wish to allow students to quiz one another about the ideas on the notes. Let them know that they should study for the upcoming quiz using the notes in this fashion.

14. NEXT DAY: Again allow students to study the notes from the day before. Now they have studied the notes two days in a row. You may do this a third day in a row (with the same notes) or you may wish to quiz them after only two days. You be the judge, but see to it that most students will have great success on the quiz. Don't throw any curve balls. Make sure that they have put away all the notes and that their desks are clear before the quiz, but quiz them on exactly what was in their notes that they have studied under your supervision. For students who have not had great success in school up until they entered your class, this will be an eye opener as they ace the quiz. The message is clear — the note-taking system works and each student *could*, using this system, become successful at learning and remembering.

15. Ask students to report on their use of the skill of making and studying two-column notes. Say — did the process of using the system and studying from it actually help you to be successful on the quiz? (Students inevitably realize at this point that, by practicing two-column note taking when reading, and studying from the notes leads to heightened understanding and better retention of information.)

16. Take the opportunity to review and reinforce the concept of well-prepared and well-rehearsed notes, in the form of Cornell Notes.

17. In the days following this exercise, use other reading strategies such as anticipation guide, paired reading, etc. for the classroom activity, but provide structured, partially completed two-column notes as a homework assignment. Thus, students will be reflecting at home or in study time on what they have read in class with the assistance of peers and teacher. By giving such structure to the homework, you make it significantly more possible to accomplish.

18. In future days, perhaps a week or two later, introduce the PQR$_2$ST+ system of note taking to help in self-analysis of content. (PQR$_2$ST+ is best taught immediately after practicing paired reading.)

Weaning Students from Your Assistance

As quickly as is possible, the process of making 2-column notes should be turned over to the students as their own responsibility. It is appropriate for the transition to take place within the first couple weeks of school. Of course, you may wish to take a few minutes at the end of class once in a while over the first months of school to go to the overhead projector or chalk board "to model just how we might organize our notes from today's reading…" but, the goal should be to help students develop a sense of autonomy regarding the notes. It should become a skill that each student has.

Of course, the quality of notes will vary, but that is to be expected in any learning experience. The development of students is a year-long endeavor for any skill, and 2-column note taking is no different from others.

Grading Notes?

People often ask me if I grade the notes. My answer comes in two parts. The first part is that I do not grade them because *it is unconstitutional to grade notes!* Because of the "double-jeopardy clause" of the United States Constitution (5th Amendment — stating that a person may not be tried twice for the same crime), it is unconstitutional to grade the notes. A person who has poor quality notes will do poorly on a test on that subject matter. Why should that person also be penalized for having poor quality notes? Though this answer is somewhat facetious, it nevertheless leads to an indirect but useful way to grade notes.

What I have had great success with is collecting notes on the day of the test. Each student is instructed to place a week or two worth of notes, stapled together with the student's name on them, in a box in front of the classroom. During the test, I look at the notes, selecting examples from among all the students so that I can make some comparisons later. I then make transparency overheads of notes of varying quality.

When I return the graded tests to the students a couple days later, I share the overheads of varying quality notes, getting students to hypothesize as to what grades they think each of the various sets of notes led to on the test. (This is, of course, done anonymously, usually using notes from another classroom if possible.) Once they see the correlation between quality notes and test grades, they usually are motivated to improve the quality of their own notes.

The second part of the answer to the question of grading is that, since 2-column notes are a daily homework assignment, it is easy to check each day to see if they are done. At the beginning of each class, students take the time to copy the day's objectives from the chalk board onto their notes for that evening. While they are doing so, they must lay on their desks the notes from the previous evening. Thus, it is easy for me to move around the classroom to place a check in my grade book for those students who had their notes for the day. These checks become part of a class participation grade for the marking period.

The dual system of comparing test grades to note quality and daily participation checks in the grade book work in tandem to help to hold the importance of the notes in front of students. My experience suggests that students gradually acquire a sense of the importance of the system for academic success. Even students who do not make quality notes learn by seeing that others are having success as a result of doing so. Acquisition occurs as a result of many concurrent influencing factors, one of which is the observation of others who are having success doing it well.

Extra Scaffolds

Many special education students have, in their IEP's, instructions that they be provided notes made by the teacher or some other person. When this is the case, you might consider having a "class log" which is a three-ring binder that can be used to collect notes that students are making. I have done this by making one person each day be responsible for that day's notes. Once submitted to me, I would make copies of the notes to be included in the class log, and I would return the notes to the person providing them. An extra copy can be provided to the student with an IEP.

Even students with such an IEP should be provided the opportunity to learn the life skill of making notes. This may mean extra consideration in the quality of notes they attempt, but they should be provided with the opportunity to learn how to take reading notes just as other students are. The emphasis in special education should be on the word *education*.

Chapter 13

Cubing

Few people think more than two or three times a year; I have made an international reputation for myself by thinking once or twice a week.

George Bernard Shaw

Motivation ✓

Acquisition

e**X**tension ✓

Cubing (Cowan and Cowan, 1980; Morgan, Forget, and Antinarella, 1996; Vaughan and Estes, 1986; Richardson and Morgan, 2003) is a writing activity that permits students to look at a subject from six different perspectives. Six labels are printed on a cube, one on each of the six sides of a square box — the cube — covered with plain paper. Each side has labeled instructions for the different levels of thinking, including description, comparison, association, analysis, application, and argument (see Appendix 4). As each side of the cube is presented to the students, they write about their topic from that perspective until the teacher calls time and moves on to the next side of the cube.

The obvious value of this activity is that it turns an otherwise abstract thinking exercise into one that is very concrete in nature, and even involves the tactile-kinesthetic activity of writing. It is not advisable to spend too much time on a single side. Rather, you should fairly quickly cover a topic from six points of view. Depending on the depth of the topic, it is advisable to spend anywhere from 2-5 minutes per side. All six sides should be used since the six sides represent the six levels of thinking of recall, comprehension, application, analysis, synthesis, and evaluation.

Cubing can be used in a number of ways, and you will find it more interesting for students if you can vary the use of this strategy. It can be used as:

1. a pre-reading activity to help students think about what they already know about a topic,
2. a post-reading activity to help students think about what they have learned about the topic,

3. both a pre-reading and post-reading activity over a longer period of study, enabling students to compare the two products to see their growth,

4. a pre-writing strategy to enable students to consider a topic for a written assignment and to begin to narrow the focus of their writing to one aspect of the topic,

5. a vehicle for discussion if used in small groups in which students turn their own cube and use it to stimulate sharing and oral discussion of ideas as either a pre-reading or post-reading activity or discussion or to review for a test.

Cubing, as a writing activity, should also be done following the cooperative learning paradigm suggested in chapter 4 in which students first commit their ideas to paper before meeting in small groups to compare their understanding of the topic, and then proceed to full-class discussion.

Teaching the Cubing Procedure

Lifelong Learning Skill(s) to be Practiced During Learning:

- Extending beyond the reading through manipulation of ideas — applying a thinking taxonomy to better understand learned subject matter.
- Writing as a tool for comprehension.

Quick Overview of Lesson:

(This strategy may be used before the learning if it is assumed that students have a good deal of prior knowledge about the subject to be studied. It is the author's experience that Cubing is best used as an EXtension activity — a tool for analysis of what has been learned.)

1. Explain and model use of the skill of higher order thinking.
2. Each student prepares to write about topic. (Paper & pencil out)
3. Use a prepared cube (Appendix 4) to help students write about the topic at each level of thinking.
4. Students share what they have written.

Materials:

- Six-inch by six-inch cube made from a cardboard box and covered with the six thinking levels of the cubing process (optional)
- Student-owned paper & writing implement
- Textbook or other reading matter
- Overhead projector (optional) and transparency of the "Thinking Cube"

Detailed version of lesson:

1. Explain to students that by using higher order thinking about a topic, they can understand it better and remember it more easily. Let them know that by using the "Thinking Cube" they can think about a topic at six different levels.

2. Show students the "Thinking Cube" either by using a transparency or by having an actual six-sided figure to manipulate in the classroom. (It is easy to make a cube of six to eight inches in diameter to be used for this purpose. Once made, it will last for years.) Model the use of the cube by thinking out loud for students as you "cube" something. You may wish to cube something concrete like a pencil, or you might wish to cube what you had studied the previous day. The important thing is not what you choose to cube as much as the idea that you are modeling the thinking process involved. *This modeling is best done by adlibbing, not with a prepared slide. This shows that thinking is not so difficult, and that it is a process, not a product.*

3. Have each student prepare to write by obtaining clean paper and a writing implement.

4. Each of the six sides should be explained carefully and you should model the thinking involved:

    A. <u>Describe it.</u> Consider/visualize the subject in detail and describe what you see — colors, shapes, sizes, memories — what does it look like?
    B. <u>Compare it.</u> To what is it similar? From what is it different? Explain how.
    C. <u>Associate it.</u> What does it make you think of? You might associate it with similar things, or you can think of different things, times, places, people, etc, Just let your mind go and see what associations you have for this subject.
    D. <u>Analyze it.</u> Tell how it is made or how it functions. If you do not know, make it up! (Used in pre-reading activities, students are making predictions.)
    E. <u>Apply it.</u> Tell what you can do with it. How can it be used? How does it work?
    F. <u>Argue for or against it.</u> Go ahead and take a stand. Be sure that you are able to substantiate your stand with reasons why you think so through reference to the text or to your prior knowledge or both.

You may wish to model the thinking involved by cubing a wooden pencil as follows:

Cubing a Pencil

A person can use this thinking strategy to think about anything from something as simple as a pencil to something as complex as the space shuttle program. Naturally, the more complex the thing or issue, the more thought that goes into it. Just for practice, let's "cube" a pencil. We will use each of the six sides of the cube to do so.

Description: A pencil is a long, cylindrical (sometimes hexagonal), device used to write on paper.

Comparison: It is different than a pen because you can erase what you have written, which you cannot do with most pens.

Association: It makes me think of drawing because I like to draw with one. (It might make you think of just about anything, such as standardized tests or sharpening before class or your book bag. There is much room for personal thought at this level of thinking.)

Analysis: Pencils are generally made of wood surrounding and supporting a thin piece of graphite, which is the substance that marks the paper. It usually has a metal cylindrical clasp at the top, which holds an eraser.

Application: It is used by rubbing the graphite tip onto a piece of paper…When an error occurs, the pencil is inverted in the hand, and …

Argument: An argument in favor of pencils is that they are efficient tools for the taking of notes or writing a rough draft of something. It is easy to make corrections if you make a mistake, simply by inverting the pencil and using the attached eraser to rub out the error. They are also light weight and convenient to carry. Arguments against pencils are that they frequently need sharpening, the graphite tips break too easily, the graphite gets all over my clothes, I always leave it at home, etc....

5. Once the topic is agreed upon (usually the main idea of the lesson you have just completed, but it could be any aspect of what was learned today or in the past) have each student write individually on each level of thinking as you either rotate a pre-made cube or refer to the various levels from a transparency or wall poster of the six levels of thinking. It is my experience that a physical cube is useful to manipulate so everyone can see each of the six sides in succession. Times may vary, but do not spend more than 2-5 minutes at each level of the cube. In some cases, depending on the topic and its complexity, you may spend as little as one minute on some of the sides. Feel this out by moving around the class to see what students are doing. *Take the time to do the same writing on your own onto a transparency so that students will, later on, be able to see how you think about the same topic. This way, **you** may get the last word if you choose.*

6. Be sure that each student understands the meaning of each of the labels from each side of the cube. Move around the classroom to look over the shoulders of the writing students to observe their thinking. Especially during the first few times you use cubing, you will want to fully define the labels and move around to assure that the correct level of thinking is taking place. Be tolerant of different interpretations, but feel free to help out an individual student, quietly whispering ideas. If it is apparent that several students are not succeeding at a certain writing/thinking level, stop the class and address the thinking by modeling. Think out loud for them so that they can see what is involved at that level of thinking. (You will only have to do this once or twice with most students. It is not that students do not know how to perform higher order thinking — it's just that they often have not had to do too much of it at school relating to academic work.)

7. Have students share by reading aloud each of their six writings of the cube process in small groups to compare notes and improve their understandings of the topic. Let them know that, by hearing others' interpretations of the learning, they will better understand the concepts themselves. Have them work to select the best description, comparison, association, etc. (or some synthesized combination of several) of the six levels of thinking *to prepare for sharing out loud with the rest of the class*.

8. Use the cube in your hands (or a cube on a transparency) to work through the six levels, randomly selecting a cooperative learning group for each level of thinking, and have that group share the response they agreed on for that level of thinking. This can be done by using the cube as a die, tossing it to see which side lands facing up, having a randomly selected group prepared to share their writing about that level of thinking. The cube can also be thrown from one group to the next, having the group catch the cube and respond to the side that ends up facing toward the ceiling. This adds a tactile-kinesthetic level of behavior that seems to engage many students, even though the real focus is on thinking. (There are many ways to run this last part of the cubing process. Be creative, and come up with your own. You may just wish to collect the students' collective writing to evaluate on your own. My experience suggests that the sharing aloud of student cubing writings is helpful in developing understanding of the subject matter.) (Figure 13-1 shows how one group in a 9th-grade algebra class cubed the slope-intercept form of linear equations.)

9. Ask students to report on their use of the skill. Ask them, "By a show of hands, how many of you felt that by thinking about this topic at six different levels, and then comparing it with the thoughts of others, it helped you to better understand what we learned in here today?" "Do you feel that you have a better understanding of the topic that was cubed than you might have had by doing a worksheet about the topic?"

10. You might extend the learning into homework by asking students to make some additional notes about each level of writing they have done, citing elaborative details, or otherwise reflecting on the learning.

Figure 13-1

CUBING THE SLOPE-INTERCEPT FORM OF LINEAR EQUATIONS:

DESCRIBE: It is the equation of a line, and it has two variables. It is written with the y-variable all by itself on one side.

COMPARE: Compared to the standard form, Ax + By = C, it is easier to use to find the line.

ASSOCIATE: It makes me think of the coordinate plane with the X and Y axis.

ANALYZE: It is y = mx + b. The y is a variable, and so is the x. The m tells the slope of the line (how steep it is). The slope, m, is the rise over run, the change in y over the change in x. The b tells where the line crosses the y-axis. It is called the y-intercept.

APPLY: For the line written y = mx + b, which has a slope of m and a y-intercept at b, there are an infinite number of solutions for x and y. For each x, there is a y, and vice-versa. An example is y = 2x + 3. The slope is 2 which means the rise in the y-value is two for every increase in the run of the x-value. The line crosses the y-axis at 3. So it looks like this:

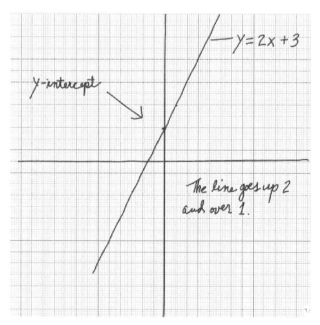

Every point on the line is a solution to the equation.

ARGUE: The slope intercept form of writing linear equations is the easiest one to be able to see the line quickly. It is better than the standard form because you don't need to change the signs or anything to calculate the slope or intercept. I can just look at the equation and picture the line in my head.

What you do after the writing is up to you. You may wish to collect them as an informal evaluation of how well the students learned the subject matter. The writings could then be used to start the next day's class by sharing some of the more accurate or more confused understandings as articulated in the cubing exercise.

The more practice students have with cubing, the easier it gets for them to do it. I recommend, after a good bit of practice, using cubing as an assessment activity on a test, in lieu of an essay question — just ask students to cube something that they have studied. It is a good idea to give them the six prompts on the test. You will see that cubing becomes a good assessment tool since they are actually easier to grade than essays. After all, you already know the outline of the answer.

Cubing may be done orally as a "last five minutes of class" activity, it can be done as a cooperative writing activity as described above, or it might be done in place of a major essay on a test. The last couple of years that I taught U.S. Government, I used cubing as a major part of my final exam. For 50% of the test grade, students had to "cube" the six principles of the U.S. Constitution. Without even considering introductory or concluding paragraphs, students were placed in a position to write 36 paragraphs for their final "essay" of the year. The shortest one, from an inclusion student, was six pages long. Most were thirteen to sixteen pages in length. I would argue that those students were much better prepared for college than students who leave high school thinking that a final exam essay is 40-50 words long.

In sum, cubing is a thinking activity that helps to apply Bloom's Taxonomy to the learning of subject matter. It works in any classroom and over just about any subject matter. Some of the concepts I have had students cube are the slope-intercept form of linear equations, federalism, physical geography of the eastern United States, group 1 of the periodic table of elements, adding and subtracting fractions, the digestive process, and many others. If you use cubing with your students, you will see that their understanding of your subject matter improves as does their ability to process new ideas.

Extra Scaffolds for Disadvantaged Readers

As in any of the classroom activities that call for individual or small group work, the teacher, in a special education or other needs classroom where heterogeneous grouping is not an option, can become more involved in the discussion. Instead of having students do individual writing before meeting in groups, the teacher might spend more time modeling by actually going through the whole process using student responses to write onto an overhead transparency or onto the chalkboard. Even in special needs classes, though, students should be weaned from dependence on the teacher as soon as possible. The fact is that cubing is a very concrete exercise, yet it allows students to perform higher order thinking without realizing they are doing so. If the teacher models cubing several times over a period of a few weeks, students of all ability levels can perform the task with relative ease (and a little one-on-one support).

Chapter 14

Fiction Prediction Sheets

The whole art of teaching is only the art of awakening the natural curiosity of young minds for the purpose of satisfying it afterwards.

Anatole France

Motivation	✓
Acquisition	✓
E**X**tension	✓

The fiction Directed Reading/Thinking Activity (DRTA) (Stauffer, 1969) helps students to set purposes for reading stories, novels, or other forms of fiction. As a class, the story is analyzed through the combination of writing and discussing student perceptions of what is happening and what they predict will happen. As is noted above, it can be used to take a group of students through all three phases of the learning framework.

Using student writing in order to get students to commit ideas to paper, the teacher facilitates a classroom discussion as to what is happening in a story, and what is going to happen. The result is that students actually teach one another the inference process without being aware that they are doing so.

A Fiction Prediction Sheet allows for students of varied ability levels to participate in a cooperative effort to be metacognitive as they read a story. By systematically stopping at times to get students to write what they individually perceive to be happening, and to share their perceptions, teachers are helping students to do, as a class, what a strategic individual reader does alone.

The two-sided "fiction prediction" sheet is the concrete prop that is used to facilitate the discussion (Figure 14-1). It is really not necessary to make Fiction Prediction Sheets for each time you use this form of DRTA. I find it reduces confusion the first few times you use the process to give a Fiction Prediction Sheet to each student. Obviously, students could make their own with their own paper once they have practiced the process. They simply need to draw a lined down the middle of a piece of their own paper in order to do so.

This activity is a classic example of why, in the cooperative learning process, we must get students to commit their thoughts to paper before discussion takes place. It is common in many classrooms for a teacher to stop a story and ask the class what they predict is going to happen next. Without students having committed to paper, the discussion is most often dominated by the thoughts of the few students who, either because of their sense of self confidence resulting from their past academic success, or because they just have a strong self concept, are willing to contribute to the class discussion. Many students become passive observers of this process in which they rarely contribute ideas.

Figure 14-1

FICTION PREDICTION SHEET	
My Prediction	What Really Happens

By getting all students to commit to paper what their own prediction is, without discussing first with others, the variety of predictions is always greater when the discussion begins. Often, students who are special needs students, or those whose grades are less than stellar, are the ones whose predictions are actually right on the target in the end. Without getting them to commit to paper, the class rarely gets to hear their contributions. On the other hand, when the teacher has gotten all students to write, the teacher can either put students in groups to compare their predictions, or go right up and down the rows, asking each student to "read what you wrote." More students become engaged in the process.

What exactly is the process? It is the process of taking the information gathered up to any given point in the story (including a preview) and using that information to infer where the author is going with the story. Through this process, students are teaching each other the process of inference without necessarily even being aware that they are doing so. By hearing each other's predictions, they also clue in to details that they may have missed in the part of the story just read. This is enhanced by the teacher's frequently asking, "Why do you think that?"

upon hearing a student's prediction. When a student answers this question, s/he is enhancing the understanding of the story for all students.

Another benefit of student writing during this process is that it affords the teacher the opportunity to observe student interpretations even before the sharing process. By moving around the classroom as students write, and looking over their shoulders to see what they are writing in each of the columns of the Fiction Prediction Sheet, the teacher can see if and when comprehension is breaking down. If it occurs with only one or two students, the teacher can stop to whisper important information to those students. On the other hand, if there seems to be a general miscomprehension occurring in the classroom, the teacher can teach the whole class to help them comprehend a confusing idea.

Fiction Prediction Procedure

Lifelong Learning Skill(s) to be Practiced During Learning:

- Previewing fiction to help establish purposes for reading
- Using self-generated predictions to help establish purposes for reading
- Maintaining thoughts through an extended piece of discourse
- Making inferences while reading to revise or verify predictions
- Referring to text to substantiate interpretation

Quick Overview of Lesson:

- Preview reading matter.
- Close book and write predictions.
- Share predictions aloud.
- Read a portion of story to verify predictions, stopping at a point predetermined by teacher.
- Write notes on actual story occurrences.
- Revise predictions in writing.
- Repeat steps 3-6 as many as two to three times with a short story.

Materials:

- A brief short story (near the beginning of the year)
- A "fiction prediction sheet" divided with a line down the middle of the page, with a heading on the left side that says "My Prediction" and a heading on the right side that says "What really happens." (Figure 14-1 and Appendix 5.)

Detailed version of lesson:

1. Introduce the content of the reading by posing a hypothetical question, reading a quotation, previewing the text, or some other interest-capturing idea to which students can react through discussion.

2. Explain to students that what they are about to do is what any skilled and strategic reader might do when reading any piece of fiction text — **previewing** to recall any prior knowledge about the topic to be read and to gather clues that might allow inferences to be made about where the story is going. This information might come from our prior knowledge or from what we have learned from the preview. Some of us will spot things that others do not spot simply because of our different experiences in life and in literature. This will allow for a variety of valid predictions to occur.

   Tell them, "Strategic readers, when reading fiction, always **make predictions** about what is going to happen. When reading a murder mystery, for example, a strategic reader might first think 'the butler did it.' Upon reading a few more pages, the reader might suddenly say, 'Wait, it could not have been the butler; it must have been the maid!' After reading a few *more* pages, the reader might again revise the prediction, suggesting, 'It could not have been the maid either; it must have been his *wife* who did it!!'"

   Tell students that what we are going to do here in class today, is, as a class, do what a strategic reader does all alone. The difference is that we are going to do it as a class. We are going to preview the story, and then we will all make predictions and then share them. Let them know that they will see how this actually helps them understand the story better.

3. Lead students through a cursory preview of the reading to be accomplished. (With fiction, you do not need to do the same form of elaborate preview as you would with non-fiction. Scan the title, look at the pictures, and read an introductory portion of the story. You must decide ahead of time how much of the story to read at this point. I usually read something between one or two paragraphs to as much as two pages of the story. How much do they need to be able to make reasonable predictions? You decide.)

4. Once the preview of the reading has been done, tell students to close their books. Give students a copy of the two-sided Fiction Prediction Sheet. (Or, you could have them make their own.)

5. Tell students to write in the left column (entitled "My Prediction") what they think the story is going to be about and what they think is going to happen. Make sure that each student writes his or her own prediction without influencing other students. Move around the classroom to facilitate the process. Make occasional positive comments like, "There are a lot of good predictions that I see as I move around the room.")

6. Once most of the students have written their predictions, allow for them to share what they have predicted. Go right around the classroom, taking a prediction from each student. If a student does not offer the logic for a specific prediction, ask why s/he made the prediction. Students sharing their thoughts out loud teach each other inferential thinking without necessarily being aware of it. (It is very important during this sharing that all students are listening to each prediction being made. At times, students will be so interested in the story that they carry on small conversations on their own that cause them to miss the predictions of some of their classmates. Be sure that, at this time, there is only one conversation going on in the classroom.)

   Make sure that you treat each prediction with a poker face so that each is considered equal to any other. This is very important in the fiction prediction process — the message is that the process itself is as important as being accurate. Make sure also that all students are listening to the others' predictions. This is critical for the development of inferential thinking. When done this way, the typical response to another student's prediction will be, "Wow, I never thought of that!" Now the collective predictions of the whole class have helped to set purpose for reading. Whether a specific student was correct in her prediction is not as important as being able to read to find out if any of the predictions were correct. (Another alternative to having each student predict aloud is to randomly select students to contribute — taking all students with a brown shirt or some other characteristic to eliminate the tedium of getting 38 predictions. Another alternative is to have students discuss in their own groups what they have written. Each group then chooses one prediction they would like to share aloud with the class.)

7. Mention to students that, when we stop reading at a certain point, they will then be writing on both sides of the Fiction Prediction Sheet. They will write on the right side to tell what is really happening, and on the left side to revise or alter their prediction.

8. Either read aloud to the students a portion of the text, or allow students to read silently to determine the accuracy of their predictions. (Make sure that it is clear how far into the story they should read if they are to read it silently. You should have the next stop point clearly marked in their books. Have them place a small pencil mark where they should stop, to remind themselves.) Tell students that they should, when they have read to the stop point, close their books and write into the right-hand column of the fiction prediction sheet a few notes about what is actually happening in the story. Instruct them to also draw a line under their original prediction and revise or redevelop their prediction based on what they have read. *Now*, what do they think is to happen?

9. Once students have done this, again go around the class to have students share their predictions. Be sure to ask frequently why they made a prediction if they don't offer the reason.

10. Continue this process throughout the story, repeating steps 5-8. Usually 2 to 3 stops is sufficient. Any more stops will lead to frustration for some students.

11. Ask students to report on their use of the skill of prediction — ask, "By a show of hands, how many of you felt that, by stopping to make predictions aloud, it actually helped to make you want to read more of the story?" Reinforce the skill of prediction by letting them know that anyone who reads fiction literature uses this method as a tool to enhance their own level of engagement in the reading.

12. Assign an EXtension activity such as writing in response to one or more of the 20 questions listed below (Figure 14-2). I find that students respond well to these open-ended questions to EXtend their thinking beyond the literal level. Further EXtension might include a review of the reading to outline the story grammar of the story, listing the setting, characters, rising action, internal response, external response, climax, and resolution. (See Chapter 21 for an easy way to get them to do this.) This is an especially appropriate homework assignment since it involves individual reflection on a reading that has already been done in class with the assistance of peers and the teacher. The class discussion the next day might start with a comparison in small groups of what the students have identified as essential story elements.

Evolution of the Process throughout the School Year

We have found that the Fiction Prediction Sheet is a process that can help students get past the fact that they do not like reading school-related stories. Something happens to students between the third grade and the ninth grade to make them avoid reading that is assigned. The DRTA, using a Fiction Prediction Sheet, can reverse that trend if it is applied properly.

Start with short stories that are only a few pages long. Read the first one aloud to the students, stopping from time to time to use the writing/predicting process as described above. Graduate to reading only a part of the story (perhaps 2/3) with stops to write/predict/discuss, leaving the last part of the story for students to read silently on their own. This silent part may be as little as a half page, but students, once "hooked" on the story through the predicting process, will read the rest no matter how long it is or what their reading grade level is.

Graduate to longer short stories, using the same process. After a few of those, graduate to the first novel. Treat the first chapter like a long short story, reading it in the classroom, sharing predictions along the way. Once finished with the first chapter, all students having shared their predictions, tell students, "You may take the novels home with you tonight, but, whatever you do, don't read past page 70." The results will be phenomenal. Students are now hooked on the story about which all their peers have made predictions, and they will read! (Your problem will be those who could not stop at page 70. What a terrible problem to have to contend with — students reading more than they are supposed to read!)

Figure 14-2

Twenty EXtension Questions to Enhance Student Appreciation of Fiction:

1. What character(s) was your favorite? Why?
2. What character(s) did you dislike? Why?
3. Does anyone in this work remind you of anyone you know?
4. Are you like anyone in this work?
5. If you could be any character in this work, who would you be?
6. What quality(-ies) of which character(s) strikes you as a good characteristic to develop within yourself over the years? Why? How does the character demonstrate this quality?
7. Overall, what kind of feeling did you have after reading a few paragraphs of this work? Midway? After finishing the work?
8. Do any incidents, ideas, or actions in this work remind you of your own life or something that happened to you? Explain.
9. Do you like this piece of work? Why or why not?
10. Are there any parts of this work that were confusing to you? Which parts? Why do you think you got confused?
11. Do you feel there is an opinion expressed by the author through this work? What is it? How do you know this? Do you agree? Why or why not?
12. Do you think the title of this work is appropriate? Is it significant? Explain. What do you think the title means?
13. Would you change the ending of the story in any way? Tell your ending. Why would you change it?
14. What kind of person do you think the author is? What makes you feel this way?
15. How did this work make you feel? Explain.
16. Do you share any of the feelings of the characters in this work? Explain.
17. Sometimes a work will leave you with a feeling that there is more to tell. Did this work do this? What do you think might happen next?
18. Would you like to read something else by this author? Why or why not?
19. What do you feel is the most important word, phrase, passage, or paragraph in this work? Explain why it is important.
20. If you were an English teacher, would you want to share this work with your students? Why or why not?

Extra Scaffolding for Disadvantaged Readers

If you are in a self-contained special education classroom, or you have a significantly large number of poor readers in your class, you may want to facilitate the process with a few extra steps. For instance, you may wish to read the story out loud to the students. If you elect to do this, you should always have the students read along silently while you are reading. (Avoid the temptation to use "round-robin" or "popcorn" reading by the students. Having students attempt to read a story out loud causes them to focus on all the wrong things about reading. See Chapter 9, FAQ 15 for more explanation on this.)

By your reading it aloud, you are allowing them to perceive the story as ideas in the form of oral language communicated through written language. They will listen and read along without focusing so much on the decoding aspect of reading. Their focus, partly because of the prediction process, and partly because of hearing the story read aloud with proper pronunciation and in a fluent manner, will be on deriving meaning from the story.

When you get to a point at which you have decided to stop, simply close your book and insist that they do so also. Then proceed through the writing and discussion process just as you would with any other group.

Chapter 15

What-I-Know Sheets

It is a miracle that curiosity survives formal education.
Albert Einstein

Motivation ✓

Acquisition ✓

E**X**tension ✓

One way to perform a Directed Reading-Thinking Activity (Stauffer, 1969) in a non-fiction reading, is to use any of a variety of formats variously called "What-I-Know sheets" (Richardson & Morgan, 2003) or "K-W-L sheets" (Ogle, 1986). As is shown in figure 15-1 and in Appendix 7, there are multiple ways of going about using this technique. These sheets act as concrete prompts to help to provoke students into first recalling prior knowledge, and then using their collective prior knowledge to set their own purposes for reading by asking questions about the subject matter before reading. In other words, the teacher is using the "what-I-know sheet" as a concrete prompt to facilitate a directed reading-thinking activity that helps students to acquire the ability to use their own curiosity as a means of setting purposes for reading.

Despite evidence that using this process helps students to learn new subject matter and at the same time acquire important learning skills, few upper grade content area teachers report using this activity in their classrooms to help students learn new subject matter. My experience in working with teachers suggests that once they recognize the steps that make it work, they are much more likely to use it in the future.

Many teachers with whom I have worked have said that they had little success with the process because their students most often had little or nothing to list in the first column — the "what-I-know" column. When I asked the teachers if they had previewed the text with the students before asking them to fill in the first column, they invariably say that they had not. Previewing the text is one of the most important elements of the non-fiction directed reading-thinking activity. It is during the previewing of the text that students pick up enough background information to make connections with their own prior knowledge, often based on what they have learned from movies, TV programs, and previous course work.

The Directed Reading-Thinking Activity simulates, in a whole-class group, what a strategic individual reader does alone. In other words, a strategic reader previews the text, and during the preview process, becomes curious as to exactly what the text will say, thus setting purposes for reading. Then, the strategic reader reads to see if these purposes are met. What is happening in a classroom where a teacher is facilitating this process through the use of a "what-I-know sheet" is that the collective thought of the class empowers all students to set more goals for the reading than any one individual might have been able to do working alone.

Figure 15-1

KWL Sheet (Ogle, 1986)

K	W	L
What I Know After Previewing	What I Want to Find Out	What I Learned

One caveat to the teacher is to expect the unexpected in terms of student questions, but be accepting of these questions. I have learned that some student questions that seem outlandish, at first, can actually lead to inferential reading on the part of most students. I not only learned to accept outlandish questions, but I learned ways to stimulate what I like to call "wild and wacky" questions (Morgan, Forget, and Antinarella, 1996). Once students set, as their purposes for reading, answers to questions that they are really interested in, they are willing to perform reading at a much higher level than when they are seeking the answers to questions from a worksheet or from the end of the chapter.

When preparing to read about electricity, one group of students with whom I was working asked questions that included:

- Why do 9-volt batteries taste bitter when you put the terminals on your tongue?
- Do cats die when you stun them with a stun gun?
- Does your brain really fry when you are electrocuted?
- If a plugged-in radio falls into an occupied bathtub, what is the life expectancy of the bather?

They asked these questions even though the reading centered on important objectives that I had to teach, such as

- What are the three conditions that must exist for an electric current to exist?
- What are the differences between AC and DC?
- How do you measure current, voltage drop, and resistance?

In this science class in which students had to read about electricity` they were instructed to recognize that their seemingly outlandish questions were good questions, but that in order to find the answers to questions such as those, they might have to "read between the lines" and actually infer the answer. I told them right up front that the likelihood of the authors stating anything about cats and stun guns in this chapter were pretty slim. Nevertheless, I recognized the validity of their questions in setting purposes for reading.

Once we had taken several minutes to read, I had students discuss their interpretations of the text to see if they had found answers. Indeed, they had been able to infer the answers to some of their questions. For others, I had to model how to make such inferences. Some questions were not answered in the reading. This is OK. At least we were reading carefully enough to attempt to find the answer. When I asked students about the objectives that they were supposed to learn from the reading (my three objectives), they had no difficulties stating clear answers to the questions. Thus, they had learned what they were supposed to learn even though, in their minds, those things were not necessarily the central focus of the reading.

My point is that by allowing students to ask questions about ideas that they are interested in, you are encouraging them to read the text in a mature way. They read unlike the way they read when they are doing worksheets, hunting for literal-level answers to questions of no interest to them. In fact, it is important to explain that this particular reading probably will not say anything about cats and stun guns, but you may be able to infer the answer to your question. What happens in this circumstance is that students read so carefully to see if they can infer the answers to their own questions, that they discover the answers to the major objectives that you are responsible for teaching! In other words, do not be afraid to be accepting of students' questions. There is more happening than appears on the surface when they open up their curiosity.

It is important for the teacher to read at the same time that the students read. Be prepared to be the model for inferential thinking the first couple times using this strategy. Students who have been raised on worksheets have little experience in drawing conclusions for which they have to actually think and interpret the text. However, the good news is that once you have modeled it for them once or twice, they take the ball and run with it. (It is a fact that on most standardized reading tests, students are asked to perform inferential thinking, and often do not do well. This reading techniques celebrates the use of inference and allows students to acquire the skills through meaningful practice.)

One way to stimulate the asking of questions that stimulate higher order thinking during reading is to use the "Question Mark" question for quality thinking bookmark (Morgan, et al., 1996) found in Appendix 6. By providing each student with one of these bookmarks and encouraging students to take advantage of the question prompts to create purpose-setting questions, you will assist them in asking the kinds of questions that require higher order thinking to occur during the reading.

One of my favorite examples of how this occurs took place in a 12th grade United States Government Class in which we were preparing to read about political philosophies of the various groups along the political spectrum in the U.S. After previewing the section of the chapter in which students had seen a graphic representation of the political spectrum as shown in Figure 15-2, one group of students worked together, using the "Question Mark" bookmark to come up with the following question from the "synthesis" level of question prompts: What would you predict or infer if God came to the United States? Would He be a Democrat or a Republican? My response, as usual, was to suggest that that was a good question, and I wrote it onto the chalkboard along with many other student-generated questions.

Figure 15-2

US Political Spectrum

Communist	Socialist	Liberal	Democrat	Republican	Conservative	Reactionary	Fascist

Once the reading was over, I probed the class for their responses to their questions, and indeed, one group of students had come up with an answer to the question about God's hypothetical party affiliation. They said that God the Father would be a conservative or a Republican — somewhere on the right side of the political spectrum. They went on to suggest that Jesus would probably be a Democrat or a socialist — somewhere on the left side of the spectrum. As I always do, I asked the students to cite the exact text that lead them to their interpretation of the answer. Without hesitation, they proceeded to cite from their textbook information regarding the right-wing belief in the death penalty, which they thought to be rather "eye-for-an-eye Old Testament-like in nature. They suggested that perhaps God the Father would therefore be on the right wing of the spectrum. On the other hand, they cited the notion that left-wingers are more in favor of higher taxes, taking wealth from the rich and redistributing it to the poor, leading them to believe that Jesus would probably be a left winger in our system.

What these students had done is to use their own prior knowledge to make sense of a concept that is not inherently interesting to 17-year-old students. What may have seemed to be an outlandish question at the outset of the class allowed students to combine the text and their prior knowledge to construct meaning in a mature, if somewhat creative way. In addition to making the reading interesting, they learned the subject matter they needed to learn, and *they* did the thinking.

Procedure for Non-Fiction Directed Reading/Thinking Activity

Lifelong Learning Skill(s) to be Practiced During Learning:

- Previewing expository text to help establish purposes for reading
- Posing questions based on prior knowledge to help establish purposes for reading
- Maintaining thoughts through an extended piece of discourse
- Making inferences while reading to answer questions
- Referring to text to substantiate interpretation

Quick Overview of Lesson:

- Preview reading matter.
- Close book and write prior knowledge.
- Share prior knowledge aloud.
- Write questions to probe the reading.

- Share questions to create an inventory of questions for all to seek answers.
- Read to find answers to the group's questions (Students write answers during reading).
- Defend interpretations of answers through reference to the text.

Materials:

- Textbook or other non-fiction reading
- What-I-Know Sheet, KWL Sheet or one of the variations on those.
- Chalkboard or overhead transparency projector

Detailed version of lesson:

1. Introduce the content of the reading by posing a hypothetical question, reading a quotation, previewing the text, or some other interest-capturing idea to which students can react through writing or discussion.

2. Lead students through a careful preview of the reading to be accomplished. (See description of the Preview Procedure in Chapter 11.)

3. Once the preview of the reading has been accomplished, tell students to close their books. Give students a copy of the What-I-Know Sheet or a KWL Sheet. (There are several variations on these. Choose the one most appropriate for your needs.)

4. Explain to students that what they are in the process of doing, as a whole class, is what any skilled and strategic reader might do when reading any piece of non-fiction text — previewing first to see the structure of the text and to get an idea of what the reading is going to be about. Mention that a strategic reader, during the preview process, actually recalls his/her own prior knowledge about the topic to be read. At the same time, s/he confronts new vocabulary and concepts that stand out in bold print or in photos or maps graphs and charts. S/he probably becomes somewhat curious about what the author might be saying in the text. Tell students that what we are going to do after the preview is, as a class, do just exactly what a good reader might do all alone in the college dormitory or on the job in industry. We are going to make a class list of what we, collectively, know about the topic. This information might come from our prior knowledge or from what we have learned from the preview. Some of us will spot things that others do not spot simply because of our different levels of prior knowledge about various things. Then we are going to allow our curiosity to help us generate some questions about the topic. Then we will read to find the answers to our own questions.

5. After the preview, tell students to close the book. Remind them of the topic of the reading. Tell students to write whatever they know about the topic in the first column of the What-I-Know Sheet. Move around the room to facilitate the writing of ideas. Encourage students to base their facts and ideas on not only what they have seen in the preview of the reading, but also on what they know from other sources such as movies, TV, other courses, etc.

6. Once most all students have written their conceptions and misconceptions about the topic on their own paper, allow for them to discuss in their own groups what they have written.

7. Now take ideas (concepts *and* <u>mis</u>conceptions) from each student and make a list of "What I Know" about the topic after previewing, but before reading. With small groups of students (fewer than 25) go right up and down each row gathering new facts. (If a student can't think of a fact to contribute, tell the student that you will come back to her and keep going.) With larger groups of students, you should have students, in their groups, share their facts that they have written, but each group should isolate one or two facts they think are most significant. Then you should ask each group to share their fact. This way, a class of 36 to 40 students in groups of 4 will have nine or ten key ideas on which the whole class may focus after sharing. All facts should go in the first column of the KWL Sheet or WIK Sheet. Do not worry about misconceptions unless students point them out. If no person questions a misconception at this point, record it as stated. These should be listed on the chalkboard or other surface for all to see and to copy onto their own What-I-know sheets. Tell students that if they do not already have a particular fact or idea on their sheet, they must copy the new ideas as they are shared aloud. This allows for each student to concentrate on what is being discussed. Mention to students that you recognize that some of the statements that are being recorded at this point may not be completely accurate, and that one of the goals of the reading will be to identify any inaccuracies from this column. Let them know that in allowing for less-than-accurate statements to be recorded at this stage of the process you are paralleling the behavior of a strategic reader who benefits from recalling all prior knowledge — accurate or inaccurate.

8. Once you have gathered the facts (?) and students have copied them onto their sheets, instruct each student independently to think about what s/he would like to find out from the reading. Tell students to write down, in the second column, one or two questions the answers to which they would like to know. This should be done independently by each student. Again, move around the room to facilitate this process. (An important enhancement to the quality of student questions may be obtained through the use of the "Questioning for Quality Thinking" bookmark available in Appendix 6. You might suggest to students that they ask some higher order questions by using the prompts available on this tool.)

9. When students have written their questions, again put them into groups for a few minutes to share their questions. You may ask them to select, from the several questions they have originated, one or two that they would share from their group to the whole class.

10. Go up and down the rows to solicit questions (or ask students in groups to select the best question(s) from their group) and make a list of questions on the chalkboard. Tell students to copy down any questions that are not already written on their own sheets at this time so that they all will have the same inventory of questions to help them focus on the reading. Frequently praise the questions as being good as you write the questions onto the chalkboard.

11. Once the list of questions has been generated, let students know that their questions are valid and interesting. Tell them that their questions are better than those at the end of the chapter because they are more interesting, and thus will make the reading more interesting. Let them know that they may not be as easy to answer as the ones found on worksheets or at the end of the chapter because they will not "jump off the page like those typically at the end of the chapter." Tell students they may need to use *inference* to ascertain the answers. Explain that inference is the skill of "reading between the lines" to find answers. Tell them that even though the answers to their questions may not be word for word on the page, that they may be found through creative interpretation of what the author(s) say(s). Model this behavior.

12. Give students a target time for them to silently read the section of text they are about to read. I usually err on the short side at this point to put some light pressure on students to read quickly. I do not always adhere to the time precisely, but rather move around the class to assess where students are in the reading. On the other hand, I usually do not wait for all students to finish the entire reading. When about two thirds to three fourths of the students have finished, I say "I know some of you have not quite finished, but we need to go to the next step," below.

13. Get students in groups to discuss the information gathered through reading. Here students will discuss their varying interpretations of what they have read. Let them know that they should be able to refer to the text to verify to others why they think their interpretations are valid. Let them know that they ought to listen to each other and help each other in the process of interpreting. Let them know that it is normal for two or more people to come away from a reading with varying interpretations, and that what each person has seen in the reading may be slightly different from others' interpretations partly because of different background knowledge going into the reading. Challenge all groups to answer all the questions, at least inferentially, and to correct any misconceptions from the first column of the worksheet. Move around the room to facilitate this process. In some cases, students will need help in finding inferences to answer the questions.

14. Conduct a class-size discussion of answers to the questions. Act as a facilitator, allowing students to compare/contrast their interpretations of answers. (Near the beginning of the year, you may need to model inferential thinking a few times to show them how to practice interpretive reading. In other words, *you* may be the only one in the room to find the answers to some of their questions. However, through your modeling of the use of inference, you are enabling them to see how it is done. The next time you do the activity, you will see more students practicing the use of interpretive reading. It is contagious. And it is fun.)

It is very important that as students defend their answers they refer to specific parts of the text. It is OK to also add reference to their prior knowledge, but the whole purpose for the activity is to practice processing the text to learn subject matter. When reference is made to a paragraph on a certain page, see that all students turn to that paragraph. Ask the defending student to read aloud the part to which s/he is referring, and ask for the interpretation. Allow for differing opinions on the interpretation, but attempt to bring the class to agreement in the discussion. Allow them to do the discussing. Act as mediator.

15. Have students report on their use of the skill — ask them, "by a show of hands, how many of you feel that, by going through the process of what a strategic reader might do to approach a piece of text such as this, it actually helped you to comprehend what otherwise might have been pretty boring…" Let them know that the process they just used collectively as a class is what any strategic reader might do when confronting such non-fiction text.

16. Assign more eXtension activity such as review of the reading for homework to seek out the seven or eight key words understanding the meaning of which would assure understanding of the topic. This is an especially appropriate homework assignment near the beginning of the year. The teacher is not demanding top quality note taking that may not have been taught yet. Instead, the teacher is allowing for success to occur through very modest assignments. The class discussion the next day might start with a discussion or debate about whose words most clearly relate to important ideas relating to the topic.

Extra Scaffolds for Disadvantaged Readers

There are, of course, many ways to alter this lesson as there are for any of the classroom activities in this book. The three major ways that I change the Directed Reading-Thinking Activity in non-fiction are

- leaving the book open during the what-I-know column activity
- reading aloud to the students from the text instead of silent reading, pausing from time to time to see if we have seen any evidence to answer any of our questions
- modeling the thinking required to make inferential answers

Each of these can enhance the process with low-performing readers. When I allow them to fill in the first column, labeled "What I Know after Previewing," students tend to continue the previewing process even while they are relating to the concepts in the text. I have found that, with low-performing readers, this can greatly enhance the "prior knowledge" that they have. This, in turn, leads to them asking better, and more focused questions.

As in any of the classroom activities in this book, the teacher's reading aloud from the text after the students have set purposes for reading can greatly enhance their comprehension of the text. As I have stated before, it is very important for students to read along silently while the teacher reads out loud. After I have read several paragraphs, I like to stop and ask if any students have seen any information thus far that points to an answer. If a student responds with an answer, I say, "*Tell us where you found that information. What page and paragraph? Read the part that says that, and tell us how you are interpreting the text.*" I then instruct all students to go to the page and paragraph to follow as the answering student cites the text by reading it aloud.

If we have read past a section of text that does have an answer, but no student spotted the answer, it could be an appropriate time to model how to find answers. In this case, I am the one to take students to the page and paragraph to "*show you how a skilled reader might interpret this.*" I like to be careful to walk the fine line between being a "teller" of information and being a *modeler* of "*how an accomplished and strategic reader might interpret the text.*"

Chapter 16

Focused Free Writes

I cannot teach anybody anything, I can only make them think.
Socrates

Motivation ✓

Acquisition

E**X**tension ✓

Free Writing is one way to get students to determine what they already know about a topic. It is useful as a pre-reading activity when students are asked to focus on the subject they will be studying. It can also be used at any point in the lesson when the teacher recognizes that an idea has been introduced about which the students may have varying opinions or with which they may have had experience — or related knowledge. At that point, the teacher can stop and ask students to focus on a question, idea, or statement and respond in writing for several minutes. By getting students to commit in writing to what they are thinking, the teacher can observe progress, and also assure more participation than if s/he simply poses an open question to the class for oral discussion. (Such discussion often tends to be dominated by a few confident students.)

Such writing can be followed by further discussion or reading to clarify students' conceptions. This can also be valuable if a class discussion is lagging and students need to get their thinking back on track. Free Writing can also be used as a culminating activity to help students reflect on what they have learned. When used in this way, students have the opportunity to synthesize the concepts they have learned in the class. At the same time, it provides an informal, but useful assessment device for the teacher. After collecting focused free writes, the teacher can scan them for understandings and misunderstandings. Normally, these should not be graded. (Regular use of non-graded reflective writing teaches the student the value of reflecting in writing, slowing down the thinking to be able to synthesize all the various components of the lesson. Eliminating the threat of a grade for this allows the student to focus on the thinking involved rather than mechanics, grammar, etc.)

The procedure is simple. State the topic, question, or statement on which you wish students to focus. Students write for a specified length of time, without stopping. The idea is for them to keep writing and thinking about the topic. If they come to a point where they can't think of anything more to say, they should still keep writing, even if they just repeat the last phrase or sentence until another thought comes. Most often, it will come.

This procedure is very effective at motivating students to write. Instead of calling it a "paragraph," which often has negative connotations to students reluctant to engage in the writing process, a "free write" sounds like something easy to do, especially when the teacher limits the time to four or five minutes. By thus minimizing the nature of the task, the teacher is making writing more palatable to many students.

Focused Free Write Procedure

Lifelong Learning Skill(s) to be Practiced During Learning:

- Writing to clarify thinking
- Summarizing thoughts

Quick Overview of Lesson:

- Instruct students in the rules of a focused free write.
- Provide the focus in the form of a statement, key vocabulary terms, or some other initiating idea.
- Set the time limit.
- Make sure that all are engaged in the free write when it begins.
- Do your own version of the free write (preferably on an overhead transparency).
- Ask for volunteers to read what they have written after the time is up.
- Collect the writings.
- Read several out loud (anonymously). Share your own as well.

Detailed version of lesson:

1. Inform students that they need to get out a clean piece of paper to be handed in when finished. (An alternative is to have students write this in their notebooks.) Tell them they are going to do a "Free Write" for ___ minutes. (I have found that 3, 4, or 5 minutes are adequate, and not overwhelming to students. You decide, though. Tell them a specific time period such as five minutes, and have a timer to be sure not to go over the allotted time.)

---

2. Inform students of the "rules" of a free write. Tell them that there are only two rules — you may not stop writing during the free write, and you must write in prose — complete sentences. If you run out of ideas, you rewrite the last phrase or sentence. On rare occasions, a person might write a statement 2 or 3 times, but that is seldom the case. Let them know that you have confidence that they know enough about the topic that they won't have to resort to that, but that it is OK if they do.

3. Let them know that they will be writing about a specific topic that you will provide. That is the "focused" part of a focused free write. If it is the beginning of class you will select a topic about which they have background knowledge, and about which the rest of the class will be concerned. If it is the end of class, the most appropriate topic is "what we learned today." (You may wish to have students include certain key vocabulary words in their free writes if it is at the end of class.)

4. Once all students are ready with paper and writing implement, tell them to begin, and start the timer. It is a good idea for the teacher to write at the same time as the students. I usually do it directly on a transparency so that I can share my writing with them afterward. Thus, the teacher is again modeling the use of writing as a tool for reflection, and the teacher gets the last word. Hopefully the teacher's free write is a precise summary of what the students should have gotten out of the class.

5. When in the last minute of the free write, let students know that they should begin to put the finishing touches on their writing as time is running out.

6. When time runs out, let students know. A few will continue to write as they finish their last sentence. That's OK. Ask if anyone would volunteer to read his/her writing. Some usually will do so. If not, simply collect them all. Then read several aloud (without telling whose they are).

7. Ask students to report on their use of the skill of writing as a tool of reflection. Ask, "Did you feel that by writing for four minutes it helped you to clarify your thinking on the subject we studied…?"

Extra Scaffolds

I often like to have a list of the key vocabulary terms on the chalkboard before writing a free write. Then I can say to students, "The focus is on what we have learned about this topic, and I would like for you to use as many of these key terms correctly in your free write as you can."

When I read some of the free writes aloud to the class, I make adlibbed corrections to those of low-performing students. If they do not write a sentence that makes perfect sense, but I can tell what they meant, I add the edits without letting anyone know that I am doing so. This is a confidence booster for very low-performing students who are developing understandings of the content, but are not perfectly articulate at stating those understandings. What they hear being read aloud is what they meant, but failed to say.

Chapter 17

Math Translation

The whole of science is nothing more than a refinement of everyday thinking.
Albert Einstein

Motivation

Acquisition

E**X**tension

Math translation is a tool that helps students to actively construct meaning from mathematical formulas and mathematical problems performed in numerals and symbols. One difficulty that many students have in mathematics classes is that they tend to minimize the nature of the mathematical "language" that is used to convey ideas. They often do not take the time to realize all the meaning that is conveyed through symbols. One way to combat this, while also getting some insight into how well students understand what is being performed mathematically, is to get students to practice math translation, the rewriting in prose of what they perceive in symbolic form.

Two column notes are an excellent medium for math translation. The formula or mathematical solution goes on the left (1/3) side of the notes. A modern American prose translation goes on the right (2/3) side. No mathematical symbols are permitted on the right side of the notes.

For a *formula*, students begin by first rewriting the formula on the right-hand side of the notes using prose text and then underlining or circling each of the mathematical words. After each mathematical word is underlined, each of the terms is then described in the student's own language. Each student should make an effort to make the prose text so clear that any other student who is to read it would be able to understand it well enough to perform the calculations on a separate piece of paper if asked to do so.

For *equations*, each step of the process is explained in detail. If you want students to do this properly, it will require some modeling. I like to use an overhead projector so that I can "think aloud" with the students observing my work. Once they get the hang of it, allow them time to practice. Be sure to reward elaboration. I often tell students that the three most elaborate and accurate ones will receive several points on the next quiz or test. This encourages them to say more (and to think more about the mathematics of the operation).

Figure 17-1a

Student Example of Math Translation of a Formula

$A = \pi r^2$	The area of a circle is equal to pi times the radius squared. Area is the amount of space inside a circle and is measured in squared dimensions. A circle is round, and is equal from all sides to the center. Equals shows two things that are the same. Pi is a Greek letter that stands for approximately three point one four (3.14). Times means multiply. The radius is drawn from the center of the circle to the edge of the circle. Squared means to multiply a number by itself: radius times radius. The formula for all of this information is only $A = \pi r^2$.

Figure 17-1b

Student Example of Math Translation of a Solution of an Equation

$2x + 3 = 17$ $\begin{array}{r} 2x + 3 = 17 \\ -3 \quad -3 \\ \hline 2x \quad = 14 \end{array}$ $\dfrac{2x}{2} = \dfrac{14}{2}$ $x = 7$	A two-step equation is given. Two operations are involved. One is addition, and the other is multiplication. To get the variable all by itself on one side of the equation, you first use the inverse operation of addition (subtraction) by taking three away from both sides of the equation. Now the variable is almost all alone on the left side, but it is still multiplied by two. So, you again use an inverse operation (division this time) to get the variable by itself. Anything you do to one side, you have to do to the other side as well, so you divide both sides by two. The equation is then solved because you have an x on one side and a seven on the other side. That is the answer.

It is a well known fact among mathematics teachers that the National Council of Teachers of Mathematics (NCTM) has long advocated the use of reading, writing, speaking, listening, and thinking in the mathematics classroom (NCTM, 2000). Yet, many mathematics teachers struggle to figure out how to get students to successfully accomplish these activities in the secondary classroom. My experiences as a mathematics teacher have shown clearly that virtually all of the classroom activities in this book work as a daily tool for facilitating the learning of mathematics. When I taught Algebra 1 to ninth grade students, I used **MAX Teaching** as the framework of instruction in which cooperative construction of meaning from mathematics text was the routine activity in the classroom. Anticipation guides, preview, paired reading, stump the teacher, two-column notes, etc. were the daily routine in a classroom in which students were quite active in processing mathematical ideas individually and interactively with others.

One of the strategies that worked very well to help students process what they were learning was Math Translation (MT). Doing MT allowed for students to slow down their thinking enough to actually process what they were doing rather than just imitate the teacher. The process of articulating ideas onto paper is one in which a person must have some clarity of thinking.

MT also allows for the teacher to see how well the student perceives new concepts. While students are doing MT, the teacher can rove about the classroom, looking over students' shoulders to observe their thinking. This affords the teacher the opportunity to intervene in cases of obvious need.

The teacher should model MT a few times before expecting great stuff from the students. For the example in Figure 17-1b, above for example, students not used to the process might try to minimize the writing by making notations like "Take away 3. Divide by 2" rather than explain that "the solution is achieved by using inverse operations, and the inverse operation for addition is……………."

Thus, the teacher should reward elaboration. I usually offer several bonus points for the most elaborate ones. Everyone has to do the process, but the most elaborate will be rewarded. This plus modeling of the process leads to students actually competing to have the most writing on the right hand side of the notes. They begin to have fun exaggerating the amount they write on a topic by thinking of more aspects of the topic.

Once you have practiced Math Translation a few times in your classroom, it is appropriate to include it on a test. Set it up with the solution or formula in the left column, and leave the right column completely blank. Let students know that they must elaborate as they had practiced in the classroom. This time, they are doing it with no notes or assistance. You will find out who really understands the mathematics processes they have been learning, and you will also find out very specifically where any understandings break down.

This is a wonderful addition to any evaluation, and it parallels what many of the statewide standardized tests are now including in their mathematics evaluations. Many states have added what they call "extended response" to the mathematics portions of their tests, and they are asking students to write about how they solved their problems. Wouldn't it be a great idea to have practiced it multiple times in the regular course of learning mathematics in the classroom?

Math Translation Procedure

Lifelong Learning Skill(s) to be Practiced During Learning:

- Comprehension monitoring while solving mathematics problems
- Paraphrasing in writing

Speed-read version of lesson:

(This strategy is primarily an eXtension activity to be used in the third step of the lesson. Students should already have learned the two-column Cornell note taking technique.)

1. Prepare two-column notes.
2. Explain and model use of the writing as a tool to help the student clarify thinking while learning new subject matter.
3. Allow students to practice writing to paraphrase their understanding of what they have learned.
4. Students compare their writings with others in their cooperative groups.

Detailed version of lesson:

1. Use any of a variety of reading/thinking strategies to help students learn the new mathematics subject matter during the **M**otivation and **A**cquisition stages of the class. Once they are at the phase of class when they show an ability to apply what they have learned about either a formula or the solution of an equation, let them know that they will now practice a writing/thinking strategy that will help them to clarify their own thinking about what they have learned in class today, and that will help them to remember what they have learned.

2. Prepare an overhead projector or a chalkboard to model the sort of thinking involved in Math Translation. Tell students that strategic learners of mathematics always perform thinking about what they are doing while performing any mathematical operation such as solving two-step equations. Tell them that they will be practicing this through writing today, using the two-column note format. Explain to them that whenever a person writes an explanation of something like a process, it helps that person to clarify his/her thinking about it. It leads to better understanding of the process. Remind them that often, we *think* that we have an understanding of a topic until the opportunity to write about it occurs. Then, when confronted with actually stating the case, we find it much more difficult than we had previously thought it would be to put our thoughts into words. Tell them that this is one reason why we are about to practice Math Translation in class. Tell them that another reason is that, along with helping them to clarify their own thinking, writing about the math will help them to remember the information in the future. In addition, tell them that this is going to be fun! Let them know that they will be surprised how their translation of math to English prose helps them to not only understand the mathematical process, but also to be able to see how others understand it.

3. The first time or two that you do this with a class, you should model the thinking that is required. Whatever the class has learned for the day is the topic for the Math Translation. Your modeling may be with the same type of math, but I recommend modeling with something they have seen before, and that you think will be generally well understood by all the students. For instance, in an algebra class, somewhat well into the school year, two-step equations should be fairly common knowledge to most of the students. I like to use this because most students are impressed by how much writing it takes to actually represent all that is happening with the solving of two-step equations. Depending on the level of students, you might do this with long division, converting numbers to scientific notation, factoring trinomial expressions, or whatever is appropriate.

4. On the chalkboard or overhead transparency, use the left column to solve a two-step equation (or whatever process you have been working on in class). Use only mathematical symbols and numbers to do so.

5. Once all the steps have been completed in the left column of the notes, and the right side is blank, tell students that you are going to model the process. Explain to them that no mathematical symbols are to be used on the right side of the notes. Explain that you are about to describe in "modern American English prose" what has taken place on the left side of the notes. Ask them not to copy, but rather to observe your thinking (or you may even encourage them to help you with the process). Begin with a detailed description of what has occurred in the left column. (Have fun with this. Don't scrimp on the details. Take the time to describe the use of inverse operations, etc. perhaps even elaborating beyond what is required. You want them to know that the process is not really about creating terse notes as is often recommended for study purposes, but rather to be as elaborate as possible so as to maximize one's thinking about the topic.) *It is important at this point to be thinking out loud so the students can hear your thoughts. This does not work if you come into the classroom with a prepared example.* Just placing the already completed transparency on the overhead projector takes away from the processing part of the operation. They need to see this in action to appreciate what it is like.

6. Once they have seen you model the process with a familiar topic, tell them that they are going to participate in doing the same thing in their own notes, and that they will be writing about the topic that was learned in class today. Thus, they might perform Math Translation about factoring polynomials, multiplying binomials, balancing equations, etc., whatever is fresh in their minds from today's class.

7. Let students know that the more they write, the better, because the writing process will help them to articulate ideas in a way that will help them overcome any confusion. Tell them that you will move around the room while they do this so that you can help them with formulating their thought. Give them one problem for the left column. Have them copy it verbatim into the left side of the notes. Tell them that whoever does the most articulate writing will be rewarded. Build them up for expanding rather than economizing on space. Allow sufficient time to get started.

8. After several minutes, have students compare notes with a partner or in small cooperative learning groups. Allow sufficient time to read aloud to one another what they have written or to exchange papers and read each others' work. Have them make any additions or changes to their writing they desire at this time.

9. Identify one that is fairly elaborate and share it aloud with the rest of the class if you wish. This can be done by having the students of one group place their chosen summary on a transparency for others to view. By seeing each others' work, students become more comfortable with the process. It can be fairly humorous to see how elaborate the Math Translation can become. Once students see that elaboration is being rewarded, they will become more involved in the process.

10. Provide a second opportunity to practice Math Translation. Use a different example from the problems in the text or a new one that you provide. Have them repeat the process of elaborating through writing. Follow the cooperative learning system of individual writing, then small group comparison, and finally classroom discussion.

11. An optional homework assignment (in addition to practice problems) is to go home and review these writings, using INSERT or Sensible Sentence Highlighting Method.

12. Once the students have completed the assignment and turned in their notes, you might want to make some copies of the finished products (without student names showing) and make transparencies of the writing to share various students' work. The process of reflecting on the work of others is an appropriate and effective eXtension of thinking beyond the text experience.

Extra Scaffolds

You may wish to have students brainstorm ideas for the process, as you stand at an overhead projector and conduct a discussion, eliciting from the students information to add to the Math Translation. This will allow for the translation to be constructed by the students, but with your assistance. In this case, it is important to really exaggerate the packing in of ideas. Let them see that simple operations and formulas carry a great deal more meaning than meets the eye at first glance. I like to go overboard to the point that they see humor in my inclusion of so many ideas.

In working with many students, you might wish to gradually lead them into the process by using interactive cloze procedure (Chapter 22) that you have already formatted in pre-prepared notes. Then gradually reduce the amount of writing that you are preparing for them in the cloze. Omit only a few key words the first time, and then, graduate to omitting much more until you are providing good structure, but leaving room for much interpretation.

Chapter 18

GIST
(Generating Interaction between Schemata and Text)

For just when ideas fail, a word comes in to save the situation.
Johann Wolfgang von Goethe

Motivation

Acquisition ✓

e**X**tension ✓

GIST, Generating Interaction between Schemata and Text (Cunningham, 1982), is a group summarization activity. Summarizing is a life-long learning skill that is necessary in order to process complex text and make ideas manageable in processing large amounts of information. In addition, summarization is a skill measured on many, if not most, of the ubiquitous standardized tests students will face throughout their academic lives. This reading/writing/thinking activity engages students, partly because of the challenge that the teacher presents in setting up the activity.

The principal challenge posed by the teacher is to summarize a passage in a limited number of words. My experiences with this activity suggest that students of all ability levels, and in all subject areas, rise to the occasion when confronted with the challenge, if it is presented properly. In addition, GIST offers activity for groups of students whose favored learning modalities are diverse. Students, during the course of the class, will be moving in and out of cooperative learning groups, reading silently, performing individual writing, discussing, and writing on the chalkboard.

I have used GIST in the mathematics classroom, having students write a 20-word summary of how to use the slope-intercept form of linear equations to graph lines, in the language arts classroom, having middle school students summarize Martin Luther King's "I have a dream" speech in 25 words, in the social studies classroom, having students write a summary of the past 2000-year history of the Arab-Israeli conflict in 30 words, and in countless other situations. What takes place in the minds of the students when they do GIST is phenomenal.

The process of working together in a small group to attempt to "capture all the main ideas" of the reading and state these ideas in a *very* short passage is what GIST is all about. It is certainly true that anyone who reads one of the short summaries that are generated in this way would not be able to glean all of the pertinent information needed to understand, for instance, why Arabs and Israelis conflict with one another, but the students who worked together to produce such a summary remember minute details from the broader reading weeks and months later! The process causes students to use a great deal of higher order thinking to accomplish the task presented by the challenge of condensing a passage to few words. They must analyze, synthesize, and evaluate throughout the process. In addition, they are experiencing multiple exposures to concepts and employing complex interactions in group discussion to determine which ideas will go together in what ways to state the case in their summaries.

As in any of the procedures described in this book, the activity below is as I have used it successfully in my own classrooms over the years since I first learned it. This does not mean that it is the only way to do GIST, and you are encouraged to adapt the process to your students' needs. All I can say is that the way it is described below works in any subject area with the vast majority of mixed-ability classes with whom I have worked over the years. Try it---you'll like it. So will your students.

GIST Procedure

Lifelong Learning Skill(s) to be Practiced During Learning:

- Summarization of complex material into brief passages
- Reading critically to identify key concepts and vocabulary
- Paraphrasing — stating things in your own words

Quick Overview of Lesson:

1. Motivation activity.
2. Discuss with students the skills of summarization (identifying main ideas & paraphrasing).
3. Assign a segment of the reading to be summarized. Limit the number of words that may be used.
4. Students read silently.
5. Groups work to summarize.
6. Repeat steps 3 - 5 for another part of the reading without increasing the word limit.
7. Repeat step 6 until entire reading is finished.
8. Student groups share on chalkboard or on large paper.
9. Students reflect on each other's work.

Detailed version of lesson:

Have students grouped in threes or fours, each group having a number corresponding to a space on the chalkboard with the same number written in it. Having student groups responsible for writing their work onto the chalkboard is a motivator that leads to quality reading.

1. Introduce the content of the reading by using a strategy that allows you to determine how much students already know about the topic while building prior knowledge. A teacher-led preview of the reading is a good idea (but not the only appropriate one). During the preview, probe for student prior knowledge on the topics covered in the reading. Keep in mind that students have not learned this subject matter yet. Be accepting of student conceptions as well as their misconceptions. Let all students know that they may change their minds about many of their ideas by the time they have finished the reading.

2. Introduce the skill of summarization. Write the word, "SUMMARIZATION" or "SUMMARIZING" on the chalkboard, explaining to students that strategic readers are constantly summarizing in their own minds what they are reading, and that strategic note takers often attempt to summarize the key concepts of a reading in as few words as possible onto paper. Mention that they do this to make it easier to remember key ideas and sometimes for the purpose of taking notes. Elicit from students the elements of summarization, and write them on the chalkboard under the word "SUMMARIZATION" in the form of a list. Though they may use different vernacular, most classes will be able to list the key elements of
   - identification of main ideas,
   - eliminating unnecessary details, and
   - restating ideas in their own words. (If they do not generate these ideas, you tell them, modeling with a summary of something they have read recently, but you probably will not have to tell them if you use wait time.) Students will also come up other items to add to the list, and I usually list those items as well, though I am really looking for the three listed above. Items that students might suggest often include "draw conclusions," "put things in order," "make a list," and others. By being accepting of these ideas, you encourage students to recognize that they know something about the process of summarizing. However, it is important that the three essential elements of summarizing are included.

3. Model use of the skill of summarization by showing summaries of varying quality on a topic they know and have recently studied. You might have a prepared summary of the previous day's lesson that is terse, yet complete. Explain to students that what they are going to do today is summarize a passage from the text.

4. Explain to students that, for today's reading, they are going to be *challenged* by limiting the number of words that students may use in their summaries. Tell them that they may not exceed 25 (or some other challenging number to be arbitrarily determined by you) words in their summary of the reading. Say, "Here is the challenge I am giving you---you must capture all the main ideas from this passage, put them into your own words, in modern American English prose (complete sentences), and you may not exceed 25 words! After you have enough time to read the passage, you need to get with your cooperative learning group and select one person to be the 'scribe,' the person who will do the writing, and work together to create your summary. Once you have written your draft of the summary, you must write it on the chalkboard in the space provided for your group." You should, at this time, expect a little groaning, but it will soon pass. Tell them that you will help them if they need help during their group discussions.

5. Model different ways to identify and gather information during reading such as the use of INSERT (Chapter 21), or creation of a word bank, note taking, or underlining, or some other method. Don't spend a great deal of time at this, but let them know that the skill of identifying important ideas has specific elements they already know and practice.

6. Direct students to the passage they are to summarize. You may apply the process to a passage as short as a paragraph or as long as two or three pages. The length of the passage should be determined by the level of complexity and/or difficulty involved. I find that most groups of students do well with one to three pages of text, depending on the complexity of the material and the level of student ability. Err on the high side. I would rather have students attempt to put the ideas from three pages into 30 words that to put the ideas of 300 words into 30. I also like for students to do the summaries on their own, in groups, rather than my leading the discussion, though that is one alternative way to do this. (See extra scaffolds, below.)

7. Allow time for students to read silently and individually to gather information. During this time, each student should gather key terms and ideas that ought to be included in a summary, planning to work with others to create a summary of the passage.

8. Now have students compare their individual notes to those of others in their cooperative groups--- with the goal of agreeing on important details and the wording of the summary for that group. Each group should select a scribe to write that group's summary as coached by the whole group. Move around the room to see that students are working to share information and that they are working to summarize in prose text. Don't be afraid to help them at this point. They may have trouble the first time they do this. Step right in and help groups word their summaries. They will appreciate it. Move from group to group to perform this service.

9. ***Optional intermediate step A:*** Choose the summary of one of the groups to place onto the chalkboard or onto a transparency to be viewed by all the class. Ask the class to help in editing the summary that has been provided. Ask them if the one you have chosen has all the important ideas that their groups' summaries had. Model the editing process by altering the one with which you are working until each member of the class is satisfied that it contains all the elements that are important from the reading. This activity requires you to think on your feet while students watch. Don't worry about getting it right the first time. Be willing to change & adapt to new ideas as they arise. Facilitate the changing shape of the summary as new ideas emerge from the class. Model the editing process, showing how to economize through the use of commas, colons, semi-colons, imperatives, etc.

9. ***Optional intermediate step B:*** Have each group put its summary in a space prepared for this purpose on the chalkboard. (I usually give each group a number and there is a corresponding number in a space on the chalkboard for that group's summary.)

10. Direct students to the next portion of the text to be read. Tell them that they will need to read this and then add new key ideas to the summary with which they have been working – *without exceeding the originally prescribed word total!* Describe this as a challenge, and express your confidence in their abilities to perform this task. This time, allow for more independence as students work on their summaries. Move around the room to facilitate the process for various groups.

11. Repeat the process as many times as needed to get through the reading. (I like to divide a typical textbook chapter section of 7 or 8 pages into two or three segments for high school classes, but the difficulty of the reading and the abilities of the students will influence your decisions.) Each time students compress more information into the prescribed limit of words, they are building complex brain programs for recalling the details of the text. The process of weeding out the unnecessary, and rephrasing the important parts by maximizing use of vocabulary terms provides opportunities for students to increase their comprehension and recall. Because of the process they went through, students' summaries of 30 or so words will recall for them much more than the 30 written down. They will retain most of the information from the whole passage.

12. Once each group of students has completed its summary, you may wish to have them write the summaries on large sheets of butcher paper or onto the chalkboard for viewing by other members of the class. By reflecting on how others phrased their summaries, students get another chance to reflect on the content of the passage, resulting in reinforced understanding of the subject matter.

13. Ask students to report on their use of the skill of summarizing. Ask "By a show of hands, how many of you felt that by working to summarize this passage into an artificially short number of words, it helped you to have to comprehend it better than you otherwise might have if you had been asked to read the same text for a worksheet, for instance?"

14. Reinforce the skill by pointing out to students that strategic readers constantly pause during reading to summarize briefly what they have read. Point out that successful readers do not always take notes at the same time, but that what students have just done is a good practice for both mentally summarizing and for note taking, since the summary they have made is what good notes are like — terse, and complete. Also point out that whenever a person summarizes like this, s/he is doing what all strategic readers do in comprehending text — identifying the main ideas, weeding out unnecessary details, and paraphrasing into ones own words.

15. You may wish to have students work to select the best summary. One way to do this is to provide each group with a ballot (index card) and ask each group to review all the summaries and come to a consensus on which two summaries do the best job of clearly stating the case for what was read in the text. Each group then submits a ballot with two numbers on it. Once the tally is made, you have identified the best. Groups each submit one ballot, and they may not vote twice for the same summary (their own).

16. You may wish to have students add the summary they have chosen as best to their notes for the day.

Extra Scaffolding

GIST can be done in much smaller portions of text, and the discussion can be led by the teacher rather than accomplished by small autonomous groups. A variation has small groups working for a time, and then reporting to the teacher as the whole class contributes to the summary with the teacher facilitating by writing on an overhead transparency while student groups contribute their thoughts. In this scenario, it might appear as follows:

Step One - Type (or enlarge from text) the paragraphs on an overhead transparency.

Step Two - Place the transparency on the overhead and display only the first paragraph (cover the other paragraphs). Put 20 blanks on the chalk board. Have students read the paragraph and instruct them to write a 20 word (or less) summary in their own words.

Step Three - As a class, have students generate a composite summary on the board in 20 or fewer words. Their individual or group summaries will function as guides for this process.

Step Four - Reveal the next paragraph of text and have students generate a summary statement of the same number of words or fewer words that encompasses both of the first two paragraphs.

Step Five - Continue this procedure by paragraph, until the students have produced a GIST statement for the entire passage under consideration. In time, they will be able to generate GIST statements across paragraphs without the intermediate steps.

Chapter 19

Guided Reading Procedure

Never give up your right to be wrong, because then you will lose the ability to learn new things and to move forward with your life.

Dr. David M. Burns

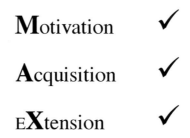

Motivation ✓

Acquisition ✓

eXtension ✓

The Guided Reading Procedure (GRP) (Manzo, 1975), is a classroom activity that is extremely language rich. It involves students reading the subject matter several times, stating ideas orally, listening to others' interpretations, scrutinizing ideas, and even writing. Yet, this activity is very engaging, and can be done in a single class period, covering a significant amount of material. Because of the repetitive nature of the activity, students end up really knowing the content of what they have read in this exercise. I like to use it with materials that are densely impacted with many and varied details. For instance, I used it to help students in a masonry class learn the U.S. Government Occupational Safety and Health Administration (OSHA) regulations for scaffolding in masonry. (This topic is very dry, and includes a wide variety of important but relatively unrelated details.) By the time we were finished with the one-hour-long GRP, each of the masonry students in this group was able to show both comprehension and retention of the many regulations involved.

Guided Reading Procedure

Lifelong Learning Skill(s) to be Practiced During Learning:

- Recall in the study process
- Paraphrasing

- Purposeful reading
- Reorganizing information for recall

Quick Overview of the Lesson:

1. Clarify important concepts and/or vocabulary terms
2. Have students make some predictions about what they will be reading
3. Place a reasonable time limit on the reading and tell students that they should remember as much as they can for later recall.
4. Silent reading.
5. Take a "fact" from each student in the room. Make sure that each student knows that the supposed facts are to be listed on the chalkboard without editing — even if the fact is wrong.
6. Correct facts through discussion.
7. Reread with limited time. (Use about ½ the time used for the first reading of the material.
8. Correct more facts and add important new ones.
9. Reorganize the information in a graphic representation or a list-group-label type activity.

Detailed version of lesson:

1. Listing four to six key terms or concepts on a transparency or on the chalkboard, conduct a brief discussion regarding what students know about the terms shown. Help them to see that the terms are important, and that they will be in the reading. (By doing this, you are focusing students on the topic, giving them a sort of preview, finding out how much they know about the topic, and building background knowledge for those who need it.)

---

2. Let students know what the title of the reading is. Have them all write (individually) a prediction of what they think the reading is about. What do they think the author will say?

---

3. Ask some students to share their predictions. Write the predictions on a projected transparency or other surface for students to be able to see. Take four to seven of the predictions from various students. Tell students that "We will come back to these after the reading to see how well we did in predicting what we were getting ready to read."

4. Tell students that the strategy we are about to use to read today's reading is one that a strategic studier might use to read something the first time, knowing that s/he is responsible to be able to recall and use the materials, but will not be able to go back over it before a test or quiz. A strategic reader who is reading for understanding and recall might look at a subsection of text that is subtitled "The Three Elements of _____", and then read that subsection, pausing at the end, and looking away from the text in an effort to recall or paraphrase what the three elements were that s/he had just read. If able to recall them, the strategic reader moves on further into the text. If the reader can only recall two of the three elements, s/he quickly scans over the text to find the third element not recalled, then looking away again, recalling all three by paraphrasing them. Tell students that we are about to practice this same strategic reading technique, but we are going to do it as a whole class.

5. Tell students that we will have *X* minutes (You decide the length of time. It should be adequate for most students to finish the reading if they read rapidly.) to read from pages ___ to ___. An appropriate length reading will vary according to reading ability of students and difficulty of the text. Tell students that when the time has expired, you will tell them all to close the book, and that, at that time, each student will have to remember a fact to list with the facts of other students. Tell them that you are going to go right around the room taking a fact from each student. Remind them that if, during the reading, a student tends to focus on only one fact, that particular fact may already have been stated by another student by the time that the teacher gets to that student. So, the thing to do is to *read while trying to remember as many facts as possible.*

6. Tell students that, during silent reading, if they run across anything that doesn't make sense, and they cannot figure it out themselves, they should raise a hand to call you over to explain a meaning of a term. Remind them of the time you have set, and tell them to begin the reading without distracting either themselves or other students through noise or movement. You should move around the room, reading silently the same passage they are reading, modeling for them what they should be doing, and dealing quietly with any classroom management problems that might occur.

7. Monitor the students' reading. When the time is expired, or about two thirds of the students have finished the reading, tell them all to close the book. Check to see that they do. You may wish to close yours in such a way that their attention is drawn to the process. Close it with a popping sound and say, "Close your books."

8. At this time you remind them that you are going to take one "fact" from each student. Tell them you will go right around the room to take a fact from each student and that you will write each fact on a projected transparency. Tell students at this point that there is only one rule to adhere to during this process – NO ONE IN THE ROOM MAY SAY ANYTHING ABOUT ANOTHER PERSON'S FACT. EACH FACT WILL BE RECORDED EXACTLY AS STATED BY THE RECALLER. Students must hold their critique of facts until later. An alternative to your writing of each fact is to have one or two students act as scribes and write the facts on the chalkboard while you elicit the facts from the students. (If you do this, you want to have students who are fast chalkboard writers or it will bog down the lesson.) You can take facts rapidly with two scribes to write on the chalkboard if they are fairly competent. If you elect to use scribes, the facts will come so fast that students in the classroom will not be able to keep up if they are trying to write the facts into their own notebooks. So don't ask them to do so when using scribes. On the other hand, if you are writing the facts on the transparency, they will be able to keep up, and each student should also write each fact into his or her notebook. This is a classroom management tool of sorts since students will be engaged while you are engaged.

If, as you go around the classroom taking facts from students, you come to a student who cannot recall a fact, don't fret or cause the student to fret. Say, "No problem — I will pass you by, but if you think of something when another student says something to remind you of a fact, raise your hand, and I will come right back to you, and we will list your fact." This lets the person off the hook, and keeps that person in the game.

The teacher can also insert a fact at any time. (I usually put in a fact that is plausible but not true. But, you could put in a fact that you feel is important, but that students omitted.)

9. Once each student has had the opportunity to have a fact recorded, you may wish to open the floor to more facts from anyone who has another. Some students will raise their hands to contribute more facts at this time.

10. Remind students that each fact was recorded as stated by the contributor, and some of them may not be perfectly accurate. Let them know that, at this time, you are opening the floor for corrections or amendments to any of the facts. (You may wish to number the facts if you have not already done so. It will be easier to refer to specific ones if they are numbered.) Allow students to make verbal corrections to any of the facts they perceive to be needing changes while you make the changes on the chalkboard or transparency. Carry on a discussion that edits the facts. You should stay out of this. Only student corrections are to be made at this time.

11. Once students have contributed corrections to the statements, tell students that, even though they have made some corrections to the list, there are other corrections or other important facts that ought to be added to the list. Let them know that "We are going to go back through this reading, but only for *Y* minutes (usually about half the original time) and that they should be reading this time to find corrections and/or to identify new important ideas that they think should be included on the list.

12. Read while students read — for the same purposes!

13. When the time has expired, open the floor for discussion of corrections or new ideas. Fix any of the incorrectly stated ideas, and list new ones.

14. When editing and adding has been done, tell students that there is one final step to this process — to organize the information into categories. This E**X**tension beyond the text will help students to perform higher order thinking about the subject matter. Tell students to study the list of ideas they have come up with and to think of the names of the three (or so) categories into which each of the statements could be grouped. Have students get into their groups to conduct a discussion of what the categories should be. Tell them, "Make sure that each of the statements on the board could fit into at least one of your categories if you were to rewrite them in similar groups." Move around the room to facilitate this process by discussing with the various groups their ideas. (An alternative to this, to save time, is for you to assign the categories, but this eliminates some important critical thinking on their parts.)

15. Once they have come up with the categories, write each group's categories onto the chalkboard. You will end up with about 18-20 categories listed. Now, ask students to look at the list of categories to see if there are three or four that stand out as super-ordinate to the others — that is, are there 3 categories from any of the many listed under which the others could all be organized? Again students will think, and they will usually spot two to three categories from this list that are clearly the best. You should facilitate this thinking.

16. Tell students that their homework is to go back through the reading one more time to list key facts under each of the three categories on which they agreed. If you have introduced Cornell Note Taking to your students, you can make the three categories the main ideas to go into the left column of the notes.

17. Go back to the original predictions that students contributed before the reading. Place a check next to any of the predictions that were correct. I usually find that about 75% of them were right on the target. This is reinforcing to students of an important reading process that strategic readers use.

18. Ask students, "By a show of hands, how many of you feel that, by reading to practice remembering with the book closed, and then going back to clarify our understandings, and doing this cooperatively as a whole class, it actually helped you to understand the reading and to be able to remember what it was about?" Remind them that what they just practiced as a class is exactly what a strategic studier would do all alone in the college dormitory, or wherever one studies, and that they can do this on their own.

Extra Scaffolds

The principle extra scaffold to this process is for the teacher to read aloud to the students while they read along silently. However, due to the nature of the activity, you will rarely, if ever, have to do this. The nature of the Guided Reading Procedure is to allow students to process the information in their own personal way to identify important ideas. Students will (as in Stump the Teacher) be poring over the material to find details that others might not find. Thus, even if I do read it aloud to the students, I still give them time to go over the text silently before closing the book.

Chapter 20

Hunt for main ideas

The fewer the facts, the stronger the opinion.
Arnold H. Glasow

Motivation

Acquisition ✓

e**X**tension ✓

Hunt for Main Ideas is an activity that teaches the writing process without the students even having to write. In addition, it allows students to acquire important metacognition skills while they are also acquiring the subject matter about which they are reading. It also provides a concrete medium through which students can interact over the content of the reading, evaluating the relative importance of ideas, and thus, performing higher order thinking without even being aware that they are doing so. What, on the surface, appears to be a fairly mundane activity—searching for the topic sentence in each paragraph—ends up helping students to deeply learn the content of the reading thanks to the multiple exposure and complex interaction in which they are involved throughout the class.

Hunt for Main Ideas Procedure

Lifelong Learning Skill(s) to be Practiced During Learning:

- Comprehension monitoring while reading
- Identification of main ideas
- Writing skills (through disassembling authors' writing)

Quick Overview of the Lesson

1. Explain and model use of the skill.
2. Students work individually to read, seeking main ideas from each paragraph noting it in the margin of the text.
3. Students work in small groups to come to consensus regarding which is the main idea of each paragraph.
4. Whole class discussion
5. EXtension activity such as Free Write

Materials:

- Textbook or other reading material organized in paragraph format (not for most mathematics text)
- Overhead transparency of one or two pages of the text (optional)

Detailed version of lesson:

1. Begin with a pre-learning concept check of key vocabulary terms. Then, preview the text.

2. Tell students that, today, we are going to work on our writing skills—only we are not going to write!!

3. Elicit from students the elements of a quality paragraph. They will point out that a paragraph has a topic sentence and other sentences that contain supporting details.

4. Ask them what is contained in the topic sentence. They will suggest that the "main idea" of the paragraph is stated there.

5. Ask them which sentence has the main idea. Usually one student will yell out, "The first sentence!" Agree, and ask, "Where else might you find the main idea sentence?" Usually someone will offer that the last sentence can be the main idea. Agree and ask them, "Where else might we find the main idea sentence?" They will admit that it could be one of the middle sentences.

6. Now that it has been established that any of the sentences in a paragraph might be the main idea of the paragraph, tell students that the focus of today's reading will be on identifying the main idea in each of the paragraphs in the reading. I usually say, "Even though *you* are not going to be doing the writing, we *are* working on our writing skills today—by taking apart the *authors'* writing." Let the students know that they need to have a pencil for this activity because they are going to be writing in the text, and that they will need to erase the marks after they are finished with the unit.

7. Model the process of identifying the main idea. Use one of the first paragraphs in the reading. Ask all students to read it silently and place a mark in the text next to the sentence that is perceived to be the one that contains the main idea. (Or, you might want to use a transparency of the first page of the text to model the thinking involved, making a mark next to the topic sentence in one paragraph, and explaining why. In either case, you should have the students practice on one paragraph without your help.) Then you should allow them to discuss in their cooperative learning groups. Be tolerant of different interpretations. If the topic sentence in the paragraph is an obvious one, there will be little discussion. On the other hand, it often is not as clear as it ought to be. This is OK. In such a case, you should share with students some strategies that you use to identify which is the main idea. One strategy is to see which sentence is more closely related to the subtitle at the head of the paragraph. Another way that I like to teach students is to say the sentence in question first—as if it is the topic sentence, and then read the other sentences to see if they make sense coming immediately after the one you read first. Try this with both of the sentences in question, and usually one stands out as better than the other. This is not always true though. Sometimes we have to agree, for instance, that one is really a restatement of the other, in which case we might decide that both of the sentences could be considered to be the topic sentence. (What a great way to get students to learn your subject matter—arguing over what the main ideas of the text are!!) Be sure to point out to students that some paragraphs have an implied main idea. Let them know that when they confront such a paragraph, they should make a special mark, such as the letter "I." Explain that, when a paragraph is structured in such a way as to, for instance, list three or four pieces of evidence about something, the main idea may be in a previous paragraph.

8. Ask students to read another paragraph silently. Practice again by having each student pencil in a small dot next to the main idea. Once they have done so, have them discuss in their groups and/or as a class to identify which was the main idea. Build their confidence through this discussion by noting positively the attempts at interpreting paragraphs. They need to know that this is not an easy task, and that there will be some disagreement when it is over, and that the teacher will help to resolve differences of opinion.

9. Once this modeling is finished, ask if everyone has a clear understanding of how the process works and is ready to try it. Be sure each student has a pencil. Remind students to concentrate on their own reading and not to distract others or themselves during the reading. Allow sufficient time for most students to finish the reading.

10. Tell students that they should now read the whole passage, reading each paragraph and trying to identify the main idea by placing a small pencil dot in the margin next to the main idea sentence for each paragraph. Tell them to be prepared to discuss their choices after the reading, and that they should be able to defend why they think the sentence they chose is the main idea sentence. Let them know ahead of time that there will be some disagreement among different students' interpretations and that they will need to be prepared to convince others of their interpretation.

11. Allow sufficient time for most students to finish the reading. Then have them discuss their findings in their cooperative learning groups. Allow time to discuss differences of opinion. Let them know that where they are already in agreement, they need not discuss, but where differences exist, they should attempt to sort those out as a group.

12. Assist in this process by moving about the room to mediate the discussions.

13. Carry out a large-class discussion comparing the findings of the various groups.

14. Point out how the main ideas, when isolated, can be developed into quality notes. If your students take Cornell Notes for homework, remind them of how easy it will be this evening.

15. Ask students to report on their use of the skill of identifying main ideas. Say—did the process of reading to find the main idea help you to concentrate and to comprehend what the authors were saying in a more effective way than if you had done a worksheet? (Students inevitably realize at this point that, by practicing the hunt, they were engaged in the reading, leading to heightened comprehension.)

16. Take the opportunity to review and reinforce the use of the skill of seeking main ideas in each paragraph. Also let them know that the skill they just practiced should help them to see not only how a paragraph is designed, but also that there are various ways to elaborate main ideas through supporting detail sentences.

17. Continue ᴇXtension through referring back to the Pre-Learning Concept Check (step 1), doing a Focused Free write, converting the main idea sentences into quality two-column notes, a free-write, homework, a quiz, etc.

Extra Scaffolds

As in most of the activities in this book, one important scaffold that is appropriate for low performing readers is for the teacher to read aloud from the text while students follow along silently in their own texts. In Hunt for Main Ideas, the teacher should do the same introduction as described above, but allow students time, after each paragraph has been read aloud, to go back through the paragraph—silently and individually—to attempt to identify the main idea in the paragraph. Thus, low performing students are getting the benefit of hearing the reading done fluently, modeled by the teacher, but then having the opportunity to reread silently immediately after hearing it aloud. This is very reinforcing of reading development since the students are now performing mature silent reading to construct personal meaning.

Chapter 21

INSERT

(Interactive Notating System for Effective Reading and Thinking)

Action springs not from thought, but from a readiness for responsibility.
Dietrich Bonhoeffer

Motivation

Acquisition ✓

e**X**tension ✓

INSERT (Vaughan & Estes, 1986) is a strategy that is used during the **A**cquisition and e**X**tension phases of the class to help students to practice metacognitive behavior while reading, carefully process new subject matter, and extend their thinking beyond the text through the process of synthesis and evaluation of ideas that they are reading. This activity is appropriate for any subject matter. I have used it in Mathematics, English, social studies, science, career/technical, and many other classes to help students process new subject matter through carefully reading it.

What INSERT does is to make concrete, by providing a tactile-kinesthetic activity, the process of constructing personal meaning from text. During the reading, the student is responsible for making decisions about his/her own reactions to the text. These reactions may reflect the student's level of comprehension or some interpretation of the text. At the same time, the student's reactions are visible to the teacher. (How many classroom activities can you think of where students are silently reading to monitor their own comprehension and, at the same time, the *teacher* can monitor their comprehension as well?) Figure 21-1 shows one of the generic variations on the INSERT process that I have used successfully with students (Vaughan & Estes, 1986). I have had a poster-sized version of that chart on my classroom wall for years. That way, any time I wish to have students perform this metacognitive skill, I simply had to refer them to the poster as a reminder of what I expected them to do during the reading.

The INSERT marks are written directly into the student's copy of the text — lightly in pencil — and can be erased at a later date after the students have moved on to another topic or another unit. There are alternatives to having students make the marks in their textbooks, but I have avoided them over the years. I feel that it is important to keep it as simple as possible so that the student is focusing on constructing personal meaning from the text rather than the mechanics of how to manipulate multiple pieces of paper or sticky notes while reading. Writing directly into the text eliminates other distractions. On the other hand, if you do not yet have tenure, you might wish to use one of the alternatives to allowing students to make marks in the text. One is to use sticky notes stuck to the edges of the page. It is possible to get rolls of tape that are of the same material as Post-It ® Notes, and place the tape down the side of the page. Another alternative is to have students use their own loose leaf paper to make the notations. They simply place a page into the crevice of the text, line up the bottom of the loose leaf paper with the bottom of the textbook page, and make their notations for the one page of reading on one side of the loose leaf paper and notations for the facing page on the opposite side of the loose leaf paper. They add a new piece of loose leaf paper for every two pages of the reading. This gets a bit more complicated for text that is written in columns, but with the appropriate level of modeling, they can handle this. (If you are going to use one of the alternative methods of tape, sticky notes, or loose leaf paper, I recommend that you model the INSERT process the first time or two with materials on which the students can write — something that you have duplicated just for this purpose. This will eliminate the complications while the students become acquainted with the process.)

FIGURE 21-1

INSERT (Interactive Notating System for Effective Reading and Thinking)

SYMBOL ------   MEANING OF SYMBOL

Symbol	Meaning
✓ ----------	I agree. This confirms what I already knew.
? ----------	I have a question about this.
?? ----------	I don't understand.
X ----------	I disagree.
+ ----------	This is new to me.
! ----------	Wow!! This is neat!
★ ----------	This is important.

Adapted from *Reading and Reasoning Beyond the Primary Grades* by Joseph L. Vaughan and Thomas H. Estes. Boston: Allyn & Bacon, Inc. (1986), pp. 136 -141.

There are many alternatives to the original model of INSERT shown in Figure 21-1. I suggest that, when you first introduce INSERT to your students that you keep it simple. I usually introduce it with only two symbols: a check mark (✓) and a question mark (?). The check represents, "I understand." The question mark represents, "I do not understand." Thus students are given a fairly simple, but important, metacognition task of monitoring their own comprehension while reading. By introducing it this way, confusion is eliminated and the task is clear and concrete to the students. Once they have practiced this once or twice, the teacher can introduce more complicated and content-specific versions of INSERT.

There are many content-specific ways to implement INSERT. My ninth grade geography students introduced the version of INSERT shown in figure 21-2 as a tool to investigate new regions of the world as we worked through a year-long course in geography. Each time we investigated a brand new region, we could use this form of INSERT to synthesize our understandings of basic geography themes with the new information we confronted. This activity inevitably led to quality discussion about essential themes of the course, and it helped students to deeply learn these essential ideas. Other forms of INSERT might include using "C" and "E" for cause and effect, or "F" and "O" for fact and opinion. Figure 21-3 shows a language arts version appropriate for having students identify elements of a story. Do not limit yourself to these. Create your own for your subject matter.

FIGURE 21-2

INSERT FOR GEOGRAPHY CLASS---THE FIVE THEMES OF GEOGRAPHY

SYMBOL ------   MEANING OF SYMBOL

L ----------	LOCATION
H ----------	HUMAN GEOGRAPHY
P ----------	PHYSICAL GEOGRAPHY
E ----------	HUMAN/ENVIRONMENT INTERACTION
M ----------	MOVEMENT
R ----------	REGION
? ----------	I DO NOT UNDERSTAND

FIGURE 21-3

INSERT FOR LANGUAGE ARTS CLASS---STORY ELEMENTS

SYMBOL ------   MEANING OF SYMBOL

S ----------	SETTING
C ----------	CHARACTER DEVELOPMENT
R ----------	RISING ACTION
I ----------	INTERNAL RESPONSE
E ----------	EXTERNAL RESPONSE
X ----------	CLIMAX
N ----------	RESOLUTION

The best way to have students use INSERT is to follow the paradigm of cooperative learning described throughout this book — individual written commitment, followed by small-group discussion, followed by full-class discussion — to get all students involved in the process. This assures interaction since each student brings something in writing (marks in the text) to the discussion. After some **M**otivation stage activity to start the class, have students read with INSERT and then discuss. Try INSERT in your classes. You will see that it really helps students learn the subject matter while, at the same time, they are acquiring literacy skills.

INSERT Procedure

Lifelong Learning Skill(s) to be Practiced During Learning:

- Comprehension monitoring while reading
- Synthesis and evaluation of subject matter ideas during reading

Quick Overview of the Lesson:

1. (This strategy requires some form of introductory activity such as a preview or a PreP before introduction of the INSERT activity)
2. Explain and model use of the skill
3. Students perform silent reading, making marginal notations to describe their thinking
4. Small-group or classroom discussion occurs based on notations
5. Large-group discussion and/or writing activity such as Cubing.

Materials:

- Textbook or some other textual matter
- Transparency of at least the first page of the text
- Poster or transparency of the INSERT notations to be used

Detailed version of lesson:

1. Introduce the content of the reading by posing a hypothetical question, reading a quotation, previewing the text, or some other interest-capturing idea to which students can react through discussion. A PreP strategy or preview of the reading might suffice.

---

2. Introduce the skill of monitoring one's own comprehension while reading. Let students know that when a strategic reader reads, s/he does not only think about the words that are on the page, but also, thinks about other things, such as whether understanding is occurring, or whether what is being read is important, or if s/he already knew it, or if s/he disagrees or agrees with the author. In other words, a good reader thinks about his or her own thinking while reading.

3. The first time or two that you do this with a class, you should model the thinking that is required. You can do so by asking to students to watch you read. Tell them that even though you are going to read aloud, you are going to read not only the words on the page, but you are going to say aloud all the thoughts that occur to you while you read. (You may want to make some marginal notes for yourself before doing this so that you will be able to perform smoothly.) Read from the textbook or other source, allowing for students to hear your thoughts about what you are reading. Show agreement, surprise, failure to comprehend, re-reading to help comprehension, etc. — all the things that good readers do to make sure they understand what they read.

4. Introduce to students the marginal notations of INSERT. You may want to keep it very simple the first time you use INSERT. Perhaps by only using two symbols — a check mark (✓) for "I understand," and a Question mark (**?**) for "I do not understand." Use a transparency of a real page from the text-book. Place it on the overhead projector so students can watch as you make your marginal notations. You may wish to read aloud at this point to show your thinking as you model making marginal notations for the students on the transparency of the text. Be sure all students have a pencil and let them know that they need to mark well out into the margin where it will be easy to erase after the lesson is finished. (Alternatives to writing in the textbook are suggested above.) Stress to students that, while reading with INSERT, they will notice how much their comprehension improves.

5. Provide guided practice with each student working independently to read the rest of the text passage while making the INSERT notations in the margin of the text. Move around the room to monitor student behavior and answer any questions students may have about the process. You should expect, at first, some reluctance to write in the text. Help students through this by coaching them quietly and individually. (They are breaking old habits by doing this activity.) As you move around the room, if you notice a student with a question mark next to something, note where it is. Continue to move around the room. If many students have a question mark in the same place, you may wish to interrupt their reading to explain a concept that will help them to comprehend the text. (This is the teachable moment.) On the other hand, if the one student is the only one with a question mark there, you might wish to whisper to the student individually to help past the comprehension problem.

6. When most students have finished the reading (or all students if you have given early finishers another task into which they could segue) call the class to your attention by beginning a discussion based on their notations. Ask students to meet with the others in their cooperative learning groups to clarify any comprehension problems related to question marks in their text. Tell them that if they are not able to help each other in solving these problems, to raise a hand and you will step in to help. (An alternative is to conduct a whole-class discussion, skipping the small-group discussion, by asking whether any student has a question mark. Have the student describe where in the text it is. Take the opportunity to address the whole class explain any unclear notions to students.)

7. Have students report on their use of the skill. Ask, "By a show of hands, how many of you felt that by practicing this comprehension-monitoring activity during reading, it actually enhanced your comprehension by helping you to think about what you were reading more than you usually do?" (Most students will admit that it did have that effect on them.)

8. Remind them that good readers always read this way, even though they don't always make marks in all the books they read. Encourage them to practice reading other texts in other classes by thinking about their own thinking while they read.

9. Follow up with some other eXtension activity such as a focused free write if appropriate.

10. Continue eXtension through Cornell Note Taking, Cubing, homework, a quiz, etc.

Extra Scaffolds

The most important scaffold in getting students to practice monitoring their comprehension through INSERT is to introduce it with as simple a format as possible. I like to use just two symbols the first time.

Chapter 22

Interactive Cloze Procedure

How often misused words generate misleading thoughts.
Herbert Spencer

Motivation ✓

Acquisition ✓

e**X**tension ✓

Many teachers are familiar with the diagnostic cloze procedure (Taylor, 1953) that has been in use for years as a tool to determine the appropriateness of text for groups of students. The Interactive Cloze (Meeks & Morgan, 1978) is different. In the diagnostic cloze procedure, every fifth (or tenth) word is removed from the passage, and students are encouraged to use semantic and syntactic clues to attempt to determine the word that the author originally used in the reading passage. With the Interactive Cloze (IC), on the other hand, only selected key terms are missing, and the passage is not necessarily the whole passage from the text. Often, the teacher can compose a summary of the entire text passage, create spaces for some of the key terms on which the students can focus in their predictions, and use this to stimulate focus on deeper meanings of words. This is a wonderful vocabulary teaching technique.

On the surface, this activity looks like the typical "fill-in-the-space" worksheet. There are two principal differences: first, the eliminated terms are something about which the students can make intelligent predictions, and second, the process is different.

Making the Interactive Cloze Sheet

The most important advice about creating an IC activity is that the eliminated terms should be terms about which the students will be able to make intelligent predictions. If the vocabulary is completely new, but the concepts are known, then they will be able to predict something close in meaning to the actual term that you want them to learn. On the other hand, if the vocabulary and the concepts are new, don't use this activity. There is no reason to frustrate students by having them attempt to "guess" new words about ideas with which they are not acquainted. That would be a waste of their time. If you wish for them to focus on precise terms or new terms for which they know synonyms, then this is a good activity. One example from a pre-algebra class I once taught is shown in figure 22-1. (This particular one was also being used as a tool to teach Cornell Note Taking. Interactive Cloze Procedure does not have to be made in the two-column format.) Students hypothesized several different words for the opposite of a number. Some said it was the same "number" from zero on the number line. Some said the same "amount" from zero. The correct and precise mathematical term is the same "distance" from zero. The point is that I knew that students would be able to predict something to complete that space.

FIGURE 22-1

INTERACTIVE CLOZE FOR ALGEBRA

Objectives 9-5-01	1. Define the opposite of a number. 2. Find the absolute value of a number. 3. Explain how to use a counterexample.
Key terms	_____ opposite _____ _____ absolute value _____ _____ counterexample _____ _____ number line _____ _____ zero _____ _____ positive _____ _____ negative _____
The opposite of a number	Two numbers that are the same _____ from zero on the number line are opposites. Examples:
Absolute value	The absolute value of a number is its _____ from zero on the number line. Absolute values are always a _____ number. The absolute value of a positive number is a _____ number. The absolute value of a negative number is a _____ number.
Symbol of absolute value	
Using a counterexample	You use a counterexample to prove that _____

Making and Using IC in the Classroom

The process of IC is also different from a typical fill-in-the-space worksheet. Such worksheets are typically used as a means to get students to hunt for correct answers. Most students do this without ever actually reading the text. If you watch them, they usually start somewhere in the middle or back of the text (It really doesn't matter.) to hunt for bold or italicized words that will help them find the right answer that fills in the space. The trick to using IC properly is to make it such that students are not able to just go hunting. They ought to process the text in a mature way, reading to see the logical argument that is being presented by the author.

The teacher, then, should make the IC passage so that the wording is somewhat different from the text, and the sequence is somewhat different. What should become obvious to the student during or after the reading is that there are precise words that carry especially important meaning related to the subject. These are the words that the teacher eliminates in the passage. They are *not necessarily the same words that are in bold print in the text*.

The process involved in engaging students in predicting the terms should follow the paradigm that we have presented in this book—individual written commitment, small group discussion, reading, small group discussion, large group discussion—so that students have the chance to interact in determining meaning from vocabulary. Done this way, IC can help students learn new subject matter and develop deeper meaning from vocabulary terms specifically related to your discipline.

Interactive Cloze Reading Procedure

Lifelong Learning Skill(s) to be Practiced During Learning:

- Predicting to create purpose for reading
- Contextual definition of vocabulary terms

Quick Overview of Lesson:

1. Give to students a copy of the Interactive Cloze passage that you have created to summarize the reading and focus on key vocabulary terms.
2. Students individually guess by writing (preferably in pencil) the terms they think will best complete the passage.
3. Small group discussion to compare guesses — students may change some.
4. Silent reading to determine better responses from the text.
5. Small group discussion to attempt a consensus on correct terms.
6. Large group discussion to achieve class consensus.

Materials:

- Summary of the reading that students are about to do—with certain key words deleted and replaced with spaces in which students can write the vocabulary terms that they predict will complete the passage.
- Transparency of the summary that students will use.

Detailed version of lesson:

1. Introduce the content of the reading by posing a hypothetical question, reading a quotation, previewing the text, or some other interest-capturing idea to which students can react through discussion. (You might skip this activity with the Interactive Cloze since it provides a preview of sorts.)

2. Give each student a copy of the interactive cloze sheet. Tell them that all strategic readers who have some prior knowledge about a topic make predictions about what they are about to read before reading. Tell them that you have provided a worksheet that will allow them to predict certain key vocabulary terms that they will find in the reading they are about to do. Tell them to attempt to guess what words go in the spaces provided on the worksheet—based on their own prior knowledge of the topic. Let them know that many clues may be found in the passage itself and that they should use as many clues as they can find. This activity should be done individually rather than as a cooperative group.

3. Model the thinking required, by reading the first few lines and allowing for conjecture by the class as to what terms might be used in one or two of the spaces. Discuss the relative merit of words offered by students. Use this opportunity to discuss connotations. Let students know that there will only be one word per space, and that they should pay special attention to punctuation, verb endings, modifying words, etc. as clues to help them predict the correct words. Tell students to do this in pencil or to write small if they do not have one, because they may wish to change their predictions once they get into the reading.

4. Move around the room to see that all students are attempting to predict the words that go in the spaces. You may need to help some of the students link prior knowledge to what they are attempting to do. Allow sufficient time for many of the students to finish their predictions, but you do not necessarily have to wait for all students to finish before the next step.

5. Now put students into their cooperative learning groups. Groups of three or four are appropriate. Remind them not to look at the reading at this point, but tell them that they should compare their predictions with one another. Let them know that they may change any prediction if they feel that another person in the group has a better one for a specific space on the IC sheet. Tell students that it is important that they explain to the others in their group why they chose the response they did for any given word. This way they are helping each other to expand the prior knowledge base they have. (At the same time, they are increasing the purposeful nature of the reading to come since they are anticipating more as a result of their discussions.)

6. Again separate students from their groups and tell them that it is time to do the reading. Let them know that they should read silently, from the beginning to the end, seeking terms that the author used or terms that are more appropriate than the ones they have predicted. Again, move around the room to facilitate this process and keep students on task.

7. When most students have finished reading, put students again into groups to compare their findings and to attempt to come to consensus on the best vocabulary terms that fit into the spaces on the interactive cloze sheet. Facilitate this by moving about the room to help in discussions, but try not to give answers. Help students to weigh the merits of various terms as they work out a consensus.

8. Ask students to report on their use of the skill. Ask them to raise a hand if they agree that, by making predictions on the cloze form and discussing their predictions with other students before the reading, that they found that their comprehension was improved over the normal way they might have read if they were just assigned a regular worksheet..

9. When at least one group has finished, you might take that group's terms and fill them in on the transparency of the cloze passage. Then conduct a class discussion to bring the whole class to consensus. Be sure to use this opportunity to focus on connotations of words, praising and otherwise discussing the alternatives that students present as opportunities to reinforce thinking about words.

Extra Scaffolding

Three major scaffolds can be used to facilitate this process for students who are low performing readers. First, you might want to do a complete preview of the text to be read. Then close the textbook and begin with the IC. Second, you might wish to conduct a whole-class discussion rather than allow for small-group discussion. Third, you might read the passage aloud to the students after all students have predicted and discussed alternatives for the spaces on the IC. If you read aloud, you might want to stop after several paragraphs to have students write in any alternatives that they now see as more appropriate than the ones they originally predicted. You might then conduct a discussion of what they now are using, asking them to cite the text to show where they are finding information regarding the terms.

Chapter 23

Paired Reading

If you would thoroughly know anything, teach it to others.
Tryon Edwards

Motivation

Acquisition ✓

e**X**tension ✓

The first thing that comes to most people's minds when I mention paired reading is the notion of one student reading out loud to another student. That is not what Paired Reading (Larson & Dansereau, 1986) is all about. As I have mentioned elsewhere in this book, when students are reading out loud, focus is on calling out words rather than on constructing personal meaning from print. By getting students to read silently to do just that—construct personal meaning—we help them to learn content while, at the same time, acquiring life-long skills. Paired reading is one way to accomplish this.

Paired Reading is one of the most engaging activities for most students, partly because it involves discussion in twosomes, a difficult place to hide and become an observer. In this activity, both students read silently the same portion of text at the same time, and once finished, close their books in order to paraphrase what they have read. There are two roles—teller and listener—and students take turns, paragraph by paragraph, working their way through text until they have read all the assigned work. Each time that they close the book, one student begins while the other listens, adding new information only when the first student has exhausted his/her knowledge of the part that is under consideration. They take turns being the "teller" who is the one to speak first each time the text is closed.

This is one of my favorite activities to use in the mathematics classroom. I have found that students who process mathematics text using paired reading tend to come away from the experience with strong understanding of the mathematical concepts. There is a slight difference in how Paired Reading is implemented in a mathematics or science classroom when there are examples involved in the text that students are reading. When students are reading the examples that are part of virtually every mathematics text, the teller writes down the problem from the example, but not the solution. Both students read the solution, and, once the books have been closed, the teller begins to duplicate, on paper, the solution to the example problem. If unable to do so, the teller passes the pencil over to the listener, who then proceeds to clarify how the solution proceeded in the text. This is very different from doing a worksheet. It is also different from watching the teacher do another example at the chalkboard. It forces students to be metacognitive while they are processing the ideas presented in the examples. The result, in my experiences, is that students really learn the mathematics!

Paired Reading Procedure

Lifelong Learning Skill(s) to be Practiced During Learning:

- Comprehension monitoring while reading
- Paraphrasing orally (the ability to say, in ones own words, what one has just read)

Quick Overview of the Lesson:

1. Explain and model use of the skill
2. Partners decide on roles of teller and listener, and decide on amount of text to read
3. Partners perform silent reading, mentally paraphrasing
4. (Books closed) Teller recalls as much as possible while listener listens
5. (Books closed) Listener then adds more information if possible
6. Both open book, scan for missed detail and discuss
7. Partners swap roles for next segment, continuing through passage until finished, swapping with each new portion read
8. Reflection activity — writing, debate, discussion, etc.

Classroom management note: be sure that students sit next to their partner as class begins so that the thought process is not disrupted when it is time to participate in the paired reading. I like to have a transparency of the pairs displayed as students enter the classroom. They simply identify who their partners are, and they sit accordingly. As has been mentioned earlier in this work, heterogeneous groups are important in all cooperative learning. In Paired Reading, it is even more important. It is not so important that you have the most advanced students with the least advanced, but it is important that you do not put two very low performers in the same group.

Detailed version of lesson:

1. Introduce the content of the reading by posing a hypothetical question, reading a quotation, previewing the text, or some other interest-capturing idea to which students can react through discussion. **M**otivate students through use of a pre-reading strategy to determine and add to students' prior knowledge.

2. Introduce the skill of mentally paraphrasing while studying. Suggest that "Strategic readers, when they study on their own, often carry on an inner dialog regarding what they read—it might sound like this if it were aloud—'The subtitle of the paragraph I just finished reading suggested that there were three key terms related to the topic. Let me see if I can recall them while looking away from the book… Let's see… There's this…and there's that…But I can't recall the third one. I've got to look back to see what it is…Oh, yeah…Now I have them.'"

Tell the class that what they are about to practice in pairs is exactly the same way of thinking, only they will have a helper in their partner. Explain that each partnership may choose how much text to tackle at a time. They may wish to take a whole page, or the paragraphs under a single subtitle, or only a single paragraph at a time. They should also decide on which partner will be the teller first. Then, they may begin.

3. The first time or two that you do this with a class, you should model the thinking that is required. You may do this by acting as the teller in a pair, asking the whole class to act as your partner, reading a portion silently with you, listening as you attempt to recall the details of the reading with all the books closed, and helping to recall what you left out in your paraphrasing of the passage. (It is OK to be human and not remember everything when you do this. In fact, it may be advantageous to do so.) When you have finished, and they have filled in as many of the details as they can after you finished, then the whole class should open their books to scan for details that all readers may have left out.

4. Once this modeling is finished, ask if everyone has a clear understanding of how the process works and is ready to try it with his/her partner. (Since student groups will finish the activity at varying times, it is a good idea to assign another activity in which students might engage when they are finished with the paired reading. This might involve creating Cornell Notes or creating a graphic representation or another appropriate eXtension activity.)

It is important at this time to make sure students know that there will be constant noise in the background since students will be finishing their readings at different times and because different students read at different speeds. Let students know that they should treat the noise in the room as if it were a motor running, and that they should not let the noise bother them while they focus on their reading and their discussion with their partners. Remind them that, at some point in the future, they will most likely find themselves in a situation where they must read thoughtfully with noise—if they are ever to study in a university dormitory, or if they are to read while working in a factory that is noisy. (By handling this objection before it occurs, I have found that later, when students are reading, it is not as much of a problem as it would have been if not addressed at all beforehand.)

(If the reading is from a mathematics text, or some form of text that has example problems to be considered, such as a physics or chemistry text, let students know that when they get to problems or examples, the teller should copy down the problem, but not the solution. Both the teller and listener read the example's solution. Then, when the book is closed, the teller should attempt to duplicate the solution on paper. If s/he is not able to do so, the listener may attempt the solution on paper. If neither can complete the process, they both go back into the text, study the example again, and close the book, trying it again. If still not able, they should call the teacher to help.)

5. Move about the room while students are performing their paired reading. Eavesdrop on their conversations. Take the opportunity to see that they are performing paired reading correctly. Some students may not have heard the instructions precisely as they were given. Some listeners, for instance, may keep their book open while the teller is paraphrasing what s/he could remember. Some listeners think they do not have to read the reading at all! They do other things while the teller prepares. The teacher's role is to spot any behavior that is not appropriate and help get students on task as quickly as possible.

   Some students will become frustrated the first time they attempt to do this. Unfortunately perhaps, no teacher has ever asked them to read at this level. Be a coach. You can support them by discussing where they are experiencing difficulty, suggesting that they try smaller segments to begin trying this, and by modeling for them personally. Let them know that they may try as little as a single paragraph, or even a part of a paragraph at first. Let them know that each effort becomes easier than the previous one. Stay with them, even joining in to model how they might be successful. If you have grouped your students heterogeneously, the partnership will succeed at the overall task with little or no support from you.

6. Once student groups have finished the assigned selection, ask them to report on their use of the skill. Say, "By a show of hands, how many of you felt, while you were reading, knowing that in a moment, you were going to close your book and tell it to your partner, it made you read at a higher comprehension level than you often do when you are, for instance, reading to fill in spaces on a worksheet?" Let students know that what they have just practiced with a partner, is exactly the way a strategic reader might read any time s/he is studying or trying to learn something important.

7. Assign an eXtension activity to take the learning beyond what has already occurred during the paired reading. This may involve either classwork, homework, or both.

Extra Scaffolds

As in most of the classroom activities in this book, the number one scaffold is for the teacher to read aloud to the students. However, with this activity, it is important that, after the teacher has read a paragraph aloud, the students have a few moments to go back over it silently to reprocess the information in a personal way. Thus, students who normally struggle with reading at a certain level are able to hear it, and, while fresh in their minds, go back over it to isolate key ideas and put them in their own words—construct personal meaning from text—before they close the book and discuss what they have read with their peer.

Doing paired reading in this fashion, with all students discussing at the same time, also eliminates one of the perennial problems associated with paired reading. Many students struggle with the noise level of a classroom full of students discussing the text. They may have difficulty reading silently while others are discussing. When the teacher is directing the process such that all students are in the silent reading phase and the discussion phases at the same time as the others, this problem is eliminated.

Chapter 24

PQR$_2$ST+

I must plough my furrow alone.

Earl of Rosebery

Motivation ✓

Acquisition ✓

e**X**tension ✓

PQR$_2$ST+ is very similar to the widely known study method called SQ3R (Robinson, 1961) . The principal differences include immediate paraphrasing *onto paper*, and the fact that the student ends up with a product that can be a useful study aid. This is an activity that I normally introduce to a class the day after we have practiced Paired Reading (Chapter 23). I do this because this activity takes advantage of the same mindset that is involved in Paired Reading: closing the book in order to immediately recall what was just read. The difference is, in using PQR$_2$ST+ (Morgan, Forget, & Antinarella, 1996), the student is doing the recall onto paper rather than saying it to another student. In fact, the student is recalling into two-column notes (Chapter 12).

PQR$_2$ST+ is a study method that can be used by a lone student learning new information. I used it throughout my graduate programs to great effect. But, it can also be used as a lesson plan: first, when you introduce it to students, and later, to reinforce the techniques. I like to use it as the principal learning tool in my classroom once every two to three weeks during the first semester, until I feel students have a good grasp of how to do it well. Thus, students are coming into class, intelligently processing text, creating notes in a system that in itself is a life-long learning skill, and *they* do most of the work! Yet, unlike a typical worksheet, they are truly processing the text in a mature way—constructing personal meaning—that leads to understanding and retention rather than just exposure to new material. They are actually reading the material from beginning to end, something students rarely do when confronted with worksheets. Instead of going on a "hunting expedition" that takes them from the middle to the end to the front of the reading, looking helter-skelter for places to find answers, PQR$_2$ST+ causes students to identify key ideas, setting them up as frame questions, and then to read the logical argument the authors are making in the same sequence in which the authors state their case. This is the kind of reading that students in grades four through twelve rarely do, yet the kind that they will find routine to their futures in either college or the real world of work. There are not too many work sheets in the work day world of the 21st century.

The procedures for using this technique are shown in Figure 24-1, below. This is from a poster that I have had on the walls of my classroom for years. Having it on the classroom wall makes it easy for me to reference it when I discuss the process with students, and it makes it easy for students to follow the correct procedure when they are doing it in class. (It is also a great reference for Previewing procedure, Chapter 11.)

FIGURE 24-1

PQR$_2$ST+

PREVIEW
Title, introduction, subtitles, pictures, charts, maps, graphs, bold print & italics, summary, end questions

QUESTION
Write a subtitle-related question on left side of 2-column notes.

READ
Read silently from the subsection, thinking about how you will summarize the passage in your own words.

REMEMBER
Summarize into 2-column notes
in your own words **with book closed**.

SCAN
Rapidly go over the same subsection of text, looking for missed details or errors in your first summarization.

TOUCH UP
Add any important details to your notes.

+

Go back and study your notes within the same day, the next day, and again the day before the test or quiz.

PQR$_2$ST+ actually includes three tools of memory that, independent of each other, each work to enhance memory. One is "chunking" information. Chunking is a widely known phenomenon wherein the person groups many details or items with a key idea or label. Whenever students are making two-column notes, they are chunking information around a main idea in the left column of the notes. A second memory tool is paraphrasing. We all know that, when we put newly learned ideas in our own words, we are more likely to remember them. This is, of course, a result of the fact that in order to do so, we have filtered the newly learned concepts through our own schemata. Another way of looking at it is that we are firing neural pathways that are unique to our own brains as we relate information to our own schemata. The result is dendritic growth within our brain. The third memory device involved in PQR$_2$ST+ is rehearsal. Anyone who has ever been involved in music, drama, or sport knows the value of rehearsal to the memory process. The plus sign in PQR$_2$ST+ signifies going back within the first 24 hours after making PQR$_2$ST+ notes and folding them over to study from the recall side.

Any of the three memory tools of chunking, paraphrasing, and rehearsal work independently to enhance a person's memory. All three are included in PQR$_2$ST+. This is why students who use the technique perform extremely well on assessments that are based on the materials that they have read. I have had great results working with advance placement students with PQR$_2$ST+. Once they begin to use the system, they realize that they are taking notes that will greatly enhance their prospects on the AP test in May. The results from students who have studied this way are tremendous. However, it is not only the AP student who can benefit from this form of note taking. All students benefit from the mature reading that it provokes and from the study system that results.

It gets better, though. PQR$_2$ST+ is a perfect assignment for make-up work when a student misses class. Even though the class activity on the day missed might have been an anticipation guide or paired reading, PQR$_2$ST+ is an excellent tool to get the student to carefully process the information that was read in class that day. The student submits to the teacher a set of notes in his/her own hand that summarize the essential elements of the reading that was done that day, and the student gets credit for the work.

It gets even better, though. PQR$_2$ST+ is the perfect assignment to leave with a substitute teacher when you cannot be in class. Once you have practiced it several times with your students, and you feel confident that they know the process, and can do it well without your help, you can feel free to take a day off without the hassle of planning ten hours to be able to take off from a six-hour school day. PQR$_2$ST+ is a meaningful activity in which students will be engaged in processing new information. It requires no significant interaction between the substitute and the students. And, it requires no interaction between students. Thus, students are engaged in continuing to learn new material (even though you are not there to assist) and what you will find on your desk when you return is a stack of each student's notes, stapled together with a name on it, written in that student's hand, ready for you to peruse to see who did the task properly, what misconceptions exist in the students' interpretations of the text, and how well they read the material. This task is the opposite of busy work in the form of worksheets. If you have prepared your students properly, they will take the task seriously and do a good job of it. I have used this as my principal substitute day activity for several years, and I have never been disappointed.

PQR$_2$ST+ Note-Taking Procedure

Lifelong Learning Skill(s) to be Practiced During Learning:

- Identifying main ideas and chunking details around them
- Taking terse and well-organized notes
- Paraphrasing as a study and memory tool
- Rehearsing as a memory-enhancing tool

Materials:

- Overhead transparency of blank two-column notes (page divided into 2 sides of 1/3 — 2/3)
- Textbook or other reading

Quick Overview of the Lesson:

(This is best introduced after having taught both Paired Reading and Cornell Note Taking.)

1. Preview the reading.
2. Explain the skill of taking quality notes—point out that many students write too much information into their notes and that you have a technique to prevent that happening.
3. Explain the procedure of PQR$_2$ST+ note taking
4. Model with the textbook.
5. Facilitate student practice of PQR$_2$ST+ note taking.
6. Have students report on their use of the skill.

Detailed version of lesson:

1. Introduce the content of the reading by previewing the text.

---

2. Explain to students that after observing the notes of many of the students, it is clear that they could improve the quality of their notes and the resulting quality of their success in preparing for tests and other measures of their learning. Discuss with them the notion that many of them take notes that are too elaborate—containing too much information—and that the skill they will practice today is of taking notes that are neither too elaborate nor lacking in important details from the reading. Let them know that they will be taking advantage of the same mental processes that they have already successfully used when they did Paired Reading.

---

3. Place on the overhead projector (or draw onto the chalkboard) a page formatted for two-column notes. Explain to students that the note-taking technique that we are about to practice is a combination of two-column notes and a particular note taking technique that will help them to understand the reading better and remember better what they have read.

---

4. Describe each of the steps of PQR$_2$ST+. Discuss the value of the steps with students. They should know that a quality preview, or survey, of a reading is extremely valuable in improving comprehension and speed of reading. They ought to know that the two-column note taking of Cornell Notes is helpful in organizing and recalling material. They should know that reading to be able to paraphrase is a tool for improving comprehension. They should know that folding over the page of two-column notes is a valuable rehearsal technique that can enhance memory.

5. Model the behavior of PQR$_2$ST+ note taking. You should have, by now, led the class through a careful preview of the material. Use an overhead transparency to set up the notes, and ask students to prepare their own paper the same way. Place a line 1/3 of the way from the left edge of the transparency, and take a moment to see that each student does the same on his/her paper. Now describe how to use the first subtitle as a tool for creating a question for the left column. Turn it into a question. For example, if it says "Formation of Glaciers," you write in the left column, "How are glaciers formed?" Now tell the class to observe you as you read the paragraph(s) under that title, close your book, and take your notes with the book closed. (Many students will copy your notes, losing the sense of what you are trying to get them to see. Do not allow them to copy at this point. Make them observe you in the process of doing the remembering onto paper.) It is not so important that you are perfect in doing this modeling. Let them see the real process of the human brain attempting to remember. Your notes will be a brief paraphrase of the text passage that was read. When you are finished remembering, point out to them that you are now ready for the scan part of this procedure. Have them scan with you to locate important details that could be added. Touch up your notes as you or the students deem appropriate. Once this modeling is finished, ask if everyone has a clear understanding of how the process works and is ready to try it alone. Explain any instructions that are not understood, and clear up any misconceptions of the task at hand. Explain that each student should read to accomplish the task without the help of anyone else.

6. Provide guided practice in reading to take notes with the book closed, using the PQR$_2$ST+ method of note taking. Move around the room to observe, help in comprehending new vocabulary if students request individual assistance.

7. You may wish to allow students to compare notes after all students have finished gathering the information from the reading. Be sure to ask students to raise a hand if they felt that, by reading to take notes with a closed book, they actually were forcing themselves to comprehend more carefully than when they read to do a worksheet, for example.

8. Remind students of the value of folding the page over to study these notes, focusing on the main idea as a reminder of the details on the right side.

9. You may wish to allow students to quiz one another about the ideas on the notes. Let them know that they should study for the upcoming quiz using the notes in this fashion.

10. NEXT DAY: Repeat the success program that you did with Cornell Notes. Allow students to study the notes they took the day before. Now they have studied the notes two days in a row. Quiz them on the material in the notes that they have studied under your supervision. For students who have not had great success in school up until they entered your class, this will be another success story as they ace the quiz. The message is clear — the note-taking system works and each student could, using this system, become successful at reading and remembering.

Extra Scaffolds

As in many of the classroom activities in this book, the principal extra scaffold is for the teacher to read out loud to the students portions of the text while they follow along silently. With PQR2ST+, this is also true, only the teacher may also help students to carry on a discussion of how to take the notes with the book closed. So, the process looks very similar to Paired Reading. In this case, the teacher reads aloud, the students and the teacher then close the book, and the students write down what they felt was important from the reading. The teacher may wish to elicit from the students their thoughts so that s/he can write some ideas on an overhead transparency for students to be able to see the note taking process. The goal, as in any special education situation, is to help students closer to the point at which they can perform the skill autonomously. The teacher must decide when and if students can do some of the PQR$_2$ST+ work alone.

Chapter 25

PreP

Ideas are like rabbits. You get a couple, learn how to handle them, and pretty soon you have a dozen.
John Steinbeck

Motivation ✓

Acquisition ✓

e**X**tension ✓

The PreP strategy (Langer, 1981) is one that allows teachers to determine the background knowledge of the students, and also to build background knowledge at the same time through hearing what their peers know about the topic. This can be used in any subject area classroom to get students to become active in the learning process. By using this procedure, the teacher assures that the learning of new subject matter is connected to the prior knowledge of students in the class. There are essentially five steps to the pre-reading part of the activity. See Figure 25-1 for an overview and example of PreP.

This activity can be used as a pre-reading activity, as its name implies, but it can also be used as a purpose setting activity to help students focus on making meaning from the text both during and after the reading. Alternatively, it can be used in the pre-reading phase of class, followed with some during-reading activity such as Paired Reading, and then used as a follow-up to the reading as students reorganize the information they gleaned from the text during the reading.

Though the overt purpose of this activity is to base the learning experience on the collective prior knowledge of the students, it is not necessarily over when the students go into the reading. Done properly, PreP establishes a base of knowledge from which the class can proceed. If, for instance, the class factstorms 20-25 ideas about what they are getting ready to learn, and then bases their reading on finding more information that fits into the pattern that they have recognized ahead of time, they are learning one of the most important skills of strategic reading—relating prior knowledge to new text to construct meaning from the text. Thus, student led through a PreP before reading are given the opportunity to acquire, through classroom practice, a life-long learning skill. The final step of the PreP is to organize the gathered information into some categories. This is a "list-group-label" type of activity, and it leads to recognition of important patterns in text. The pattern that students recognize during the PreP can be used as the purpose for reading. Students read to find new information to be added to the categories they have created. The final e**X**tension phase of the class can be used to compare notes, sharing newly discovered ideas that fit the pattern and enlarge the knowledge base from which the activity began.

FIGURE 25-1

PreP (Pre-reading Plan)

Steps of the PreP	Sample Classroom Scene: Algebra
1. Initial associations with the concept – Students are asked to jot down what comes to mind when they think of _____ (a word or phrase written on the chalkboard).	**Teacher**: Everyone get out a piece of paper and jot down whatever comes into your mind when you think of the term 'slope.' Teacher moves around the classroom to view what students are writing, and to assure student involvement.
2. Sharing – Students are then asked to share what they wrote. The teacher goes up and down each row to be sure that each student has a chance to get his/her idea listed on the chalkboard or overhead transparency.	**Teacher**: Lets make a list of what we have. Jennifer, what did you write?
	Jennifer: I said snowboard.
3. Reflecting on initial associations – If students do not offer a rationale, the teacher asks each student to tell why s/he made that particular association. This added discussion helps to build background knowledge for the other students in the class.	**Teacher**: Why did you say that?
	Jennifer: Because when we went skiing, it was hard to learn how to snowboard on the steep parts.
	Teacher: Thomas, what did you have?
4. Organizing conceptually – Once each student has had an opportunity to get his/her association on the chalkboard, students are put into groups to consider how they might organize the terms they have generated. **	**Thomas**: I had rise over run, because of what we read yesterday about the y-axis and the x-axis.
	Teacher: Takeesha, what did you have? ..... (The teacher continues to probe each student's idea to add to the list the class is generating.)
5. Teacher leads a full-class discussion to narrow down the thinking of the various groups. What has really occurred here is a cooperative effort to determine and to build the prior understandings of all students about the topic to be learned in the reading. Even students who at first thought they knew little or nothing about the topic now have learned through peer discussion that they did really know something. A typical sentiment expressed by students when they hear the comments of their peers is, "Yeah, I knew that! I saw that same movie!"	**Teacher**: From the list you have collectively generated, it looks like we already know a great deal about the concept of 'slope!' What I would like for you to do now is to get into your cooperative groups and see if your group can come up with the names of three categories under which all these neat facts might be organized.
Students are now prepared to read – By the time students have finished a PreP activity, they are really in a frame of mind to learn from the reading to come.	The teacher leads a discussion to help students see how the common threads of their ideas connect until they have isolated 2 or 3 categories. Students are then asked to use these to help them comprehend the reading. Typical categories are *meaning of slope, how to calculate slope, and how to use slope.*
**A quicker alternative is for the teacher to name the categories and have students rewrite the list.	*Optional – Students use the categories they generated to reflect by taking notes for homework.

Detailed version of lesson:

1. Begin the class by writing a word or concept on the chalkboard.

2. Explain to students that strategic readers always think before they read new subject matter about how much they already know about the subject to be studied. Tell them that what we are going to practice as a class is what an individual might do all alone in a dormitory room at the university or preparing to learn something new on the job.

3. Ask each student to write whatever comes to mind when s/he thinks about the concept written on the chalkboard. Encourage students to write as many things as they think of. You might model the thinking involved by suggesting what comes into your own mind. Allow time for students to think. Move around the room to see that each student participates in writing. Encourage reluctant students by making quiet suggestions to stimulate their thinking.

4. After a few moments, when it appears most students have something to contribute, move to the chalkboard and begin at one side of the room taking ideas from each student, giving each student the opportunity to contribute his/her idea. Be accepting of all ideas, frequently asking, "Why did you say that?" if it is not clear what logic has led to a student's contribution. (This helps all students to build background knowledge about the topic. It also allows the teacher to determine what students know before the learning. At times, a seemingly inappropriate response will prove to be correctly related to the topic once the student explains his/her reason for stating it.)

5. Once each student has had the opportunity to contribute his/her idea, open the floor to any new ideas that relate to the topic. Usually students will have some more to add at this time. Then, ask students to get together in their cooperative groups to determine the names of two, three, or four categories into which all the terms they have listed could be organized. Tell them that "...miscellaneous is not a category!" (An alternative activity is for the teacher to name the categories and have the students rewrite the terms into the categories as they see fit. This can be done as a group or individual activity.)

6. If you have elected to have students name the categories, again, share onto the chalkboard, making another list, this time accepting each group's categories. Conduct a discussion leading to recognition of the two or three super-ordinate categories under which all the other categories could be organized. Let students know that they will be using these categories to set purposes for the reading they are about to do. (This activity is easier than you might think. You will usually find it fairly easy to get students to recognize the three that you already had in your mind. I usually circle some of the categories that are obviously related. Soon students will see patterns, and they are ripe for the reading yet to come.)

7. You may wish to employ another classroom activity for the students to use during reading. They could create word lists under the categories they have created. An alternative is to use a modified version of INSERT (Interactive Notation System for Effective Reading and Thinking). Using a different symbol for each of the categories, they could make marginal notations in their text each time they find information relating to one category.

8. You may wish to use an altogether different strategy for the reading portion of the class. Paired reading, GIST, etc. could be employed at this time. Or you may wish to use the structure you have created from step 6 of the PreP Strategy to gather information by having students list key terms from the reading under each of the categories they have created in the form of a graphic representation. A post-reading discussion could then be conducted, first in small groups, then as a class, as suggested in step 9.

9. Final reflection should relate back to the original three (or so) categories the students created in the pre-reading phase of class. An appropriate assignment is to have students assemble key vocabulary words from the reading under the appropriate categories as a homework assignment. This can be done in two-column notes.

10. As always, there are various EXtension activities you could use to reflect further on what students have learned. Suggestions include Cubing, Free Writes, First-Person Summaries, etc.

Extra Scaffolds

No extra scaffolds are required for this activity.

Chapter 26

Extreme Paired Reading
(Reciprocal Teaching)

Education is not filling a bucket but lighting a fire.
William Butler Yeats

Motivation

Acquisition ✓

EXtension ✓

Reciprocal teaching (Palinscar & Brown, 1984) is an activity that helps students to focus on the four essential strategies that good readers use to make sense of text:

- prediction
- clarification
- questioning, and
- summarization.

By getting students to practice these four strategies in a formal and structured format, teachers are allowing for students to acquire the strategies for themselves. Repeated use of this activity in the classroom not only facilitates reading of difficult materials, but it allows students to perceive themselves as successful readers and thinkers—an important step in overcoming the ubiquitous aversion many students have to reading difficult text.

I have chosen to call it "Extreme Paired Reading" for two reasons. Students these days identify with the hip term, "extreme" as it is applied to many sports that go "outside the bounds" of the normal. If students have practiced paired reading a few times, they are willing to go a step further with this activity. It should be noted that, even though the pattern of activity in Extreme Paired Reading (EPR) is one that starts out going back and forth from teacher to student and back again, the ultimate goal of this activity is to have students practice it in small groups or in pairs on their own with teacher acting as facilitator and supervisor of student-centered thinking. It takes a while to get to that point, but the work is worth the effort.

The second reason why it is called EPR is that it is a logical eXtension beyond the activity known as Paired Reading (Chapter 23). Once students have practiced paired reading a few times, they have a sense of confidence in themselves as persons who can paraphrase text that they have read. The new part, then, is the discussion that follows the paraphrased summary of what has been read. In Paired Reading, the students simply paraphrase and follow with a rescan of the text to see if they have captured the key ideas. In EPR, on the other hand, students are now empowered to go beyond recall to clarification, curiosity, and prediction.

My experiences with this activity suggest that students actually thrive on the interaction once they have gotten used to the pattern of behavior involved. At first, though, you should expect little participation on the part of students. They have become inured to the idea that, if they did not get it the first time, they are stupid. They do not know that, even the best readers and thinkers often wonder about the meaning of certain pieces of text. EPR allows for the institutionalization of the process of making meaning from text through conversation with others.

When I first introduce this to students, it is after they have had success with several others of the reading activities that I use in the classroom. This leads to an open mind about the process. Even then, many students will be reticent to ask questions when offered the opportunity. This is OK. I use a great deal of wait time. Sometimes, even that does not work at first. I might have to be the one who first asks for clarification on certain items in the text. I might say, "Why do you think that the author said it this way?" or some other open-ended question to get students to recognize a key idea. My experience suggests that, once you break the ice, students will "get on board the train" and become involved. Essentially, you are institutionalizing the idea that it is *OK to not know* exactly what is meant by the text, and that it is *OK to ask* to find out. Believe it or not, these are not things that we are reinforcing in the traditional way of presenting materials to students.

I usually suggest to students that this is the way that experienced students and teachers discuss what they are reading with other people. They have a conversation that allows them to wonder about things. I point out that it is OK to not understand on the way to attempting to understand. This is a major breakthrough for some students who have been taught (implicitly) that they are stupid, and that other students are smarter than they are. It is important for teachers to model the idea of making sense of text.

Extreme Paired Reading Procedure

Lifelong Learning Skill(s) to be Practiced During Learning:

- predicting
- clarifying
- questioning
- summarizing

Quick Overview of the Lesson:

1. Explain the process.
2. Preview reading.
3. Students write & share predictions.
4. Read a portion of text.

5. Teacher summarizes.
6. Students and teacher ask one another questions for clarification or curiosity.
7. Repeat steps 3 & 4.
8. Student summarizes.
9. More clarification & curiosity questions.
10. Repeat steps 3-9.

Detailed version of lesson:

1. Use the PreP procedure to introduce this activity the first time you do it. (After that, any Motivation-stage activity will suffice, and you may skip steps one and two of this detailed description.) Ask students to write down on their own paper what strategies they use when they must read something that they know is difficult, and perhaps dry and boring as well. Tell them to write down whatever they do to try to help themselves to be able to get through such a difficult reading that they know that they have to do. Allow a couple of minutes for them to do this. Move around the classroom to see that they are writing something. Then follow the PreP process of taking contributions from students, frequently asking them why they said that.

2. Once the chalkboard is full of their responses, ask them if they see any pattern to the responses. Point out to them that they have identified the four things good readers do all the time when they are reading to make sense of text: predicting, clarifying, questioning, and summarizing. Show them how their responses really fit into these categories, even though it might not be obvious at first. Show them how their responses fit into the categories of predicting, clarifying, questioning, and summarizing. (This should be easy to do. Some of their responses will not fit perfectly, but you can make a case that they fit into one of the categories.) The most important thing is that you are establishing what good readers do. It is possible that you will be adding to what they offer rather than translating. That is OK.

3. Tell students that, as a class, we are going to practice Extreme Paired Reading, which just happens to use the four characteristics we have identified. Tell them that as we first do this activity, we will do so by going back and forth between teacher and students, but that in the end, it is expected that small student groups will participate in doing this activity on their own.

4. Tell the students, "We will be taking turns with this activity. We will first predict what is coming in the next portion of text, then read it silently, then summarize it in our own words, and then ask clarification and curiosity questions to attempt to make sense of what we are reading. You may ask the questions of me, and I may ask them of you. Then we will again predict what is to come in the next subsection of text, and we will repeat the process."

5. Do a careful preview of the reading.

6. Tell students how much of the reading that is to be done in the first subsection. Let them know that the teacher will be the first summarizer upon finishing the reading. Now ask students to close their books and write a prediction of what they think that subsection will be about. Allow for a few seconds for them to do this, and then ask several students to read what they wrote. Be upbeat and positive about all of the predictions. (Get into the process yourself if you have not read the piece.)

7. Allow sufficient time for most of the students to read the piece. Then, summarize it as best you can, in your own words.

8. Allow for students to ask clarification questions and/or other questions about which they are curious. You might want to give them the bookmark in Appendix 6 to enhance the quality of questions they ask you at this stage of the lesson. Be sure to ask them questions that will help to clarify important concepts in the lesson.

9. Once there has been sufficient time for the questions to take place, ask students to once more write a prediction of what they think the next part will say. Allow sufficient time for their predictions to be written, and then solicit several from students, being accepting of what they offer.

10. Remind students that, after this next piece is read, one of them will be randomly selected to summarize the passage. (You may want to tell them of the method of choice—drawing names from a hat or whatever.)

11. Allow sufficient time for the reading to occur. Move around the room, reading from your own book as you do so.

12. When sufficient time has elapsed, name a student to summarize "in your own words" what you read. Remind the student that, unlike Paired Reading, it is OK to look at the book while you are giving your summary. When the student has finished, ask if anyone else would add to what has been summarized.

13. Open the floor to clarification and curiosity questions. Ask some of your own to help students to see the important concepts in the reading.

14. Repeat steps 6-13 until the reading has been accomplished.

15. Ask students to report on their use of the skill. Say, "By a show of hands, how many of you feel that, by reading using the four essential strategies of good readers—predicting, summarizing, clarifying and being curious—you actually got more out of this reading than you would have if you were assigned to just read it or were given a worksheet to use to read it?"

16. Continue e**X**tension through any of a myriad of activities to reflect on what had been read.

Extra Scaffolds

Extra Scaffolds are built into this activity. I have had great success with Extreme Paired Reading with students from a broad range of English language learners all the way to advanced placement college-bound students. This activity works with very difficult readings because the activity builds in the idea that "we are all struggling to make sense of this." As always, the teacher might read aloud to very low-performing readers to enhance their ability to see the print as language.

Chapter 27

Sensible Sentence Highlighting

Learning is finding out what you already know.
                    Richard Bach

Motivation

Acquisition ✓

E**X**tension ✓

Sensible Sentence Highlighting (or underlining) is a reading and study strategy that I created for myself when I was in college. Watching other people use highlighters in their books, I could never understand what logic was behind highlighting whole paragraphs, or even whole pages! When a person highlights a large section of text in that way, reviewing the reading will require rereading the entire highlighted passage. I knew that there must be a more economical way to highlight the material for a more efficient and economical review. I thought that there must be a way to do it so that the important concepts can be highlighted such that, upon review, they can be seen at a glance and still make clear sense.

Knowing that every paragraph is composed of a main idea and several elaborating details, it would seem that the key ideas are, in one way or another, repeated enough in the paragraph that a logical arrangement of terms could be identified such that, by highlighting only selected words, a thought could be expressed as a sentence (or pseudo-sentence) if the highlighted words were read in sequence. Furthermore, if it could be done for a paragraph, it could likely be done for a subsection of text containing several paragraphs. Figure 27-1 shows what it would look like for the paragraphs you have just finished reading.

As can be seen from Figure 27-1, the highlighted words clearly capture the key ideas from those two paragraphs. On reviewing the text by reading the highlighted terms in sequence, a reader is reminded of the whole context, even though it takes only moments to read a whole page this way. In fact, a person can reread an entire 4-500 page book in about 15 minutes if it has been highlighted this way—something that certainly cannot be done in a text that has had entire pages or whole paragraphs highlighted. The reader does not have to reread unnecessary amounts of text and decide a second time what is important and what is not so important. If an entire page is important because the reader wants to focus on all the details and presentation of that page, then you just run the highlighter down the side of the page, indicating that all the information is to be reviewed carefully.

Figure 27-1

Sensible Sentence Highlighting

Sensible Sentence Highlighting (or underlining) **is a** reading and study **strategy** that I created for myself when I was in college. Watching other people use highlighters in their books, I could never understand what logic was behind highlighting whole paragraphs, or even whole pages! When a person highlights a large section of text in that way, reviewing the reading will require rereading the entire highlighted passage. I knew that there must be a more economical way **to highlight** the material for a more efficient and economical review. I thought that there must be a way to do it **so** that the **important concepts can be** highlighted such that, upon review, they can be **seen at a glance and still make clear sense**.

Knowing that every paragraph is composed of a main idea and several elaborating details, it would seem that the **key ideas** are, in one way or another, repeated enough in the paragraph that a logical arrangement of terms could be **identified** such that, **by** highlighting only selected words, a thought could be expressed as a sentence (or pseudo-sentence) if the **highlighted words** were read **in sequence**. Furthermore, if it **could be done** for a paragraph, it could likely be done **for a subsection** of text containing several paragraphs. **Figure 27-1 shows** what it would look like for the paragraphs you have just finished reading.

Rereading only the highlighted words in the two paragraphs in Figure 27-1, one reads as follows:

"Sensible Sentence Highlighting is a strategy to highlight so important concepts can be seen at a glance and still make clear sense. Key ideas identified by highlighted words in sequence could be done for a subsection. 27-1 shows."

This form of review allows the reader to get the main idea and read massive quantities of text rapidly. This system is better than taking reading notes because, if necessary, the reader might stop to read more detail if something is not clear in review. The reader is already right there in the text. There is no need to hunt around for the right location to get more detail if the reader feels the need.

Why SSH Helps Students Learn New Subject Matter

This procedure can be used in a content area classroom to help students process new text. Obviously, a decision must be made by the teacher as to whether students can write in their textbooks. Many teachers teach this strategy in the last year of their textbook adoption process, knowing that the textbooks will be discarded at the end of the year. Other teachers use the process with duplicated materials so that they need not worry about writing in the book.

What this process does for students is it gives them clear and concrete purposes for reading the text. In order to do this highlighting properly, a student must practice metacognition. The student will actually be reading and rereading the text to make decisions about which terms to highlight. The result will be that the student really

Acquires the subject matter by the time s/he is finished with the reading! In addition, the student has Acquired, without even being aware of it, the ability to be metacognitive while reading---monitoring one's own comprehension while reading.

Sensible Sentence Highlighting/Underlining Procedure

Lifelong Learning Skill(s) to be Practiced During Learning:

- Comprehension monitoring while reading
- Paraphrasing text
- Creating a valuable study tool for review

Quick overview of Lesson:

1. This strategy requires some form of introductory activity such as a preview or a PreP before introduction of Sensible Sentence Highlighting (SSH).
2. Use a transparency to model SSH to create paraphrased sentences.
3. Allow students to practice highlighting/underlining to shorten the reading.
4. Students compare their newly created sentences with others in their cooperative groups by reading aloud only the highlights to others in their group.

Detailed version of lesson:

1. Ask students if they have ever wondered if there is another way, other than by taking notes, to effectively summarize lengthy passages of text for later reviewing. Let them know that what you are going to practice today is just such a system.

2. Use a preview of the text or some other means of preparing the students to read.

3. Explain that by either highlighting or underlining text, anyone can create a means of shortening the text to be reread for reviewing. Explain that the problem is deciding what should be highlighted and what should not. Explain that many studiers get carried away, and highlight entire pages — a practice that uses up a great deal of ink and, at the same time, leaves the student with the entire page to reread upon review — defeating the purpose of highlighting! Explain that a well-highlighted text highlights only key words that will jog the memory of the reader so that s/he will recall what was originally read.

4. Display on overhead transparency of the first page of the text to be read. Use overhead transparencies of some text that you have duplicated in advance for the students. A five to seven page reading is appropriate. You might use a section of the same textbook that you normally read in class. Be sure that students have a copy on which they can write without defacing their real textbooks. (I used to teach this technique using the textbook itself on the last year before adopting a new text.)

5. Tell students that they should focus on the overhead transparency as you read aloud to them. Read the first paragraph. Discuss what it said, noting the key idea. Go back and highlight terms that are key to the meaning of the main idea(s) and highlight them in such a way as to make sense if the highlighted words are read in sequence.

    For the above paragraph, it might look like this:

    Tell <u>students</u> that they should <u>focus on</u> the overhead <u>transparency</u> as you read aloud to them. <u>Read</u> the first paragraph. <u>Discuss</u> what it said, noting the <u>key idea</u>. Go back and <u>highlight</u> terms that are key to the meaning of the main idea(s) and highlight them in such a way as to <u>make sense</u> if the highlighted words are read <u>in sequence</u>.

6. Once they have seen you model the process with a page or two of text, doing a paragraph at a time, tell them that they are going to practice doing the same thing in their own reading that you have reproduced for them. Remind them that they must read, deciding on what is important, and how they might highlight it in such a way that they will be able to reread and get the main idea. Let them know that, once finished, they will read their highlights to others in their groups to share how they made sensible sentences out of the highlighted words.

7. As always, remind students that if they run across words or concepts that they are not able to comprehend, to raise a hand and you will come over to explain it to them. Move around the classroom to facilitate as students perform the reading and practice the skill.

8. After several minutes, have students compare their highlights with a partner or in small cooperative learning groups. Allow sufficient time to read aloud to one another what they have highlighted or to exchange papers and read each others' work. Have them make any additions or changes to their highlighting they desire at this time.

9. Identify one that is fairly well done and share it aloud with the rest of the class if you wish. This can be done by having the students of one group highlight a transparency page that you had prepared for this purpose for others to view. By seeing each others' work, students become more comfortable with the process.

10. Continue the process through the whole reading, having students read aloud only their highlights to one another in the end. Ask for a group to volunteer one of theirs that they think is particularly good at logically summarizing in the fewest words what the text said. Read it to the entire class. Ask students to report on the use of the skill. Ask them, "Did reading this way — attempting to find the main ideas and to make sensible sentence highlights — help you to improve your comprehension? Do you feel that you will be able to study well from these kinds of highlights? Tell students that you will have a quiz on the subject matter tomorrow, and that you will give them only two minutes to study before the quiz!

11. Continue eXtension beyond the text through a free-write, homework, a quiz, etc.

Extra Scaffolds

As in most activities in this book, the best scaffold is to do everything exactly the same for all students except when it comes to the silent reading phase, at which time, it is most appropriate for the teacher to read aloud to the students while they read along silently in the text. The teacher stops from time to time to allow students to process individually. This is very important in Sensible Sentence Highlighting since even the best readers go back over the paragraph to process how to organize the highlighting. thus, the teacher who reads aloud to students should give adequate time for them to go back and reread for highlighting purposes.

Chapter 28

Student-Generated Graphic Representation

Learning is what most adults will do for a living in the 21st century.
Bob Perelman

Motivation ✓

Acquisition ✓

e**X**tension ✓

Student Generated Graphic Representations of Text

When students construct their own graphic representations of difficult and complex text, they create visual images that show relationships that are often too difficult to visualize mentally. Students thus create concrete images of complex and often abstract ideas. They are able to see the relationships of ideas and focus on the vocabulary that is so important to understanding any subject area concept.

What Are Graphic Representations?

Graphic representations are visual summaries of prose text. There are many different forms that they may take — network trees, fishbone diagrams, compare and contrast matrices, spider maps, two-column organizers, three-column organizers, human interaction diagrams, and many others, including hybrid combinations of some of these (Jones, Pierce, & Hunter, 1988). They are collections of key vocabulary terms organized in a visual diagram that allows the viewer to see relationships between important words and ideas. A well-made graphic representation is a holistic picture that groups related terms to summarize text.

Figure 28-1: Nine Generic Graphic Representations

1. The Network Tree: Shows a hierarchy of related ideas. The main idea goes at the top, and subsidiary ideas go into the areas below. It can have many levels of subtopics stemming from the lower levels.

2. Spider Map: Shows main idea in the center and subsidiary ideas branching out from there.

Items to be compared/contrasted	Attribute A	Attribute B	Attribute C
Item 1			
Item 2			
Item 3			

3. The Compare & Contrast Matrix: Can be used to compare or to contrast the various attributes of several things, such as human cultures, plant types, rock types, bacteria types, etc.

4. The Cycle Graph: This can be used to show any cyclical pattern of events such as the life cycle of plants, the biological process of mitosis in cells, historical cycles of events, etc.

5. Series of Events Diagram: Can be used to show the sequence of events in history, in a chemical reaction, or any sequential pattern that might occur in a process of any kind.

6. The Continuum Scale: This graphic representation can be used to portray a time line, political orientation on a political spectrum from left wing to right wing, a number line, or anything that can be represented as a continuum.

7. Fishbone Diagram: Ribs identify factors that contribute to the result. The result could be an election outcome, the resolution of a story, a mathematical concept such as the product of two binomial expressions, or any other result of contributing factors.

8. Venn Diagram: This can be used to compare similarities and differences in two different things such as comparing schools today with schools 100 years ago. The similarities would go in the overlapping parts of the two circles. The characteristics of 100 years ago would go in the non-overlapping portion of one circle, and the characteristics unique to present schools would go in the non-overlapping part of the other circle.

Essential Characteristics	Non-essential Characteristics
Concept	
Examples	Non-examples

9. Frayer Model: The Frayer Model is a tool used to help students develop vocabulary and conceptual understandings. Students write a particular word in the middle of a box and proceed to list essential and non-essential attributes, examples, and non-examples.

Why Use Graphic Representations?

Graphic representations can help students to comprehend, summarize, and synthesize complex and difficult text passages (Jones, Pierce, & Hunter, 1988). Many teachers are not aware of the fact that graphic representations can become the primary purpose-setting tool for student reading of difficult and complex text. By helping students to see that text written by others can be deconstructed into a visual graphic that not only shows complex interrelationships of concepts from the text, but is also easy to study, teachers are helping to make difficult reading easier for students to handle. The systematic use of graphic representations for the purposes of motivating readers to tackle difficult text, acquiring new understandings, and extending beyond the text can be taught to students through actual use in processing textbook or other readings in the classroom. Students who practice reading this way will better learn the subject matter at the same time they are developing lifelong learning skills.

Teaching Students to Construct Graphic Representations

Teachers should follow a two-step process in teaching this to students. They should first model the process to familiarize students with the thinking that goes on in creating a graphic representation from text. In doing so, they should be willing to allow students to see the thinking that goes on in their (the teachers') own minds. They should, in other words, be prepared to think out loud as they model the process. It is OK to make mistakes, going back to change some of the understandings they originally make on the graphic they construct onto a chalkboard or on an overhead transparency. In fact, this modeling of thinking and hypothesizing about relationships is important for students to see. It is important that the teacher discuss procedural processes at this time, explaining to students why they organize things the way they do, and allowing student input as to how portions of the graphic relate to one another.

Second, teachers need to provide opportunities for students to work cooperatively to construct graphic representations with coaching by the teacher. It may be appropriate, when first introducing the concept, to lead a class discussion about selecting a particular graphic model for a reading. Then students, working in small teams of three or four, can work to construct a graphic representation from the reading they do. It is important that the format follow the cooperative learning format of individual written commitment on the part of each student, followed by small-group discussion to construct meaning, and then large-group discussion to clarify and extend the conversation beyond the text.

Lesson Plan: Using Graphic Representations to Read New Subject Matter

Once students are familiar with the process, the five steps of the lesson plan for constructing student-generated graphic representations are as follows:

1. Preview the text.
2. Each group of students cooperatively hypothesizes as to which graphic representation might best portray the content of text. (At first, students should have a set of generic graphic representations from which to choose. You may use the ones in Figure 28-1.)
3. Each student reads individually, gathering information on his/her own draft of the graphic representation the group has selected.

4. Small-groups meet again to discuss and construct meaning, and to agree on the format for assembly of a large poster-sized version of their graphic representation.
5. Student groups present to the class. (An alternative is for each student to write a summary.)

When student groups are presenting to the class, the teacher may ask any of the students who are part of the group to take over the presentation at any time. This encourages all members of a group to develop strong understandings in the earlier stages of the project and prevents one or two students in a group from doing all the work. Thus, the graphic representation process provides for each student to bring prior knowledge into consciousness before reading, read purposefully to acquire and organize new information, and then construct meaning cooperatively within the parameters of a small-group discussion. Each student has the opportunity to use prediction to set purposes for reading, and then to construct, individually at first, and then through cooperative sharing, the meaning of complex text. The group construction afterward is an opportunity for students to perform higher order thinking with the assistance of competent peers. When using this process, students tend to end up with superior understandings of relationships that no teacher could ever have given them through lecture or any other method. They have learned it on their own, in their own unique ways of perceiving.

Evolution of the Process throughout the School Year

At the beginning of the year, the teacher may want to be more involved in the process of creating a graphic representation as a class. Depending on the level of students in the class, they may need more or less help in first becoming acquainted with the process, but quickly, they will be able to do this in small groups.

Once students have been coached, as a full class, in selecting appropriate graphic representation models to represent prose text, they should be given more autonomy in selecting how to represent text. After the teacher has led a class discussion once or twice to select the graphic to be used by the whole class, it is time to let small groups determine how they wish to represent text.

Often, different groups within the same class will choose different ways of graphing the same information — and each of the methods they choose may be appropriate. I once had a world history class of 32 students work in small groups after the preview process to select graphic representations from several graphic models to which they had been exposed beforehand. They were preparing to read about four Middle Eastern civilizations over a 1500 year period from 2500 BC to 1000 BC. Different cooperative learning teams, working in groups of four, selected the graphic representation models they thought to be most appropriate. They ended up choosing five different models — and each was appropriate in its own way! After the reading, small-group discussions, and constructions of presentable models, they all learned from the other groups' presentations of how *they* had chosen to represent the same material differently.

Independent Learners

If students are not familiar with the process, you may wish to take charge of step two and lead the discussion of which graphic would be most appropriate for the reading that will take place. Advanced students, who show aptitude for the process, will require much less coaching than other students. As with all of these reading/writing activities, you must be the judge of how much autonomy to give them in class. Don't be afraid to put responsibility on students. They will rise to the occasion. It is worse to err on the side of not trusting that they can perform. In my experience, it has always been easier to back up and say, "I may have given you guys more than you can handle. Let me show you how you might have approached this." leading to modeling of the thought processes that would have aided them in thinking through the problem. Babying students and assuming that they cannot perform at a certain level is a real turnoff to many students. You will be surprised at how well most students do with graphic representation.

Use the generic graphic representations in Figure 28-1 to introduce your students to the concepts. Make a copy of the page for each student's notebook. Encourage students to be creative and design their own graphic representations once they are comfortable with the process.

Lifelong Learning Skill(s) to be Practiced During Learning:

- Previewing to determine probable structure of the text before reading
- Using prediction as a means of developing purposes for engaging in reading
- Reading critically to clarify interpretation of text
- Visually representing text
- Using key vocabulary terms to show important relationships

Quick Overview of Lesson:

1. Preview the text.
2. Students cooperatively hypothesize as to which graphic representation best might portray the content of text.
3. Students read individually to gather information for graphic representation.
4. Small-group discussion to discuss/agree on assembly of GR.
5. Student groups present to the class.

Detailed version of lesson:

1. Introduce the content of the reading by posing a hypothetical question, reading a quotation, previewing the text, or some other interest-capturing idea to which students can react through discussion.

---

2. Discuss the skill of visually representing text as a tool for interpreting complex ideas and their relationships. Show how the textbook has done this by referring to some graphic representations in your text, or refer to a graphically-represented concept on the wall of the classroom. Show how you or someone else has already used a form of graphic representation.

---

3. Model the way a strategic reader might look at a passage of text, see a probable format for visually representing the passage, and use it to create both the purpose for reading and also as a tool for organizing the content during and after reading. You might refer to a reading the class had done very recently to show how the thinking might have occurred prior to the reading, and then during the reading. (This gives you a chance to review recent learning even while you are introducing a new skill.)

4. Explain to students that, for today's reading, we are going to preview the text, discuss possible ways of graphically representing the passage, and then read, silently and individually, to gather information to be included in a personal draft of a graphic representation. Explain that after some time to read, we will get into groups to compare our interpretations of the passage, and to create a group-version of a graphic representation of the text. Explain why strategic readers benefit from both parts of the process — previewing to determine text structure — and reorganizing the reading's main ideas visually for easy reference.

5. Lead students through a careful preview process.

6. Pass out copies of the generic graphic representations from Figure 28-1. Allow students to discuss with their group to determine which graphic representation might best fit the information contained in the passage they are about to read.

   (The first few times, the teacher might want to conduct a classroom-sized discussion to make sure that students understand the process of interpreting what was learned in the preview to create an appropriate structure. It is equally important, *after* the first few times, to allow the students a good deal of leeway in selecting their own format for representing the text. Allowing students to see how others have chosen to represent the same passage in a different way can be helpful in constructing meaning from the text in the present circumstance as well as in future ones.)

   Move around the room to facilitate the discussions of the various groups. Some groups will need more help than others, especially the first few times they try this activity. However, it is important that students be allowed to be creative. Some, for instance, may want to create a "hybrid" form of graphic, combining the characteristics of two or more of the generic forms. Assist in the logic used, but allow for creativity. (Your main job at this point is to make sure that no group chooses something that is inappropriate to represent the text.)

7. Once each group has decided upon which format it will use, tell students that now is the time to read. Remind them that each student is reading to create a personal "draft" of the graphic representation in the format of the one their group has decided upon. Then, when they are finished, the group members will compare notes on their individual drafts, discussing the best way to assemble a final draft. Allow adequate time for most students to complete the reading. It is important at this time that the room is quiet, with all students reading silently, making notes for later sharing. The teacher should model by reading the same passage while students do so. The teacher should move quietly around the room while reading, stopping to quietly assist any students who might have questions or comprehension problems, and to observe the progress of individual students as they gather information.

8. When about three quarters of the students have completed the reading, allow the groups to again come together, this time to agree on the final draft of each group's graphic representation. (Remind those who have not finished the reading that they should be able to finish it for homework. Some will continue to read even while their group discusses. It is OK if they elect to do so.) Allow for each group to have access to large paper and markers for production of a large final product to be presented to the rest of the class. Move around to facilitate this. Tell students that they are responsible for describing to the class, and defending their group's representation of the information. Also, you may wish to allow some movement of students around the classroom to see what others are doing. Often, this is an important part of the learning experience. The teacher's job at this point is to see that students are on task, help students through disagreements, and generally facilitate the thinking that is occurring in the classroom. Typically, this is a fairly noisy period of time — yet very productive — since students are helping one another to construct meaning from the text. (Have an activity for groups that finish well before others. This could be writing a summary of the passage, writing a cinquain, etc. This will help in classroom management.)

9. Once each group has completed the graphic representation, the products should be posted for all to see. Each group should present its own justification for its method of representing the information. (You may wish to select which person is the presenter for each group. You may also change the presenter from one student to another during the presentation process. By telling students you will do this before they even begin constructing their finished product, they will all have more incentive to stay on task and participate in the process.)

10. Ask students to report on their use of the skill of graphically representing text. Ask them to raise their hand if they felt that the process enhanced their ability to comprehend and remember what they have read. Remind them that skilled readers often use graphic representations as pre-writing tools. (You may wish to tell them that the ones they have created today will remain on the wall during the upcoming test that will include an essay on the topic about which they have read today. Later during the school year you might wish to give extra credit to students who use a graphic representation as a pre-writing tool when taking a test. This helps them in two ways — in systematic planning for their writing — and in receiving an extra few points for the effort.)

11. Remind students that they can use graphic representations in any class, to learn any subject matter.

12. Assign a homework assignment that allows for reflection on what was learned in the reading. This could be writing a summary (which some had started in class) or it could be in the form of some kind of note taking exercise.

Extra Scaffolds

The major additional scaffolds for this procedure are four:

- providing direction in selecting appropriate graphic representations for specific text
- providing partially filled in graphics for students to complete
- directing whole-class discussion to create a graphic representation
- reading aloud to students from the text, pausing from time to time to conduct discussion regarding the development of the graphic representation.

Especially near the beginning of the year, the teacher who uses this lesson plan to help students process text should lead the preview process from the front of the classroom, and then assist students in deciding, as a class, which graphic representations would be appropriate to use to reorganize the information in the reading. Most low-performing readers have little concept of structure in text. By leading the discussion on structure as a part of the preview process, the teacher allows students to develop a sense of how to identify structure, and to recognize the various structures that they might confront in text.

Modeling identification of structure is best done while previewing or immediately after previewing. I like to use an overhead projector to "think aloud" as I shape the structure as I see it. Sometimes, I even make mistakes! On those occasions, I make adjustments to the structure as needed. This process of thinking aloud while thinking through a complex process such as creating graphic representations is useful for students who have done most of their school work with dry, boring, and less-than-stimulating worksheets that required little or no thinking.

Providing partially-filled-out graphic representations makes it much easier for students to identify patterns in the text. However, as soon as they are able to do so, groups of students ought to be given the opportunity (with support of the teacher) to make some decisions regarding selection of graphic representation. One way to begin this process is to provide two or more partially-filled-out graphic representations, each of which is appropriate for the text to be read. This will give students a sense that there is more than one correct way of doing it.

All students can benefit from "deconstructing" the text by creating graphic representations of what they read. Even though some students may, at first, need more help from the teacher, they will all benefit from the process — knowing more about the content of the lesson as well as more about the organizational skills of writing.

Chapter 29

Think-Pair-Share

In the course of your work, you will from time to time encounter the situation where the facts and the theory do not coincide. In such circumstances, young gentlemen, it is my earnest advice to respect the facts.
Igor Stravinsky

Motivation ✓

Acquisition

e**X**tension ✓

Think-Pair-Share (TPS) is a very engaging activity that follows the paradigm of cooperative learning that has been the method used in virtually all of the activities in this text. Effective cooperative learning follows the pattern of first, individual written commitment on the part of each student, second, and attempt at small-group consensus, and third, large-group discussion seeking consensus. The focus in this activity is that TPS is very rapid, and may be used either in the pre-reading phase or post-learning phase of class.

TPS is a very structured way to engage students cooperatively to simultaneously develop and assess their understanding of a topic. It is useful for grammar, vocabulary, concept development, mathematical practice, or whatever learning that you wish to either assess or develop through practice with immediate feedback. The best thing about it is that it takes little or no time to prepare to use it, yet it is a powerful tool to help students understand concepts about which they have read or learned.

As in any cooperative learning activity, TPS works best if the groups are heterogeneous in nature. I sometimes go from individual work to paired comparison to foursomes with two pairs comparing notes on their answers. On other occasions, I go from individual to pair to whole-class sharing. How you do it will depend on the nature of the task and how much time you have.

218

Think-Pair-Share Procedure

Lifelong Learning Skill(s) to be Practiced During Learning:

- Cooperation in solving problems
- Analysis, synthesis, and application of subject matter ideas after reading

Quick Overview of the Lesson:

1. Teacher poses problem and individuals attempt to solve.
2. Individual students compare notes with partners—attempting to resolve differences if any exist.
3. Partnerships compare notes with larger group.

Materials:

- Pencil
- Paper
- Brain

Detailed version of lesson:

1. You may use this activity either to assess and to build student knowledge before a learning experience or to assess, practice and apply the learning after the learning experience. The first step is to have students heterogeneously grouped.

2. Explain to students that they need to have paper and pencil in order to do this. Suggest that what we are about to do is to find out how much you know about…(whatever your topic is)

3. Explain the process by saying, "I have you partnered with another student with whom you will compare answers. I am going to pose a problem, and you are to write your answer on your own paper. When I say, "Now, compare." you should compare what you have written with what your partner has written. If you have the same answers, raise your hands to let me know. If you have different answers, explain to each other why you think you are correct, and make a decision, if possible as to who is right, and why. If, after that discussion, you have the same answers, raise your hands."

4. Either pose orally, write on the chalkboard, or assign from the text, a single problem relating to what should have been learned. Tell students to "do this on your own, without looking at your neighbor's paper or discussing it with your neighbor."

5. Move around the room, looking over students' shoulders, giving positive encouragement for attempting to solve the problem. Do this briskly. Depending on the nature of the problem, you might have as little as five seconds to do this, or you might have 30 seconds to a minute or more.

6. When you feel that students are ready (not necessarily when they all have solved the problem), tell them, "Now, compare notes with your partner." Allow sufficient time for this. Watch to see how many hands go up to show agreement.

7. At this point, depending on how you had explained the process before you started, you might ask a partnership to share with the whole class, or you might say, "Now compare notes with your other partnership." (pre-assigned by the teacher).

8. When groups are ready, poll a group to see if they have a correct answer. If others have the same answer, they have learned the concept. If there are problems, you have the teachable moment.

9. Repeat steps 4-8 as often as required, or as time permits.

10. Continue eXtension through Cornell Note Taking, Cubing, homework, a quiz, etc.

Extra Scaffolds

The major scaffold that a teacher might add to Think-Pair-Share (a scaffold in itself) is to become a temporary partner in some of the groups as they perform the activity.

Chapter 30

Stump The Teacher

It is important that students bring a certain ragamuffin, barefoot, irreverence to their studies; they are not here to worship what is known, but to question it.
Jacob Bronowski

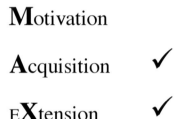

Motivation

Acquisition ✓

e**X**tension ✓

Stump the Teacher/Stump the Student is a name that I have given to an activity known as ReQuest (Manzo, 1969) which stands for reciprocal questioning. This is one of the most motivating of all the activities in this book. Like any activity in this book, if a teacher uses it too frequently, it gets old. That is one reason why I recommend to teachers that they use a wide variety of classroom activities to help students acquire content and skills. This activity, however, is one that is very motivating even to the lowest performing readers in your class.

"Stump the Teacher" needs to be preceded by some **M**otivation-stage activity such as a preview of the text to be read. Once ready to read, the teacher explains the process, and all classroom participants read the text silently to think of questions that might stump the other side of this equation. The teacher reads, and the students read. Both focus on a small segment of text, usually one to two pages. Then the teacher closes the book, and students leave theirs open and begin to quiz the teacher for a pre-set time segment. (I often use either two or three minutes, timed with a timer on my watch.) As students pose questions through raising a hand to be recognized, the point is for them to ask a question that the teacher might not be able to answer correctly. I usually award a few, but significant amount of, bonus points (usually five) on the next test as a reward if a student asks a question that I am not able to answer correctly. (After all, I went to college to learn this stuff!)

Once the timer goes off, the students close *their* books, and I get to pose questions of *them*. However, there is no penalty for a wrong answer; only positive rewards for contributing to a correct answer. I usually award one bonus point to the responding student for each correct contribution at this phase of the activity since it is easy to contribute some small part of a more complex answer, and many students usually will contribute something to the answer of any one question that I ask.

Student behavior in this activity usually follows a set pattern. Once the task is understood, and it is time to read, students will read carefully to attempt to find something that the teacher might not get. The result is that they read fairly thoroughly. But, they don't stop there. Once the teacher has closed the textbook, the students continue to have theirs open. Even students who do not consider themselves readers, and who are not normally motivated to participate in academic work, will continue to pore over the text looking for remote ideas and facts that the teacher might not be able to recall. The result is that students who otherwise never read, except to "hunt for answers" on worksheets, pore over the text seeking the remotest ideas. The result is that they learn the subject matter through reading!

It gets better, though. Once students have their books closed, during the second timed questioning period in which the teacher poses questions of the students, the teacher asks higher order thinking questions. (I always ask analysis, synthesis, application, and evaluation questions of the students.) But the teacher never puts one student on the spot to create an embarrassing situation. The teacher just offers up the question, and students volunteer contributions to the answer. *Collectively, the class constructs meaning from the text.* Normally, several students each earn one or more points for this behavior. The level of participation is very high, and all students "stay tuned" during this because of the motivating nature of the activity.

The activity is repeated as the class works through a section of text, and is usually followed by some other eXtension activity such as a Focused Free Write or Cubing or Two-Column Note Taking. Stump the Teacher is an activity that I use once every two to three weeks, and its primary focus is to learn new subject matter, not as a review of already learned substance.

One career/technical teacher that I know tells the story of his recent experiences with this activity in his classroom. For the first eleven years of this teacher's career, he had struggled with getting his students to read his textbook at all. Two years ago, this teacher began to use content literacy instruction to engage his students in reading for learning in his classroom. He reports that the change has been phenomenal, and one of the strategies that he reports to be responsible for the success is Stump the Teacher. He described to me one recent occasion in which students were quite frustrated that they were not able to "stump" him throughout an entire reading. He mentioned to them that he planned to do the same activity the next day. *Even though he assigned no homework, several of his students took the book home and read ahead into the next chapter just so they could stump him! They were successful too!*

Stump the Teacher/Stump the Students Reading Procedure

Lifelong Learning Skill(s) to be Practiced During Learning:

- Comprehension monitoring while reading
- Studying with a study buddy
- Higher-order Thinking

Quick Overview of the Lesson:

1. This lesson requires a Motivation activity. Using a Preview or PreP procedure is good. Any quality anticipatory activity can suffice.
2. Explain the format for the game.

3. Silent reading of a portion of text.
4. Students quiz teacher whose book is closed for a set time period.
5. Teacher asks questions of students whose books are closed for a set time.
6. Repeat steps 3-5.
7. Further eXtension can be done through note taking, etc.

Materials Required:

- Textbook
- Timer

Detailed version of lesson:

1. Introduce the content of the reading by posing a hypothetical question, reading a quotation, previewing the text, or some other interest-capturing idea to which students can react through discussion. A preview is ideal.

2. Introduce the skill of studying with a friend. Suggest, "What we are going to practice in here today is a study strategy that someone might use if that person has a 'study buddy' with whom to work." Point to a student near to you, and say, "If you and I were study buddies, we might say to one another, 'Let's read this whole first page, and then, let's take turns closing the book and quizzing each other about what we have read.' This is what we are going to do in this classroom today, only we are going to make kind of a game of it. We are going to play 'stump the teacher; stump the student. We are going to do, as a class, what two study buddies might do working together in a college dormitory or on the job to help each other learn."

3. Explain the nature of Stump the Teacher, assigning a reading of appropriate length (I like to use from one to three pages, depending on the complexity of the text.). Tell students, "We are all going to read this same piece of text, and after we have had sufficient time to read this passage, I will give you X minutes (I usually use 2-3 minutes.) to quiz me on this. If you can stump me — if I cannot get the answer right, even though my book is closed and yours is open, the person who posed the question will receive X points (I usually use 5 points; after all, I went to college to learn this stuff, and I am hard to stump.) on the next test. Ask for a person to volunteer to be the scorekeeper. Give a several-point award for doing that. Let students know how much time they will have to quiz you, explaining that when the time is up, they will close *their* books, and you will open *yours* to ask *them* questions for the same duration of time. Mention to them that they may not ask questions like, "How many words are in the third paragraph?" or "How many times does the word 'the' appear in the passage?" Let them know that they must ask questions about the content of the reading. Remind students that you will be reading at the same time they are.

4. Remind them again of the size of the subsection of the text. Make a decision as to what amount of time is appropriate for the questioning period to follow the reading. (If the time does not work well first period, try a bit more or less second block.) Allow sufficient time for most students to read the passage.

5. When most students have finished, close your book and set the timer for the amount of time allotted for student questions. Remind students that your book is closed and that they may keep theirs open, and that they may ask questions by raising a hand to be recognized. Begin taking questions. (Keep in mind that you will not get them all correct. Expect to give out a few points. Also keep in mind that here is your chance to really clarify some ideas about your subject matter with a completely rapt audience!) The first few times you do this activity, expect questions that are primarily literal in nature. Students will ask about the details from pictures, graphs, etc. You will get quite good at remembering everything that is on the page (especially by third block). Eventually, you may wish to have students improve the nature of their questions by using the "Question Mark" bookmark (Appendix 6) for quality questions. But don't add that complication the first time or two.

6. When their questioning time has expired, tell students that now, they must close their books, and that you will pose questions of them. Again, they must raise their hands and be recognized in order for their answers to count. They may not just yell answers out. Let them know that a partially correct answer may still be awarded a point. Now — begin by posing a question that is of a nature as to get them thinking. (In fact, now is the chance to get them to perform higher order thinking over the subject matter!) I almost always begin with an "analysis" question—saying, "Let's analyze this. What was this all about? Can someone paraphrase the passage by putting it in your own words?" If a student gives a partial answer, say "That's worth a point, but can anyone add to it?" Gradually, students will cooperatively reconstruct the passage without realizing that they are doing so. (Everyone learns from this activity.)

7. Continue while your time remains to ask higher order thinking questions such as "How does what we just read relate to what we studied in the last chapter?" (synthesis) or "What would you predict would happen if …?" (application) or "Do you agree that…?" (You should use the Appendix 6 bookmark to assist you in asking higher order thinking questions.)

8. Continue through the reading, doing a portion of the text at a time. (Alternative process: You may alter the order of who closes the book first after the reading. The first portion of the text, the teacher closes the book first for three minutes, followed by the students closing the book. Then the students—with the second portion of the reading—close the book first, and so on until the reading is done.)

9. After the reading is complete, ask students to report on their use of the skill. Say, "By a show of hands, how many of you felt that the process of reading to ask questions of me, and to remember with the book closed when it was your turn, actually helped you to comprehend what the passage was about?" (Students inevitably realize at this point that, by practicing both the questioning of the teacher and the reading to remember with the book closed, they were engaged in the reading, leading to heightened comprehension.)

10. Now you should proceed to another eXtension activity such as a focused free write or practice in two-column note taking about the same text passage. (This could also be homework.)

11. Continue reflection through homework, a quiz, etc.

Extra Scaffolds

As in most of the activities in this book, the principal scaffold to assist low performing readers with the task of constructing meaning from the text is for the teacher to read aloud to the students while they read along silently. If this is done before the teacher closes the book, it allows students to immediately reprocess the text silently while the teacher's book is closed.

Chapter 31

Three-Level Study Guides

Man's mind stretched to a new idea never goes back to its original dimensions.
Oliver Wendell Holmes, Jr.

Motivation

Acquisition ✓

E**X**tension ✓

Three-Level Study Guides (Herber, 1970) are very similar, in some ways, to anticipation guides. They are composed of a list of statements to which students react during and after the reading of some piece of text. Therein lies the chief difference: though it is sometimes useful to have students anticipate the reading through the anticipatory reading of 3-level guides, just as if they were anticipation guides, in most cases, they are better used during and after the reading. Thus, they are **A**cquisition and E**X**tension level activities, and require some pre-reading **M**otivation activity to start the lesson. (I usually use a preview of the reading.)

Three-Level Study Guides are made up of statements that relate to the reading. Students, as they do with anticipation guides, read to find evidence that proves or disproves the statements. The three different levels are composed of statements that the teacher has arranged into the three categories of "literal interpretation," "inferential interpretation," and "synthesis or application level interpretation" of what is being read. Appendix 3 has several 3-level study guides as examples.

By using these guides, students are explicitly empowered to perform higher order thinking. Once explained to students, they know that it is OK to think outside of the lines in the text. They knowingly stretch their interpretation, with the knowledge that the teacher is encouraging this behavior. Unfortunately, this is the opposite of what is normally expected in many classrooms. All too much effort is placed on listening to how the teacher interprets what is important, or looking for answers to place in spaces on worksheets, all at the literal level of interpretation.

To make a three-level study guide, Richardson & Morgan (2003) recommend creating level-two statements first, then looking back through the text to find level-one statements that can point students in the direction of discovery of the ideas in level two, and finally adding level-three statements to help students to think beyond the text. In creating level-two statements, I find that the methods mentioned in chapter 10 of this book for making anticipation guides are helpful. Each statement is a plausible rephrasing of a key idea in the text, and you want to provoke thoughtful discussion and/or argument.

I recommend using three different pieces of paper, each labeled 1, 2, or 3. Have them on the desk while reading the piece of text you are planning to use with the students. As you read, focus on level two, but jot down statements on any of the three sheets of paper that represent each of the three levels of thinking. It is easier to do it this way because they do not always appear in the sequence you wish. Literal statements are the easiest because you are taking the statements pretty much from the text.

Level two statements involve "reading between the lines." They are inferential statements — those things that you would like students to infer from the reading if they were really accomplished readers, but you know they would not probably spot those things on their own.

Level three statements are your opportunity to apply what you know about Bloom's Taxonomy. These involve "reading beyond the lines." Level three statements get students to have to extend beyond the text by performing thinking that has them synthesize, apply, analyze, or argue. At this level, you might make statements that relate the reading to what was learned in the previous chapter or something in the news. It is also good to use famous adages at level three.

Using three-level study guides is one more way to get students to perceive themselves as persons who can and do perform higher order thinking over what they read. Again, the keys to accomplishing this are the concrete props of the text and the 3-level study guide that the teacher has constructed to facilitate the process.

Classroom Procedures for Three-Level Study Guides

Lifelong learning skill(s) to be discussed with students and practiced during the process:

- Reading critically to clarify interpretation of text
- Thinking at the literal, inferential, and application/synthesis level

Materials:

- 3-level guides — one per student,
- Textbook or other reading,
- Transparency of 3-level guide

Quick Overview of lesson:

1. Motivation activity to start discussion — PreP, fact storm, Previewing, etc.
2. Introduction of thinking at three levels
3. Silent reading, seeking evidence for interpretations
4. Discuss — small groups
5. Discuss — whole class

Detailed version of lesson:

1. Capture the students' interest. Introduce the content of the reading by posing a hypothetical question, reading a quotation, previewing the text, or some other interest-capturing idea to which students can briefly react through discussion.

2. Introduce the skill of thinking at three levels. It is a good idea at this point to model thinking at three levels by doing so on a topic that was recently covered in class. This can also bring students up to pace with a brief review. Show students how, after reading a paragraph or two, you literally interpret what it says. Then show how you might infer a meaning into it. Then think out loud about how it might apply in the real world. Let them know that this is the way they will be thinking concerning today's reading, but that you have helped them do so by separating the statements on the three-level study guide into the three levels of thinking.

3. Ask students to scan the statements on the study guide to see what they are about. Tell them that, unlike an anticipation guide, they do not have to check the statements they think to be true ahead of time. Instead, they will do so during or after the reading. Allow a few moments to scan the 3-level guide.

4. Explain to students that, for today's reading, we are going to use a different type of study guide to help us comprehend the reading, so we can practice what strategic readers routinely do to make reading more understandable. Tell them that the three-level study guide has many statements on it, and that some of the statements will have evidence in the textbook that supports them, some will have evidence that negates them, and some may have evidence that is conflicting, and about which students will probably argue.

5. Students should begin individual silent reading at this time. Remind them that they should keep the three-level guide on the desk for reference while they read, and that they ought to use all levels of thinking while they read. Tell them that they must interpret what they are reading in order to determine whether a statement should be checked or not, and that they must be able to refer to specific parts of the text to verify their beliefs. It is good to have students list page-column-paragraph notations under the statements they wish to verify or refute. (Their notations might look something like this: 251-2-4, meaning that information to support or negate a particular statement can be found on page 251, column two, paragraph four.) Move around the room to monitor progress and support students in their work. It is also good at this point to read silently along with the students, with the goal in mind that you may later need to model some of the thinking that goes into thinking at the different levels.

6. When most students have finished reading, tell them to get into their small groups to discuss the three-level guide, attempting to come to a consensus within their groups about whether a statement should be checked or not. Here, they compare their various interpretations of what they have read, referring to evidence in the text to support those interpretations. Move around the room to assist in this process, making sure that students are referring to the text to support their opinions. Allow several minutes for the discussions to occur.

7. When at least one group has come to a consensus on the three-level study guide statements, use their decisions to conduct a whole-class discussion to attempt to achieve a classroom consensus. Make sure that students are able to support their beliefs either through direct reference to the text or through their interpretation of specific text. It is very important during this phase of the lesson that the teacher act as a mediator or arbitrator, avoiding telling students answers. Intellectual ownership must be in the minds of the students as they collectively construct meaning from the text. Near the beginning of the year, some teacher modeling of higher order thinking and reading might be necessary, but students will quickly take ownership of the process, and they will surprise you with their thoroughness of analysis.

8. Ask students to report on their use of the skill of thinking at three levels. Say — did the process of thinking at literal, inferential, and application/synthesis levels help you to comprehend what you read more than when you are doing a worksheet? Did it help you focus and stay focused while you were reading? (Students inevitably realize at this point that, by practicing higher order thinking while reading, they were engaged in the reading, leading to heightened comprehension.)

9. Take the opportunity to review and reinforce the use of the skill of thinking while reading. Point out to students that they can use the skill of thinking at the literal, inferential, and application levels in any reading that they do in any subject area to engage themselves, make the reading more interesting by setting a purpose for reading, and by keeping that purpose in mind during the reading.

10. Continue reflection through a free-write, homework, a quiz, etc.

Extra Scaffolds

The extra scaffolds for 3-Level Study Guides are the same as those used with anticipation guides (P. 107). In addition, if the teacher chooses to read aloud to the students, s/he should stop from time to time to discuss whether any information has been cited that would cause students to be able to prove or disprove any of the statements *in any of the three levels* of the guide.

Chapter 32

Pre/Post-learning Concept Checks

Personally I am always ready to learn, although I do not always like being taught.
Winston Churchill

Motivation ✓

Acquisition

E**X**tension ✓

The Pre-Learning or Post-Learning Concept Check (Richardson & Morgan, 2003) is simply a list of terms that are important to the day's reading. Students are asked to react to the terms before the reading has taken place, and again, after the reading. The number of terms included may range from two to ten or more, depending on the type of reading and the level of students in the class. It is a fairly simple activity that, nevertheless, has a tremendous impact on how well students learn new vocabulary terms that are important to understanding the content of a particular reading. I frequently use it along with one or more other content literacy activities. A typical class might include a pre-learning concept check, a preview, paired reading, a post-learning concept check and a focused free write that is focused on using the terms that were in the concept check.

There are many benefits to using these concept checks. One is the fact that it is a low-threat way to find out how much students know about a topic before they begin the learning experience. It takes almost no classroom time to do. Another advantage is that it gets students focused on key terms without necessarily knowing what those terms mean yet. After the reading, it can be used as a writing prompt for reflecting on what was learned in the class that day; all this from an activity that takes at most one to two minutes of class time.

This activity is usually done on the students' own paper. The teacher simply walks into the classroom, writes five or six terms onto the chalkboard (as in figure 32-1), and asks students to copy the terms onto their own paper. Then the teacher asks students to rate themselves on the terms as to how well they know the words. Later, the students are referred back to their papers in order to, once again, rate themselves on the same words. The result is that students see their own progress. They see themselves as responsible for their own learning, and they see how the words relate to the overall topic of the day.

FIGURE 32-1

Pre- & Post-Learning Concept Check

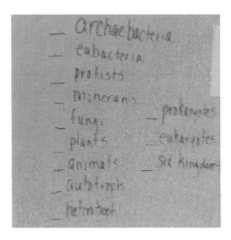

Pre/Post-Learning Concept Check Procedure

Lifelong Learning Skill(s) to be Practiced During Learning:

Focusing on key vocabulary before reading new materials
Self-monitoring of comprehension of terms

Quick overview of Lesson:

1. Students copy several key terms onto their own paper.
2. Students use a symbol system to rate themselves on the terms, making marks on the left side of each term.
3. The learning experience takes place with other activities involving reading/writing to learn.
4. Students refer back to the list they made, rating themselves a second time on the right-hand side of the terms.
5. Often, more eXtension takes place in the form of writing.

Detailed Version of the Lesson:

1. Write several key terms on the chalkboard (or on an overhead transparency) for students to copy onto their own paper. (When I have more than six or seven terms, I usually type them up ahead of time to save valuable classroom time.)

2. Have students get out a piece of paper, and have them copy the terms onto their paper near the top of the page. Tell them that you have written key vocabulary words on the chalkboard, and that what you are doing is to help you find out how much they know about the important words and ideas from today's lesson.

3. Move around the classroom to see that they are copying the words. When most of the students are finished copying the terms, tell students to place a little space right to the left of each of the terms. (Do this yourself on the chalkboard. Make little blank spaces to the left of the terms you have written on the board.)

4. Now tell students that you are going to ask them to rate themselves as to their knowledge of these key words. Tell them you just need to find out how well they already know the words. Ask them to use one of the three symbols, a plus (+), a check (✓), or a zero (0) in the space to the left of each of the words.

5. Write on the chalkboard the following three items so that students can see them

+ = expert

✓ = heard of it

0 = do not know it

Explain that a plus sign means that you consider yourself an expert on the term—you could explain the term to any other person in this classroom, and that person would then know what it means—in other words, you could *teach* it.

Explain that a check means that you have heard of it, but you do not consider yourself an expert on the term.

Explain that a zero means that you do not yet know the word or term.

6. Ask students to rate themselves on the terms. Move around the room to see what they are writing. Mention to them that "This is good news to me; there is room for learning in here."

7. Mention to students that, once we are finished with the learning experience, we will come back to these terms to rate ourselves one more time. This time, we will rate ourselves on the *right-hand* side of the terms.

8. Now go about the learning experience. This could include any of a number of activities.

9. Once the learning experience—**M**otivation, **A**cquisition, and e**X**tension has occurred, again have students rate themselves on the list of terms—this time, on the right side of the words. Again, move around the classroom to see how the students report their progress.

10. If appropriate, and time permits, e**X**tend further by using the terms for a writing exercise such as a focused free write.

Extra Scaffolds

One could read aloud the terms in this exercise. Another scaffold is to have students meet in small groups to discuss the terms before they mark their knowledge assessments.

Appendix 1

Daily Lesson Plan Format

DAILY LESSON PLAN: TOPIC _____ DATE _____

OBJECTIVES:

MATERIALS:

KEY VOCAB. TERMS:

MOTIVATION:

ACQUISITION:

eXTENSION:

Appendix 2

Selected Anticipation Guides

The anticipation guides included here are examples from many different disciplines. If you wish to view more anticipation guides visit **http://www.maxteaching.com** and click on the term "Anticipation Guides" at the bottom of the home page. The best anticipation guides are those that you make yourself, but it is hoped that you can see from these the kinds of statements that will lead to sound understandings of course content. (Note that in foreign language classes the guides can be made in English for less experienced students preparing to read in the target language, or they can be in the language for advanced students.)

Anticipation Guide : Automobile Charging Systems

Name_____ Date _____

Before reading pages 63-71: In the space to the left of each statement, place a check mark (✓) if you agree or think the statement is true.

During or after reading: Add new check marks or cross through those about which you have changed your mind. Keep in mind that this is not like the traditional "worksheet." You may have to put on your thinking caps and "read between the lines." Use the space under each statement to note the page(s), column(s), and paragraph(s) where you are finding information to support your thinking.

_____1. The charging system has four parts, and it usually supplies all needed current to the system when the engine is running.

_____2. The generator rotor turns at about the same number of revolutions as the crankshaft.

_____3. The output of the generator is in AC current.

_____4. It would be fairly easy to build an electrical generator from scratch if you had a magnet and a few other items.

_____5. The output of a generator increases as the speed of the engine increases.

_____6. A charge indicator light that is on may be an indication that either the voltage is low, or that the voltage is too high.

_____7. Power is generated by a magnetic field cutting across near a group of conductors, and the amount of power generated depends on the strength of the magnetic field.

_____8. The electrical current that is produced in a generator is passed out of the generator through spinning brushes that are touching a rotating ring to receive the current.

_____9. There is an important reason why two diodes are used for each phase winding of the stator.

_____10. A generator can ruin the car's electrical system.

_____11. The voltage produced by an electrical generating system is not smooth, but modern systems have several components to smooth out the voltage ripple that might occur.

Anticipation Guide for *Mendel's Laws of Heredity (pp. 259-268)*

Name_____ **Date**_____

Before reading: In the space to the left of each statement, place a check mark (✔) if you agree or think the statement is true.

During or after reading: Add new check marks or cross through those about which you have changed your mind. Keep in mind that this is not like the traditional "worksheet." You may have to put on your thinking caps and "read between the lines." Use the space under each statement to note the page, column, and paragraph(s) where you are finding information to support your thinking.

____1. Garden pea plant reproduction is similar to human reproduction – both involve gametes.

____2. You can tell the genotype of a plant from its phenotype.

____3. Everyone in this classroom is a hybrid, but no one here is a monohybrid.

____4. Whenever you cross a tall pea plant with another tall pea plant, you will get a tall plant as a result.

____5. There is a clear mathematical relationship between the appearances of genetic traits such as height, color, and size in offspring.

____6. If your grandfather had red hair, and your mother and father both have brown hair, and your hair is red, then you have a recessive gene inherited from your grandparent.

____7. Mendel developed ways to prevent chance cross-pollination so he could observe the genetic nature of the reproductive process.

____8. Trihybrid plants are those that differ from each other in three or more traits.

____9. Monohybrid crosses have different Punnett squares than dihybrid crosses.

____10. Mating two plants that are heterozygotic will lead to the same results each time the experiment is conducted – a three to one ratio of the dominant trait.

____11. There is no way for you to find out if the single pea plant you have in front of you at any given time is homozygous or heterozygous.

____12. Gregor Mendel must have been one lonely guy.

Anticipation Guide : Turbulent Centuries in Africa

Name_____ Date_____

Before reading pages 398-402: In the space to the left of each statement, place a check mark (✓) if you agree or think the statement is true.

During or after reading: Add new check marks or cross through those about which you have changed your mind. Keep in mind that this is not like the traditional "worksheet." You may have to put on your thinking caps and "read between the lines." Use the space under each statement to note the page(s), and paragraph(s) where you are finding information to support your thinking.

____1. Most of the Africans who were captured and sold as slaves between the years 1500 and 1870 were shipped to North America to support tobacco, sugar, and cotton plantations.

____2. The Portuguese were the first traders to participate in the trade of human beings.

____3. Greed makes people take advantage of other people for their own profit.

____4. Fifty percent of Africans shipped across the Atlantic Ocean never made it to the new world.

____5. First Arabs, then Portuguese, then Spanish, and then English and other Europeans bought and sold African slaves in the new world of the Americas.

____6. African rulers supported the slave trade.

____7. There were similarities between many African kingdoms and those of Europe during the period from 1600 to 1800.

____8. If the triangular trade never had been established, both Africa and America would have been very different today than they are.

____9. Many Africans became converted to the Muslim religion in the past few hundred years.

____10. Technology was a major factor in the defeat of Africans in South Africa.

____11. If Africans had not fought so much among themselves, they might not have lost so much of their land and people to Europeans.

Anticipation Guide : Digestion Problems

Name_____ **Date**_____

Before reading pages 118-120: In the space to the left of each statement, place a check mark (✓) if you agree or think the statement is true.

During or after reading: Add new check marks or cross through those about which you have changed your mind. Keep in mind that this is not like the traditional "worksheet." You may have to put on your thinking caps and "read between the lines." Use the s pace under each statement to note the page(s), and paragraph(s) where you are finding information to support your thinking.

_____1. Digestion problems are caused by people themselves.

_____2. If you are allergic to certain foods, it is because your body th inks those foods are a disease or virus that it must deal with.

_____3. Diarrhea is the opposite of constipation.

_____4. If you have constipation, you should drink more water.

_____5. If you have diarrhea, you should drink more water.

_____6. You can die from constipation.

_____7. You can die from diarrhea.

_____8. People actually cause allergies in some other people.

_____9. Food intolerance and food allergies are pretty much the same thing.

_____10. Ham and bacon are not good for you.

_____11. Food kills.

Anticipation Guide : Figurative Language

Name_____ **Date**_____

Before reading: In the space to the left of each statement, place a check mark (✓) if you agree or think the statement is true.

During or after reading: Add new check marks or cross through those about which you have changed your mind. Keep in mind that this is not like the traditional "worksheet." You may have to put on your thinking caps and "read between the lines." Use the space under each statement to note the page, column, and paragraph(s) where you are finding information to support your thinking.

____1. When an author uses figurative language, s/he writes about things that are easy for the reader to picture in the mind.

____2. Figurative language always compares two things that are not alike.

____3. A writer who uses figurative language can describe something in fewer words than a writer who just describes something by telling as many details as possible.

____4. Middle school students usually don't use figurative language in their writing.

____5. It is possible to describe the red sky of early morning by reference to an animal.

____6. When someone interprets something *literally*, it means that s/he is telling what really happened or what something is really like in real life.

____7. A one-word description of something might use figurative language.

____8. You might actually describe something or someone by saying that it is something else.

____9. Figurative language is creative.

Name_____ Date _____

Guía de Predicción – **La Vida sin Gravedad**

Antes de leer, pone un cheque (✓) al lado de cualquier declaración que usted crée será verdad en la lectura. Entonces, durante o después de lee r, usted puede cambiar su mente por cambiar cualquier simbolo por cruzar por los originamente checado o chequar los que quiere. Sea preparado para defender su interpretación por referencia específica al texto – especificamente cual párrafo y cual frase en que se encontró la información . Utilice el espacio bajo cada declaración para escribir la página y dividir en párrafos donde usted encuentra evidencia.

____1. No es fácil vivir sin gravedad porque nuestros cuerpos se han desarrollado para la supervivencia en un ambiente con la gravedad de la tierra.

____2. Es diversión estar en un ambiente sin gravedad.

____3. Los astronautas consiguen a menudo enfermos cuando están en espacio porque el cuerpo humano no se diseña para existir en un ambiente ingrávido.

____4. La ingravidez puede hacer al cuerpo humano actuar de maneras extrañas.

____5. Los astronautas vomitan con frecuencia cuando están en espacio porque su sentido del balance se pierde.

____6. Una ventaja de ser ingrávida es que una persona puede uti lizar más del espacio dentro de un cuarto que si él estuviera en la tierra.

____7. Los astronautas tienen que ejercitar raramente en espacio.

____8. Es difícil beber en espacio porque el líquido no permanecerá en el vaso, y cuando usted derrama el líquido, es difícil limpiar.

____9. Cuando un astronauta vuelve a la tierra, ella se sentirá probablemente apenas tan enferma como ella lo hizo cuando ella llegó en el ambiente ingrávido del espacio.

Name _____ Date _____

Prediction Guide: '*Spiderman* Bate Récords'

Instructions: Before reading the article from *El País*, place a check mark (✓) in the space to the left of each of the statem ents with which you agree. Then, during or after the reading, cross through those you wish to change, and check any new ones you find to be true. BE SURE YOU ARE ABLE TO REFER BACK TO THE READING TO PROVIDE EVIDENCE FOR OR AGAINST EACH STATEMENT.

____1. The film, *Spiderman* broke the ticket office record for making money when it opened in the US.

____2. Spiderman is a millionaire superhero who is covered with spiderwebs .

____3. The first-day box office receipts of the film surpassed those of *Harry Potter and the Sorcerer's Stone* by millions of dollars .

____4. Euros are worth slightly more than dollars .

____5. Spiderman was written by someone named Lee, produced by someone named Raimi, and stars Tobey Maguire .

____6. The ACNielson Company is the agency t hat rates new films when they come out.

Anticipation Guide : Pastels

Name_____ **Date**_____

Before reading: In the space to the left of each statement, place a check mark (✓) if you agree or think the statement is true.

During or after reading: Add new check marks or cross through those about which you have changed your mind. Keep in mind that this is not like the traditional "worksheet." You may have to put on your thinking caps and "read between the lines." Use the space under each statement to note where you are finding information to support your thinking.

____1. Pastels are sticks of ground pigment mixed with chalk.

____2. Just as paints can be mixed on a palette to blend colors, you can blend pastels the same way.

____3. Whenever you have small fragments of pastels, you should not throw them away – you can recycle them.

____4. You can make your own pastels; it's easy to do.

____5. You can buy pastels in several hundred colors.

____6. When comparing painting with oils or pastels, there are more similarities than there are differences between the two.

____7. Though pastels have been used for thousands of years, one famous modern artist really advanced the medium to the level of complexity it has achieved today.

____8. When working with pastels, you should draw the picture with pencil first.

____9. With pastels you apply layer after layer to get a blending effect and you sometimes paint with your fingers or other tools.

____10. Some pastels are harder than others, and there is a reason why an artist would choose one over the other.

Name_____ Date _____

Prediction Guide – Transforming Formulas

Before reading, place a check mark (✓) next to those statements you think will be true in the reading on pages 175-177. Then, during or after the reading change any that you wish by crossing through checked ones you think not to be true, and by checking any new ones you now agree with. Be prepared to defend your interpretation by specific reference to the text. Use the space under each statement to note page and paragraph or diagram you are referring to in order to prove your interpretation.

____1. When you solve an equation, you end up with the variable on only one side of the equal sign.

____2.Solving for a variable always leads to some number on the other side of the equal sign from the variable.

____3. A formula always shows a relationship between two variables such as Celsius and Fahrenheit temperatures.

____4. The addition property of equality says that if you add a quantity to both sides of the equation, the sides are still equal to each other.

____5. The subtraction, multiplication, and division properties are similar to the addition property.

____6. Solving an equation sometimes does not give you a number – sometimes you get one or more variables on the other side of the equal sign.

____7. All formulas are literal equations.

____8. You can solve $Ax + By = C$ for any of the variables in this equation.

Appendix 3

Selected 3-Level Study Guides

NAME_____ DATE_____

THREE LEVEL STUDY GUIDE: THE RENAISSANCE

INSTRUCTIONS: Scan the statements on this study guide before reading pages 326 - 331. Then, during or after reading, place a check mark (✓) in the space next to each statement with which you agree. Be sure to be able to refer to the text to support your choices whether you agree with a statement or not.

LEVEL I: RIGHT THERE ON THE PAGE

____1. Music, architecture, sculpture, essays, history, and philosophy are all manifestations of culture.

____2. Wealthy renaissance women were well educated like wealthy men of the time.

____3. Before the 15th century, the only books were hand written manuscripts in Latin.

____4. One of the first books widely read by thousands of people was about how narrow-minded many educated people were in the early 15th century.

LEVEL II: READING BETWEEN THE LINES

____5. Most people in the 1300's were aware that it was late in the middle ages.

____6. Rich people in 14th century Italy imitated the cultures of people who had lived more than 2000 years earlier.

____7. One carry-over from the middle ages was the strong desire for power on the part of political leaders.

____8. The average person's awareness of the world expanded enormously as the manufacture of books became inexpensive and relatively easy to perform.

LEVEL III: READING BEYOND THE LINES

____9. The pen is mightier than the sword.

____10. When people today say "That person is a real renaissance person," they mean he/she is a smart, athletic, witty, and generally interesting person.

____11. It is an insult to be called "machiavellian" in the way you deal with other people.

____12. America is a utopian society.

NAME_____ DATE_____

THREE LEVEL STUDY GUIDE: Branches of Earth Science

INSTRUCTIONS: Scan the statements on this study guide before reading. Then, during or after reading, place a check mark (✓) in the space next to each statement with which you agree. Be sure to be able to refer to the text to support your choices whether you agree with a statement or not.

LEVEL I: RIGHT THERE ON THE PAGE

___1. The four main branches of earth science are astronomy, geology, meteorology, and oceanography.

___2. Geologists use scuba diving to learn about the earth, and oceanographers study volcanic activity and mineral formations to learn about the earth.

___3. Meteorologists study meteors that fall to earth from out er space.

___4. Astronomers study not only the stars, but also the planets, asteroids, and other bodies of the solar system.

LEVEL II: READING BETWEEN THE LINES

___5. Being an earth scientist is often dangerous.

___6. Scientists who study volcanism, seismology, and paleontology study many of the same exact things.

___7. Scientists do not know very much about the floor of the oceans.

___8. The study of astronomy helps us to learn more about the earth.

___9. All scientists gather number data to cond uct their research.

LEVEL III: READING BEYOND THE LINES

___10. Of the four special branches of earth science, ecology, geochemistry, environmental science, and geography, one of them is obviously more valuable to mankind than the other three.

___11. You could make a great living and earn a lot of money being an earth scientist.

___12. The quality of life for all citizens of the planet earth is improved by the work of scientists.

NAME_____ DATE_____

THREE LEVEL STUDY GUIDE: The Benefits of Exercise

INSTRUCTIONS: Scan the statements on this study guide before reading pages. Then, during or after reading, place a check mark (✓) in the space next to each statement with which you agree. Be sure to be able to refer to the text to support your choices whether you agree with a statement or not.

LEVEL I: RIGHT THERE ON THE PAGE

____1. Fitness means being physically healthy.

____2. Through exercise, you can build strong muscles, prevent stiffness, and become more coordinated.

____3. Exercising with other people helps you to keep going even when you are tired.

____4. Certain types of exercise make you stronger, while others help you to bui ld endurance.

____5. Exercise causes your brain to change chemically and helps you feel relaxed & sleep better.

____6. You can burn calories and lose weight through exercise.

LEVEL II: READING BETWEEN THE LINES

____7. People who are in good shape can get more done than people who are out of shape.

____8. If you are nervous, you might not be getting enough exercise.

____9. The more you exercise, the more tired you feel most of the time.

____10. People in Japan are more aware than most Americans of the be nefits of exercise.

____11. If you stayed inactive for fifteen days, you would not be able to move.

____12. People who play soccer are more physically fit than those who play football, and those who run cross country are more physically fit than those who play soccer.

LEVEL III: READING BEYOND THE LINES

____13. I can tell by observing my friends who exercise and play sports that what is in this chapter is true.

____14. Early to bed and early to rise makes a man healthy, wealthy, and wise.

____15. I should take my physical education class seriously – it's the best way to get myself in shape and live a healthy life.

NAME_____   DATE_____

THREE LEVEL STUDY GUIDE: *The Road Not Taken*, by Robert Frost

INSTRUCTIONS: Scan the statements on this study guide before reading pages. Then, during or after reading, place a check mark (✓) in the space next to each statement with which you agree. Be sure to be able to refer to the text to support your choices whether you agree with a statement or not.

LEVEL I: RIGHT THERE ON THE PAGE

____1. The narrator is at a fork in the road.

____2. Only one of the two possible roads had been used prior to the time the narrator describes.

____3. Both roads had about the same amount of use by others in the past.

____4. The scene takes place in the summertime.

LEVEL II: READING BETWEEN THE LINES

____5. If a person makes a wrong choice, s/he can always go back and start over again.

____6. Regardless of which decision is made, a person may always wonder if it was the right decision.

____7. The narrator is pleased by his own life choices he made in his past.

LEVEL III: READING BEYOND THE LINES

____8. Hindsight is 20/20.

____9. A poem should "begin in delight and end in wisdom."

____10. Doing what "everyone else" is doing is the easiest short -term strategy, but may, in the long run, prove to have been foolhardy.

Three Level Study Guide: Finding customers

Read Section 3.2 on page 38 and follow the directions under each of the three levels of thinking.

Part 1: The Facts
Directions: Read the statements below. Check column A if the statement is true according to the problem. Then go back and check column B if the information will help you solve the problem.

A   B

_____   _____   They surveyed 100 people.
_____   _____   They called only people they knew
                                might take a bike tour.
_____   _____   Majority of customers surveyed were
                                willing to pay as much as $350.
_____   _____   They would make more profit with
                                65 people at $300 than if they had 59
                                people at $350.

Part 2: Math Ideas
Directions: Read the statements below, check the ones that contain math ideas about this problem.

_____   As the price increases the number of people willing to buy goes
            down.
_____   The higher the price, the greater the profit.
_____   The more the customers, the greater the pro fit.
_____   A graph of the data on page 38 will not be a straight line.

Part 3: Ways to find the answer
Directions: Below are possible ways to get an answer. Check those that will help or work this problem. Write a statement under each explaining why you think so.

_____   Find the best price by drawing a graph.

_____ $250 x 71

_____ $300 x 65

_____ $350 x 59

_____   ($300 + $350) x 62 divided by 2

Appendix 4

The Thinking Cube

Fold under and glue.

DESCRIBE

Look closely.
Describe what you see.
(Colors, shapes, sizes, etc.)

COMPARE

To what is it similar?
or different?

f
o
l
d

g
l
u
e

ARGUE

Tell why it is positive or
why it is negative.
(Or tell why it is important
to know about it.)

Give specific reasons.

ASSOCIATE

What does it make
you think of?

APPLY

Tell how it works.
What can you do with it?

f
o
l
d

g
l
u
e

ANALYZE

What is it made of?
What are the
component parts?

Appendix 5

FICTION PREDICTION SHEET	
My Prediction	What Really Happens

Appendix 6

Question Mark
(Book Mark for Quality Questioning)

QUESTION MARK

BOOKMARK FOR QUALITY QUESTIONS

Knowledge — Identification and recall of information
Who, what, when, where, how _____ ?
Describe _____ .

Comprehension — Organization and selection of facts and ideas
Retell _____ in your own words.
What is the main idea of _____ ?

Application — Use of facts, rules, principles
How is _____ an example of _____ ?
How is _____ related to _____ ?
Why is _____ significant ?

Analysis — Separation of a whole into component parts
What are the parts or features of _____ ?
Classify ____ according to _____ .
Outline/diagram/web _____ .
How does _____compare/contrast with _____ ?
What evidence can you list for _____ ?

Synthesis — Combination of ideas to form a new whole
What would you predict or infer from _____ ?
What ideas can you add to _____ ?
How would you create/design a new _____ ?
What might happen if you combined _____
_____ with _____ ?
What solutions would you suggest for _____ ?

Evaluation — Development of opinions, judgments, or decisions
Do you agree _____ ?
What do you think about _____ ?
What is the most important _____ ?
Prioritize _____ ?
How would you decide about _____ ?
What criteria would you use to assess _____ ?

Appendix 7

What I Know Sheet Variations

What I Know Sheet			
What I Know After Previewing	What I Need to Find Out	What I Learned	What I Still Need To Find Out

What I Know Sheet			
What I Know Before Previewing	What I Know After Previewing	What I Need To Know	What I Learned

What I Know Sheet			
What I Know After Previewing	What I Need To Know	Where I Can Find The Information	What I Learned

What I Know Sheet			
What I Know After Previewing	What I Need To Know	What I Learned	My Reaction

Appendix 8

Introducing Anticipation Guides to Students

The first time you use an anticipation guide with students, you will need to explain how this activity differs from the typical "worksheet" that they all know so well. I usually begin by asking the students if they have ever done a worksheet. Once they respond, I explain the differences between anticipation guides and a normal worksheet. This explanation is important because a well-made anticipation guide can truly empower students to perform true reading – thoughtful construction of meaning from the text – if they realize that it is very different from a worksheet. The monologue usually goes as follows:

"Before we begin this reading, I need to clarify with you people how you use an anticipation guide during the reading. By a show of hands, how many of you have ever done a worksheet?"

Once they all raise their hands and suggest that they have done thousands of them, I say, "The anticipation guide you are about to use is like a worksheet *in that it is on paper – and that is where the similarity ends. An anticipation guide is the opposite of a typical textbook-published worksheet.*

First of all, it does not have questions! Rather, as you have already noticed, it is made up of statements – hypothetical truths – about which you already have opinions. As I walked around the room and listened to your discussions, I noticed that you have differences of opinion on several of the statements on the anticipation guide. This is a good thing. When we get into the reading in a few moments, I want you to read to seek information that supports your beliefs.

But there are two other important differences between this anticipation guide and a typical worksheet. With most worksheets, you can find the answer to a question in one place in the text. And, normally, the question on the worksheet is worded just about the same way as the answer is worded in the text. The result is that you never have to really read the text to find the answers. Instead, you simply go on a little hunting trip – starting in the middle or back of the reading – skimming and scanning, to stalk bold print or other clues that will help you locate "the right answer" without ever seeing the logical presentation that the author is making. You all have been taught writing techniques, and you know that a well written work has some logic to the way it is organized, stating key ideas and then supporting those ideas with elaborating details. Mature readers who want to understand a new idea don't skim & scan except to preview the reading. Once they begin to read for understanding, they read from the start to see the author's logical presentation of ideas. This is what I am going to ask you to do with this reading today. You need to read this from the beginning, and work straight through it. You will see that, because you have made the predictions you made, and because you have discussed these things with other students, you will find that you are able to make good sense of the reading. It will be easy for you to read.

So you need to keep a couple of things in mind at this time:

1. You will not find anything in the text worded exactly the same way the statements on the anticipation guide are worded. So, if you attempt to go on a skim & scan "hunting trip" through the reading, you will become frustrated fairly quickly. Instead, you will have to put on your thinking caps and read interpretively. You may have to infer the data that support your beliefs. (I usually model inferential thinking here.)

2. Another big difference between this activity and a worksheet is that, in order to support or negate some of the statements on this anticipation guide, you may have to assemble an argument, using information from more than one paragraph, possibly from two or more different pages.

In other words, you may have to behave like attorneys behave – gathering as much evidence as you can to support your case – preparing to convince a jury of what you believe to be true.

So here is how you will gather the information:

Let's – just for demonstration purposes – suppose that I had checked statements 1, 3, 5, and 7 on this anticipation guide. (At this point, I place check marks on the overhead transparency of the anticipation guide.)

As I said earlier when you were first making your individual predictions, you could change any of the check marks as you read the text if you were to find your prediction to be incorrect. Here is how you would do so:

If, as I were reading, I found that number 1 should not be checked, I could just cross through the check mark like this. (I draw a line through the original check mark perpendicular to the line of the mark.) You do not need to get out a bottle of "White-Out" or wear down your eraser. Just cross through it, and it will be just as if you never checked it. *But it is important that you make note of where you found information that leads you to think this way.* You can do so by noting the page, column, and paragraph where you found information that you are interpreting to support your beliefs. You place the information right on the anticipation guide like this. (I write on the transparency to model the gathering of information.)

Suppose that, during the reading, I change my mind and I feel that number two should be checked. No problem; I just place a check mark next to it like this. (I put a check next to the statement on the transparency overhead, and I make sure to write a page, column, and paragraph indicator under the statement.)

Does everyone understand now how to gather information to prove your case? Remember that you are acting like attorneys – gathering as much information as you can to support your case, and preparing to present your interpretation to the jury – and the jury, in your case, is your cooperative learning group.

Let's go into the reading now. (I allot some reasonable time to read.) My final instruction: Please do not distract yourself or others during this reading time. If you have a habit of tapping your pencil on the desk or clicking your pen or some other distracting behavior, I am asking you to forgo that at this time. Let's make this a library-like quiet place to read. Also, you might – since you have already discussed some of these ideas with your peers – feel the need to poke your neighbor in the shoulder and say, 'Look. Here's number three. I told you!' Please refrain from doing that. We will have time to discuss our findings in our groups immediately after we finish the reading. So please don't distract yourself or others. Let's begin…sshhh"

References

Ammann, R. & Mittelsteadt, S. (1987). "Turning on turned off students." *Journal of Reading*, 30(8), 708-15. [EJ 350 581]

Alvermann, D. & Phelps, S. (1998). *Content reading and literacy*. Boston: Allyn & Bacon.

Anderson, L., & Krathwohl, D. (2001). *A taxonomy for learning, teaching, and assessing : a revision of Bloom's taxonomy of educational objectives*. New York: Longman.

Atkinson, J. (1964). *An introduction to motivation*. Princeton, NJ: Van Nostrand.

Atkinson, J. (1987). *Michigan studies of fear failure*. In F. Halisch & J. Kuhl (Eds.), *Motivation, intention and volition* (pp. 47-60). Berlin: Springer.

Atkinson, J., & Raynor, J. (1974). *Motivation and achievement*. New York: Wiley.

Atwell, N. (1987). *In the middle; Writing, reading, and learning with adolescents*. Portsmouth, NH: Heinemann.

Bartoli, J. (1995). *Unequal opportunity: Learning to read in the U.S.A. language and literacy series*. New York: Teachers College Press.

Bloom, B. (1956). *Taxonomy of educational objectives (cognitive domain)*. New York: McKay.

Brown, A. (1987). "Metacognition, executive control, self-regulation and other more mysterious mechanisms." in Weinert, F. & Kluwe, R. (Eds) *Metacognition, motivation and understanding*. Hillsdale, NJ: Erlbaum.

Brown, A., Bransford, J., Ferrara, R. & Campione, J. (1983). Learning, remembering, and understanding. In J Flavell & E. Markham (Eds.), *Handbook of child psychology*. New York: Wiley.

Brozo, W. (2003). Making word learning memorable. *Thinking classroom*. Vol. 4, no. 4. Newark, DE: International Reading Association.

Caine, R., and Caine, G. (1991). *Teaching and the human brain*, Alexandria, VA: Association for Supervision and Curriculum Development.

Cardoso, S. (Ed.)(2003). Brain and Mind: Electronic Magazine on Neuroscience. http://www.epub.org.br/cm/n05/mente/estados_i.htm

Csikszentmihalyi, M. (1990). *Flow: The psychology of optimal experience.* New York: Harper & Row.

Collins, N. (1996). Motivating low performing adolescent readers. *ERIC Digest.* ED296365. Bloomington, IN: ERIC Clearinghouse on Reading English and Communication.

Cowan, G. & Cowan, E. (1980). *Writing.* New York: Wiley.

Cunningham, J. (1982). Generating interactions between schemata and text. In J. A. Niles & L. A. Harris (Eds) *New inquiries in reading research and instruction.* Thirty-first yearbook of the national reading conference. Rochester, NY: National Reading Conference.

Dewey, J. (1933). *How we think: A restatement of the relation of reflective thinking to the educative process.* Boston: Houghton Mifflin.

Dixon-Krauss, L., (1996). *Vygotsky in the classroom.* New York: Longman.

Dole, J. A., Duffy, G. G., Roehler, L. R., & Pearson, P. D. (1991). Moving from the old to the new: Research on reading comprehension instruction. *Review of Educational Research,* 61, 239-264.

Draper, J. (2002). School mathematics reform, constructivism, and literacy; A case for literacy instruction in the reform-oriented math classroom. *Journal of Adolescent & Adult Literacy. 45:6.* Newark, DE: International Reading Association.

Duke, N. & Pearson, D. (2002). Effective practices for developing reading comprehension. In Alan Farstrup & S. Jay Samuels (Eds.) *What research has to say about reading instruction.* Newark, DE: International Reading Association.

Estes, T, & Vaughan, J. (1986). *Reading and learning in the content area classroom.* Boston: Allyn and Bacon.

Flavell, J. (1979). Metacognition and cognitive monitoring: A new area of cognitive-developmental inquiry. *American Psychologist, 34,* 906-911.

Forget, M. (1991). *The effects of a content area reading curriculum on senior high school students.* Unpublished paper presented in partial fulfillment of the Certification in Reading, Old Dominion University. Norfolk, VA.

Forget, M., Lyle, N., Reinhart-Clark, K., & Spear, M. (2003). Convincing All Teachers to Use Reading and Writing to Learn in Their Classrooms – A Successful Paradigm. Unpublished presentation, International Reading Association Annual Conference, May, 2003. Orlando FL.

Forget, M., & Morgan, R. (1997). A brain compatible learning environment for improving student metacognition, *Reading Improvement*, v 34, no. 4, Winter, 1997.

Forget, M., Morgan, R., & Antinarella, J. (1996). *Reading for success: A school to work approach, instructors manual.* Cincinnati, OH: ITP South-Western Publishing.

Gallimore, R. & Tharp, R. (1990). Teaching mind in society: Teaching, schooling, and literate discourses. In L. C. Moll (Ed.). *Vygotsky and education: Instructional implications and applications of sociohistorical psychology.* New York: Cambridge University Press.

Gardner, H. (1983). *Frames of mind.* Boston: Basic Books.

Gardner, H. (1991). *The unschooled mind: How children learn and how schools should teach.* Boston: Basic Books.

Gardner, H. (1993). *Multiple intelligences: The theory in practice.* Boston: Basic Books.

Georghiades, P. (2000). Beyond conceptual change learning in science education: focusing on transfer, durability and metacognition. *Educational Research, 42,* No. 2, 119-139.

Greenleaf, C., Schoenbach, R., Cziko, C., and Mueller, F. L. (2001). Apprenticing Adolescent Readers to Academic Literacy. In *Harvard Educational Review*, Vol. 71, Number 1, Spring 2001.

Gunstone, R. (1991). Constructivism and metacognition: theoretical issues and classroom studies. In: Dutt, R., Goldberg, F., & Niedderer, H. (Eds) *Research in physics learning: Theoretical issues and empirical studies.* Bremen: IPN

Hart, Leslie (1975). *How the brain works.* New York: Basic Books.

Hart, L. (1983). *Human brain and human learning.* New York: Longman.

Healey, J. (1990). *Endangered minds: Why our children don't think.* New York: Simon and Schuster.

Herber, H. (1970). *Teaching reading in the content areas.* Englewood Cliffs, NJ: Prentice Hall.

Johnson, D., Johnson, R. and Holubec, E. (1993) *Circles of learning cooperation in the classroom.* 4th edition. Edina, MN: Interaction Book.

Jones, B., Pierce, J., & Hunter, B. (1988). Teaching students to construct graphic representations. *Educational Leadership.* Vol. 48, no. 4. Alexandria, VA: Association for Supervision and Curriculum Development.

Keller, J. (1983). Motivational design of instruction. In C.M. Reigeluth (Ed.). *Instructional design theories and models: An overview of their current status.* Hillsdale, NJ: Erlbaum.

Kiewra, K., (1993). An Embedded Curriculum Approach for Teaching Students How To Learn. In Sandra L. Christenson and Jane Close (Eds.). *Home school collaboration: Enhancing children's academic and social competence.* Silver Spring, MD: Nat. Association of School Psychologists.

Krashen, S. (1996). *Every person a reader: An alternative to the California's Reading Task Force Report.* Culver City, CA: Language Education Associates.

Krashen, S., & McQuillan, J. (1996). *The case for late intervention: Once a good reader, always a good reader.* Culver City, CA: Language Education Associates.

Langer, J. (1981). From theory to practice: A prereading plan. *Journal of Reading,* 25, 152-156.

Larson, C., & Dansereau, D. (1986). Cooperative learning in dyads. *Journal of Reading,* 29, 516-520. Newark, DE: International Reading Association.

Lotan, R. (2003). Group-worthy tasks. *Educational Leadership.* Vol. 60, no. 6. Alexandria, VA: Association for Supervision and Curriculum Development.

MacLean, P. (1978). A mind of three minds: Educating the triune brain. In J. Chall & A. Mirsley (Eds.), *Education and the brain.* Chicago: University of Chicago Press.

Manzo, A. (1969). The request procedure. *Journal of Reading, 11,*123-126.

Manzo, A. (1975). The guided reading procedure. *Journal of reading.* Vol 18, 287-291.

Manzo, A., & Manzo, U. (1997), Factor analysis of Teachers' responses to why they don't use published reading-teaching methods and what would cause them to do so. *Yearbook of the American Reading Forum.* Rochester, NY: American Reading Forum.

Marzano, R. (2001). *Designing a new taxonomy of educational objectives.* Thousand Oaks, CA: Corwin.

Marzano, R., Pickering, D., and Pollock, J. (2001). *Classroom instruction that works: Research-based strategies for increasing student achievement.* Alexandria, VA: Association for Supervision and Curriculum Development.

Marzano, R. (2003). *What works in schools: Translating research into action.* Alexandria, VA: Association for Supervision and Curriculum Development.

McQuillan, J. (1998). *The literacy crisis: False claims, real solutions.* Portsmouth, NH: Heinemann.

Meeks, J., & Morgan, R. (1978). New use for the cloze procedure: Interaction in imagery. *Reading Horizons,* 18, 261-264.

Miller, G. (1977). *Spontaneous apprentices: Children and language.* New York: Seabury.

Morgan, R., Forget, M., and Antinarella, J. (1996). *Reading for success: A school to work approach.* Cincinnati, OH: ITP South-Western Publishing.

National Center for Educational Statistics. (1998). Reading *report card for the nation and the states.* Washington, DC: Educational Testing Service.

National Center for Educational Statistics. (2003). The NAEP reading achievement levels. *The nation's report card, 2003.* http://nces.ed.gov/nationsreportcard/reading/achieveall.asp#grade12.

National Council of Teachers of Mathematics. (2000). *Principles and standardsfor school mathematics.* Reston, VA: Author.

Ogle, D. (1986). KWL: A teaching model that develops active reading of expository text. *The Reading Teacher.* 39, 564-570.

Opitz, M., & Rasinski, T. (1998). *Goodbye round robin; Twenty-five effective oral reading strategies.* Portsmouth, NH: Heinemann.

Palinscar, A., & Brown, A. (1984). Reciprocal teaching of comprehension-fostering and comprehension-monitoring activities. *Cognition and Instruction. 1,* 117-175.

Paris, S., Lipson, M., & Wixon, K. (1983). Becoming a strategic reader. *Contemporary Educational Psychology*, 8, 293-316.

Paris, S. G., Wasik, B. A., & Turner, J. C. (1991). The development of strategic readers. In R. Barr, M. L. Kamil, P. B.Mosenthal, & P. D. Pearson (Eds.), *Handbook of reading research. 2,* (609-640). New York: Longman.

Paris, S., Wasik, B., & Van der Huizen, G. (1988). Metacognition: A review of research on metacognition and reading. In J. E. Readance, R. S. Baldwin, J. P. Konopak, & P. R. O'Keefe (Eds.), *Dialogs in literacy research,* Thirty-seventh yearbook of the National Reading Conference, (143-166). Rochester, NY: National Reading Conference.

Pauk, W. (2001). *How to study in college.* Boston: Houghton Mifflin.

Pearson, P., & Fielding, L. (1991). Comprehension instruction. In R. Barr, M. Kamil, P. Mosenthal, & P.D. Pearson (Eds.), *Handbook of reading research, 2,* 815-860. New York: Longman.

Peck, R. (2003, April 5). The writer's almanac. (Garrison Keillor, ed.). From http://emd5.rdg.com/u?e=mfVXq7xV2c3gg&a=17ms&b=7.html

Powell-Brown, A. (2004). Can you be a teacher of literacy if you don't love to read? *Journal of Adolescent and Adult Literacy*, Vol. 47, no. 4. Newark, DE: International Reading Association.

Rasinski, T., & Hoffman, J. (2003). Theory and research into practice: Oral reading in the school literacy curriculum. *Reading Research Quarterly,* Vol. 38, No. 4, 510-522. Newark, DE: International Reading Association.

Raths, L., Jonas, A., Rothstein, A., & Wasserman, S. (1967). *Teaching for thinking: Theory and application.* Columbus, OH: Charles E. Merrill.

Readance, J., Bean, T., & Baldwin, R. (1981). *Content area reading: An integrated approach.* Dubuque, IA: Kendall/Hunt.

Richardson, J. & Morgan, R. (1994). *Reading to learn in the content areas.* Second edition. Belmont, CA: ITP Wadsworth.

Richardson, J. & Morgan, R. (2003). *Reading to learn in the content areas.* Fifth edition. Belmont, CA: ITP Wadsworth.

Robinson, F. (1961). *Effective study.* New York: Harper & Row.

Schoenbach, R., Greenleaf, C. L., Cziko, C., & Hurwitz, L. (1999). *Reading for understanding.* Jossey-Bass Publishers: San Fransisco.

Shefelbine, J. (2002). The hidden role of academic language in meeting standards. Unpublished presentation from The Conference on Adolescent Literacy, California Department of Education, March 7-8, 2002.

Sinatra, R. (1986). *Visual literacy connections to thinking, reading, and writing.* Springfield, IL: Thomas.

Slater, R. (2002). Brain Compatible Classroom Practices. Unpublished presentation, 16th Annual *High Schools That Work* Staff Development Conference, Nashville, TN.

Slavin, R. Synthesis of research on cooperative learning. *Educational Leadership,* 48 (February 1991): 71-82.

Smith, F. (1983). *Essays into literacy.* Portsmouth, NH: Heinemann.

Smith, F. (1986). *Insult to intelligence: The bureaucratic invasion of our classrooms.* New York: Arbor House.

Smith, F. (1988). *Joining the literacy club.* Portsmouth, NH: Heinemann.

Smith, F. (1994). *Understanding Reading.* Fifth edition. Hillsdale, NJ: Lawrence Erlbaum Associates.

Stahl, R. (1992). A Context for 'Higher Order Knowledge:' An Information-Constructivist (IC) Perspective with Implications for Curriculum and Instruction. *Journal of structural learning,* 11, 189-218.

Stack, J. (1995). Literacy and the inner city child. Paper presented at the Annual Conference of the International Association of School Libraryship.

Stanovich, K. (1986). Mathew effects in reading: Some consequences of individual reading differences in the acquisition of literacy. *Reading Research Quarterly, 21(4)*, 360-406.

Stauffer, R. (1969). *Directing reading maturity as a cognitive process.* New York: Harper & Row.

Taylor, W. (1953). Cloze procedure: A new tool for measuring readability. *Journalism Quarterly,* 30, 415-433.

Tovani, C. & Keene, E. (2001). *I Read It, but I Don't Get It: Comprehension Strategies for Adolescent Readers.* Portland, ME: Stenhouse.

Vacca, R. (2002). Making a difference in Adolescents' school lives: Visible and invisible aspects of content area reading. In Alan Farstrup & S. Jay Samuels (Eds.) *What research has to say about reading instruction.* Newark, DE: International Reading Association.

Vaughan, J., & Estes, T. (1986). *Reading and reasoning beyond the primary grades.* Boston: Allyn & Bacon.

Vygotsky, L. (1978). *Mind in society.* Cambridge, MA: Harvard University Press.

Whitehead, D. (1994). Teaching literacy and learning strategies through a modified guided silent reading procedure. *Journal of Reading*, 38, no. 1. Newark, DE: International Reading Association.

Worthy, J., & Broaddus, K. (2002). Fluency beyond the primary grades: From group performance to silent, independent reading. *The Reading Teacher.* Vol. 55, no. 4, 334-343. Newark, DE: International Reading Association.

Zingraff-Newton, A. E. (1995). The effects of content-area reading strategies on the achievement of secondary mathematics students. Unpublished MA thesis at Old Dominion University, Norfolk, VA.

Zinsser, W. (1988). *Writing to Learn.* New York: Harper & Row.

Zintz, M. & Maggart, Z. (1984). *The reading process: The teacher and the Learner.* Dubuque, IA: Wm. C. Brown.

Index

About the Author

Dr. Forget (pronounced forjáy) has been a teacher and coach from 1974 until the present. He has taught at the elementary, middle, high school and university levels. The vast majority of his teaching experience is in the high school (19 years). He has successfully applied the pedagogy of content area reading and writing instruction in the teaching of algebra, trigonometry, statistics, American history, American Government, geography, earth science, world history, health and physical education, and, as a reading teacher, in many other content areas, as a guest teacher. He has taught undergraduate and graduate courses in content area reading instruction for over ten years at Old Dominion University, in Norfolk, Virginia, and at the University of Findlay, in Findlay, Ohio. He is the co-author of *Reading for Success: A School to Work Approach*, published in 1996, and principal author of the accompanying instructor's manual. He has also published many articles about reading instruction and brain-compatible learning, and is a nationally-recognized staff developer in the field of content area literacy. You can learn more about Dr. Forget through the *MAX Teaching* web page, at **http://www.maxteaching.com**.

ISBN 141200992-8

9 781412 009928